THE WESLEYAN THEOLOGICAL HERITAGE

A Francis Asbury Press Book

ESSAYS OF
ALBERT C. OUTLER

THE WESLEYAN THEOLOGICAL HERITAGE

EDITED BY
THOMAS C. ODEN &
LEICESTER R. LONGDEN

Zondervan Publishing House
Academic and Professional Books
Grand Rapids, Michigan

A Division of HarperCollins*Publishers*

The Wesleyan Theological Heritage
Copyright © 1991 by Thomas C. Oden and Leicester R. Longden

Requests for information should be addressed to:
Zondervan Publishing House
Academic and Professional Books
1415 Lake Drive S.E.
Grand Rapids, Michigan 49506

Library of Congress Cataloging-in-Publication Data

Outler, Albert C., 1908-1989.
    The Wesleyan theological heritage : essays of Albert C. Outler /
2medited by Thomas C. Oden and Leicester R. Longden.
        p.   cm.
    Includes bibliographical references and index.
    ISBN 0-310-75471-2
    1. Wesley, John, 1703-1791. 2. Methodist Church—Doctrines—History. I. Oden, Thomas C. II. Longden, Leicester R. III. Title.
    BX8331.2.092 1991
    230'.7—dc20   90-45268
                                                                        CIP

Designed by James E. Ruark
Cover Design by Allie Design

Printed in the United States of America

91   92   93   94   95   96 / CH / 10   9   8   7   6   5   4   3   2   1

Contents

SPIRIT AND CHURCH IN THE WESLEYAN TRADITION

EPILOGUE: VISIONS AND DREAMS

THANK YOU FOR ORDERING THE FREE

GOOD NEWS BULLETIN INSERTS! WE TRUST THAT

YOU HAVE BEEN ABLE TO USE THEM AS PLANNED.

ENCLOSED IS THE COMPLIMENTARY BOOK WE

PROMISED TO SEND TO YOU FOR PLACING YOUR

ORDER. WE HOPE THAT YOU WILL ENJOY IT!

Introduction

—┼—

The central purpose of this book is to make accessible a core series of influential essays that all who wish to enter the arena will instantly recognize as crucial to all further serious conversation about Wesley. Albert Cook Outler has provided a pivotal reformulation of the scholarly questions in this entire field.

This book presents the substantive contributions of Outler to contemporary Wesley studies. It is for those who have already developed a taste for Wesley studies, yet want to take that taste into more precise levels of discrimination. It is also for novices who wish a preliminary introduction to key issues of current inquiry into Wesleyan theology and tradition. This introduction seeks to clarify the crux of Outler's achievement, its relevance to current audiences, and why Wesley is still a viable model of evangelical theology.

WHO WAS ALBERT OUTLER (1908–1989)?

A leading interpreter of Augustine, indefatigable Protestant observer at Vatican II, teacher par excellence, ecumenical expert, eminent patristic scholar, key figure in the shaping of Methodist doctrinal teaching in this century, editor of Wesley's Sermons in their definitive edition, leading American historical theologian— all these descriptions are true. But in this book we focus upon Outler as leading interpreter of John Wesley's theology.

If one had nothing else but Outler's comic perception of theology, this would make these essays a happy read. It is rare in theological works to find the humorous angle so constantly at play. It seemed hard for Outler to write a single paragraph without turning something in a comic direction, or looking for some amusing angle of vision or some element of play.

Not only is Outler a delight to read. He is also the one interpreter most acutely aware of the richly nuanced historic antecedents of Wesley's theology in Puritanism, Anglicanism, medieval theology, and more importantly in the ancient church tradition. No one offers a better focused picture of Wesley's sources and context.

Outler was forever attentive to the practical moral and religious formation of the communities to which he was accountable: the scholarly world of historical theology, the Faith and Order movement in ecumenism, and the Wesleyan theological and church traditions. He served many years as delegate to United Methodist General Conferences and as the leading theological advisor of Methodist bishops. For decades he played the delicate, difficult role of chief theological and intellectual mentor in his church. He courageously involved himself in sticky decision-making processes of the church even when it became a costly act that diverted him from his wide-ranging scholarship. When the Methodist Church united with the Evangelical United Brethren, Outler more than anyone formulated the theological basis for the Plan of Union in 1967, shepherding it through the 1968 General Conference.

It is difficult to think of any American who has contributed more substantively to the theological development of the ecumenical movement. Outler was long closely associated with leading ecumenists such as George Florovsky, Edmund Schlinck, Robert Calhoun, Paul Minear, and W. A. Visser t' Hooft. The ecumenical movement today remains deeply imprinted by his former students and close associates: John Deschner, Hans Frei, Bard Thompson, George Lindbeck, John Leith, Richey Hogg. His ecumenical credentials remain untarnished by reckless or partisan political activism. It is he who first made Lutherans aware of how deeply committed Wesley was to justification by faith, and Roman Catholics aware of how deeply Wesley was committed to faith active in love. What finally eventuated in Lima in the Faith and Order Report on *Baptism, Eucharist and Ministry* was deeply indebted to Outler.

Outler served as president of his own guild of scholars, the American Society of Church History, which now offers an Albert C. Outler prize. He exercised strong influence among the Kent Fellows, Danforth Fellows, Society for Values in Higher Education, the brilliant "Duodecim" group of theologians, the Hazen and Lilly Foundations, and the Foundation for Theological

Education. In the sensitive Faith and Order discussions of Tradition and Traditions, Outler was key drafter and formulator.

He was engaged lifelong in the reappropriation of tradition, not slavishly or archaically repristinating traditions, but mining them anew in ways pertinent to the contemporary situation. As an historian, he sought to show the complex layers of causality in the historic transmission of cultural and religious traditions.

Outler's footnotes save a mountain of labor and time for scholars who wish to penetrate the sources of Wesley. Anyone who plans to be a preacher or leader in the Wesleyan tradition of church bodies, whether British Methodist, or United Methodist, or Free Methodist or Wesleyan or Nazarene or Salvation Army or AME Zion, or whatever, will be helped immensely by Outler to understand the dynamics of these traditions. He will help them understand historically why various ecstacies, despairs, glories and absurdities persist. In good spirit he caringly analyzed common self-deceptions, sources of identity formation, and unconscious motives. Outler was a brilliant storyteller. In his essays we discover a consummate professional in succinct re-counting of complex historical movements, periods, and figures. Outler learned well the art of communicating highly differentiated ideas and descriptions in novel, plausible, often amusing ways. It is a marvelous gift that is worth savoring whether one is interested directly in Wesley or not. Anyone seeking a model of how to write and think historically can hardly find a better one than here. In these essays we see how a brilliant historical scholar patiently worked to introduce a figure and his ideas even to resistant audiences. He is similar to Macauley or Carl Becker or Reinhold Niebuhr in his ability to take dense complexities and express them sharply and accurately.

WHY OUTLER'S AUDIENCE IS GROWING

What audience is ripening for this book? Those of any evangelical tradition who want to understand better what has been happening in the world of Wesley scholarship in this century, and the directions in which it is headed; those from any of the Wesleyan family of church traditions who are now seeking freshly to reappropriate Wesley's message for today. Anyone serious about ordination in the Wesleyan tradition owes it to him or herself to discover what makes this tradition tick and cohere, even while there remains much room for debate and dialogue as to details. Outler offers a road map for this discovery. But the audience is wider and growing. Why? Who are finding him edifying and illuminating?

- ☐ Anyone seeking better to understand the historical roots of charismatic Christianity, pentecostalism, and the holiness traditions.
- ☐ Evangelical pastors, lay readers and scholars interested in building a usable bridge between Reformed and Wesleyan evangelical traditions.
- ☐ Anyone who wishes to see how the Wesleyan evangelical tradition fits into the modern ecumenical stream, both in its development and contemporary expressions.
- ☐ Anyone who seeks to illuminate the hidden roots of evangelical pietism in the traditions of Eastern Orthodoxy and patristic Catholicism.
- ☐ Anyone who wishes to see through the fog of sentiment in Wesley scholarship and discover the actual textual-documentary heritage of the Wesleys.
- ☐ Anyone who seeks to preach from a deliberately Wesleyan vantage point.
- ☐ Anyone who wishes to offer intelligent criticisms of the Wesleyan tradition or of other related traditions of theology and ministry.

One need not be a Wesleyan or Methodist to benefit. There is no doctrinal test for savoring these gems. One may be Catholic, charismatic, pentecostal, or mainline-oldline, and never once be bored.

The Francis Asbury Press imprint of Zondervan is hereby especially inviting thoughtful evangelicals to reconsider the theological bearings of the Wesleyan branch of evangelicalism. Conservative evangelicals and neo-evangelicals have much catch-up work to do to enter this arena. Those who mark Wesley out as Semi-Pelagian or Enthusiast or crypto-Catholic will quickly find such stereotypes corrected.

Outler's interpretation is a good cure for the quiet malaise and uneasy tension which has brewed for two centuries between Calvinists and Methodists. Outler was an informed student of Calvin and the Calvinist tradition, particularly its Puritan phase. In Outler conservative evangelicals find a historian whom they can use as an accurate mirror for getting better in touch with their own church traditions. He will help them see how the various Protestant traditions of piety, mission, and testimony complement each other creatively. Conservative evangelicals misjudge Outler if they pigeonhole him too quickly as "liberal" Methodist, for he thought of himself as postcritical and postliberal. Evangelical readers are invited to study him openmindedly, not prejudging, to behold afresh this expression of evangelical faith. We can no longer afford to assume that there is little more to be said between Calvinists and Wesleyans. Roman Catholics are already better in touch with Outler's effort than are conservative evangelicals. He has taught Protestants how they can be in dialogue with Catholics and Orthodox without surrendering evangelical credentials.

A scholarly pastor or theologian who occasionally chafes at the absurdities of his own ecclesial traditions will have much to learn from this model of interpretation. Most historians struggle with hagiographical or antiquarian romanticisms, and seek to reengage with the font of traditions. Outler provides a temperate, good-spirited, balanced model of how this may be done.

WHY A REAPPRAISAL OF WESLEY NOW?

A vast reappraisal of the theological heritage of John Wesley is already proceeding apace. Wesleyan theology is currently undergoing a major recrudescence. Outler is central to it. The Wesleyan doctrinal standards are being more carefully attended in the last quarter of this century than any previous quarter. Outler is an important part of that rediscovery. Those who wonder why this is happening do well to attend to Outler's work.

The current rediscovery of Wesley as theologian is a wide-ranging undertaking of persons of varied perspectives: evangelicals and liberals, charismatics and postcritical biblical scholars; historical scholars interested in evangelical revivalism; all those associated with the Wesley Bicentennial Works project; college, university and seminary teachers in Wesley studies (as seen in the Wesley Studies Section of the American Academy of Religion); evangelical scholars associated with the rapidly growing Wesleyan Theological Society, and Wesleyans in the Evangelical Theological Society; and Methodists and Wesleyans of many denominations interested in the recovery of doctrinal standards.

Wesley is being rediscovered as a well-tempered theologian of astonishing influence. The events of his biography are being thoroughly reassessed in relation to his theological sources and development. We are belatedly beginning to understand in greater detail just how the doctrinal standards of Wesleyan traditions were derived, refashioned, and transmitted. We are only now beginning to realize in this post-Outlerian phase just why Wesley remains a pivotal player in the history of Protestant theology and in ecumenism, as one who wished to resynthesize and embody the subtle tensions of ancient ecumenical Christianity. This is why many pastors and teachers from varied quarters will find this collection useful and edifying.

Wesley's teaching was strongly focused upon bringing the Christian life into practical personal and social actualization. There are steady moral dimensions in this entire theological enterprise. With Wesley we are not dealing with an aloof speculative mind that makes no practical difference in the way one lives one's life. Outler helps readers to discover their own identity within their community of faith. Selfhood and faith are seen in the context of historical process and living community.

It was Outler more than any other who identified, refined, and developed the notion of a quadrilateral Wesleyan theological method (relating Scripture as primary source of revelation to tradition, experience and reason)—now a matter of general debate and generally wide reception in Wesleyan circles. Though there remain controversies concerning this theological method, it is difficult to talk with Wesleyan scholars anywhere without hearing the language of quadrilateral, which suggests that it has already become something of a theological staple. Outler was its original and major expositor, and the one who helped us see how Wesley's method is still usable and highly pertinent. The Wesleyan-based churches have all been deeply affected by this discussion.

Through Outler's eyes, we have come to see that Wesley is a complex, multifaceted, intriguing figure pertinent to Protestants of many stripes. Wesley remains a significant figure not simply for popular religiosity or denominational nostalgia, but for theological substance as a practical reappropriator of the Christian tradition to an early modern audience, and, I believe, to a post-modern audience. In Wesley we have the most important theologian of the Anglican evangelical tradition—no small claim. There is a richer Wesley than we have known when we were nostalgic, a better mind than we had known before Outler introduced us to its deeper nuances. I think of Outler as the inveterate Wesleyan spelunker, introducing the reader to the cavernous stretches of Wesley's mind.

Oxford in the eighteenth century was a place where the revival of patristic studies was actively proceeding before Wesley appeared on the scene. We now know that Wesley was a serious reader of the classical Christian tradition, and especially of Eastern ascetic piety. He was drawn to ancient ecumenical theology, especially of the writers of the first three pre-Constantinian centuries.

We have in Wesley a thoughtful and educated theological mind, yet because he was constantly searching for simplicity in plain speech, it is easy to treat his effort merely as popular sermonizing. Outler helps us see the underlying richness and fabric. Wesley hid his Oxford scholarship in order to reach out in plain speech for plain people, with no fancy airs. It took someone like Outler to notice and define how finely nuanced were his practical appropriations of the classic Christian tradition. The Oxford don clearly had gifts of scholarship, as an excellent Latinist and Greek scholar. The decision to leave Oxford to engage actively in the "street work" of the evangelical revival rather than to remain an Oxford don was an irreversible vocational decision for Wesley. Yet from his early years onward he continued reading Cicero in Latin, Clement of Rome in Greek, and translating hymns of Gerhard and others from the German, and managed a vast publishing operation for the poor. A lifelong learner and teacher, he wanted his ordinary hearers—the miners, the urban poor, the Cornwall villagers—not to be intimidated or blocked by his scholarly competencies. He sought to communicate to them the classic tradition through a vast publication project including a library of Christian classics.

When I first met Outler, I was a pacifist, theoretical socialist, liberal political activist. He challenged all that, but more so, helped me examine historically some of my reasons for my hasty commitments. Later when I became a post-liberal transplant into paleo-orthodoxy, I learned to appreciate him even more, without having to deny the best moral resources of the liberal tradition by which I had been spawned, whose strengths and weaknesses he enabled me to assess. He was at home in pluralistic democratic processes. He saw no reason to be defensive amid them. But that does not imply that his work does not have evangelical force or rootage in the orthodox tradition.

We study Outler today because he helps us grasp the neural and muscular connections between the Wesleyan tradition and Protestant, Catholic and ecumenical theology. With Outler Wesleyan studies have ceased being parochial. Outler has helped us see Wesley as a lively embodiment of piety and vital religion, who for two centuries has provided Protestantism with high energy resources for its American and international journeys.

To students of Wesley I say without hesitation: read this. You will enjoy it. Your faith, hope, and love will be deepened. It is hazardous to hold on to your ecclesial identity too tightly or defensively. Outler will help you become less defensive, more tolerant of others in the twenty centuries of Christian tradition. As this century wanes, we miss the finely-construed judgment, delightful realism, and unsinkable humor of Albert Outler.

We commend Outler's volume on John Wesley in the Library of Protestant Theology series as a companion in this study for neophytes in Wesley, and his four-volume commentary on Wesley's Sermons for those who wish to probe further. These essays are best read as commentary upon and supplement to the Wesley text itself.

These essays have been edited with Outler's permission and full cooperation. He was actively engaged in the project up to the point of his death, September 1, 1989. The modest editorial intent has been to make the essays accessible as a sequential argument. Although the entire volume has been a cooperative effort of editing at every turn, Oden has taken major responsibility for drafting the Introduction, while Longden has taken major responsibility for drafting the discrete introductions that bridge essay to essay, and for annotations and scholarly apparatus. The overall organization and sequencing of the essays has been throughout a joint effort. The editors' notes appear in brackets.

The essays fall naturally into two parts, first, those that discuss the antecedents of the Wesleyan theological heritage in Wesley and his sources. In Part One, "Wesley as Theological Mentor," we have selected essays that show the development of Outler's project for the recovery of Wesley by establishing a critical text, by releasing Wesley from the Methodist cocoon, and by formulating his distinctive understanding of theology. In Part Two, on "Spirit and Church in the Wesleyan Tradition," we have selected essays that focus upon the consequences of the Wesleyan theological heritage for theology, society, ecumenicity, and contemporary ecclesiology.

Special thanks are due to the libraries of Perkins School of Theology, Southern Methodist University, and Drew University, for many kindnesses in this project, and to Dirk Rodgers for linguistic-philological assistance, and to Carla Outler for many acts of thoughtfulness in encouraging this project.

Easter 1990
The Drew Forest

Acknowledgments

We would like to acknowledge the following for permission to reprint the essays listed:

Abingdon Press
"Do Methodists Have a Doctrine of the Church?" From THE DOCTRINE OF THE CHURCH edited by Dow Kirkpatrick. Copyright © 1964 by Abingdon Press. Used by permission.
"Methodism's Theological Heritage: A Study in Perspective." From METHODISM'S DESTINY IN THE ECUMENICAL AGE edited by Paul Minus, Jr. Copyright © 1969 Abingdon Press. Used by permission.
"A New Future for Wesley Studies: An Agenda for 'Phase III.'" From THE FUTURE OF METHODIST THEOLOGICAL TRADITIONS by M. Douglas Meeks. Copyright © 1985 Abingdon Press. Used by permission.

The Committee on Archives and History of the United Church of Canada
"John Wesley's Interests in the Early Fathers of the Church." *The Bulletin* 29 (1983).

The Consultation on Church Union
"The Mingling of Ministries." *Digest of the Proceedings of the Eighth Meeting of the Consultation on Church Union*, ed. Paul A. Crow, Jr. (1969).

The General Commission on Archives and History of the United Methodist Church
"John Wesley as Theologian—Then and Now." *Methodist History* 12 (July 1974).

Perkins School of Theology
"Towards a Re-Appraisal of John Wesley as a Theologian." *Perkins Journal* 14 (Winter 1961).

"Pastoral Care in the Wesleyan Spirit." *Perkins Journal* 25 (Fall 1971). "A Sermon for the Uniting Conference of the United Methodist Church" [reprinted here under its orginal title "Visions and Dreams: The Unfinished Business of an Unfinished Church"]. *Perkins Journal* 27 (Spring 1974).

The Scarecrow Press

"The Place of Wesley in the Christian Tradition." Reprinted by permission from *The Place of Wesley in the Christian Tradition: Essays delivered at Drew University in celebration of the commencement of the publication of the Oxford Edition of the Works of John Wesley* by Kenneth Rowe (Metuchen, N.J.: Scarecrow Press, Inc. 1976). Copyright © by Kenneth Rowe.

Theology Today

"John Wesley: Folk-Theologian." *Theology Today* 34 (July 1977).

University of Illinois Press

" 'Biblical Primitivism' in Early American Methodism." *The American Quest for the Primitive Church*, ed. Richard T. Hughes (1988).

The United Methodist Publishing House

"A Focus on the Holy Spirit: Spirit and Spirituality in John Wesley." *Quarterly Review* 8 (Summer 1988).

The World Methodist Historical Society

"Methodism in the World Christian Community." *Dig or Die*, ed. James S. Udy and Eric G. Clancy (1981). This address was delivered at the World Methodist Historical Society Wesley Heritage Conference at Wesley College within The University of Sydney, Australia, 10–15 August 1980. Used by permission.

Wesleyan Theological Journal

"The Wesleyan Quadrilateral—in John Wesley." *Wesleyan Theological Journal* 20 (Spring 1985).

Abbreviations

COC   Philip Schaff, ed. *The Creeds of Christendom.* 3 vols. New York: Harper, 1919.

HMT   Heiko A. Obermann. *The Harvest of Medieval Theology.* Cambridge, Mass.: Harvard University Press, 1963.

JWJ   Nehemiah Curnock, ed. *The Journal of the Rev. John Wesley, A.M. . . . Enlarged From Original Manuscripts.* 8 vols. London: Charles H. Kelly, 1909–16.

JWL   John Telford, ed. *The Letters of the Rev. John Wesley.* 8 vols. London: Epworth, 1931.

JWLB   Frank Baker, ed. *Letters of John Wesley.* Vols. 25–26 in *The Works of John Wesley.* Oxford/Bicentennial Edition. Oxford: Clarendon Press, 1975–83; Nashville: Abingdon, 1984–.

JWO   Albert C. Outler, ed. *John Wesley.* A LIBRARY OF PROTESTANT THOUGHT. New York: Oxford University Press, 1964.

JWW   Thomas Jackson, ed. *The Works of the Rev. John Wesley.* 3d ed. 14 vols. London: Mason, 1829–31.

WJWB   *The Works of John Wesley.* Oxford/Bicentennial Edition. Oxford: Clarendon Press, 1975–83; Nashville: Abingdon, 1984–.

Wesley as Theological Mentor

The Wesleyan Quadrilateral— in John Wesley

—✝—

[1985] The lead essay in this collection sets forth Albert Outler's lifelong conviction: the evangelical and ecumenical resources of John Wesley's theology have yet to be fully claimed by the heirs of the Wesleyan tradition. Outler shows that Wesley guided the Methodist movement by means of a distinctive theological method using Scripture as "pre-eminent norm" in conjunction with an "interactive" appeal to tradition, reason, and experience. Although not completely satisfied with the term "quadrilateral," which he coined to describe this method, Outler remained convinced of its significance for contemporary theologizing and acknowledged his own debt to Wesley as tutor and spiritual guide.

For five full decades, John Wesley served as theological mentor to "the people called Methodists," with no peer and no successful challengers. Throughout that half-century, he was embroiled in one doctrinal controversy after another—with Anglican priests and bishops, with Calvinist partisans (clerical and lay) and with occasional dissidents within his own "connexion." Doctrinal consensus was a prime concern with him and a prerequisite for stability in the Methodist Societies. Thus, at the outset of his first "conference" with his "assistants" (1744), the first questions posed for discussion were:

(1) *What* to teach?
(2) *How* to teach?
(3) What to *do* (i.e., how to regulate our doctrine, discipline and practice)?

There was, of course, no question in anyone's mind as to who would have the final word in these conversations, but everyone agreed that these were the right questions for a religious society within an established church.

EARLY METHODISM'S THEOLOGICAL CHARTER

As the Methodist movement spread and matured, Wesley supplied it with reams of theological and ethical instruction, in different *genres:* sermons, letters, tracts, exegetical notes, a huge *Journal,* even a full-length monograph (*The Doctrine of Original Sin*). But—and this, of course, is my point—there is only one instance in all of this of anything resembling a doctrinal credo (in his open "Letter to a Roman Catholic," 1749) and even this was an obvious borrowing from Bishop John Pearson's classic *Exposition of the Doctrine of the Creed*—the bishop's counterpart to the Westminster Confession and Shorter Catechism. Wesley seems never to have toyed with the notion of a *summa theologiae*—not even a catechism. What then did he expect his people to identify as their "standards of doctrine"?

His first move had been to abridge the first four Edwardian *Homilies* (of 1547) into a brief theological charter: *The Doctrine of Justification according to the Church of England* (cf. *Journal*, Nov. 12,

1738). Then as the Revival gained momentum, he turned to the method of conciliar dialogue, gathering his assistants together by invitation. He himself recorded the upshot of their discussions and published this in a cumulative set of *Minutes of Conversations Between the Rev. Mr. Wesley and Others* (1744 et. seq.). The theological substance of these "minutes" reflects the mind and spirit of early Methodism very well indeed. A version of them ("The Large Minutes") was accepted by the fledgling Methodist Episcopal Church in America and so may be considered as included within the scope of that notoriously ambiguous phrase in "The First Restrictive Rule" (1808) in the Methodist *Book of Discipline* concerning "our present existing, and established, standards of doctrine."

In 1763, in what came to be known as "The Model Deed" Wesley proceeded to stipulate the *negative limits* of Methodist doctrine—viz., that preachers in Methodist chapels were to preach "no other doctrine than is contained in Mr. Wesley's *Notes Upon the New Testament* and four volumes of *Sermons.*" This provided his people with a doctrinal canon that was stable enough and yet also flexible. In it, the Holy Scriptures stand first and foremost, and yet subject to interpretations that are informed in "Christian Antiquity," critical reason *and* an existential appeal to the "Christian experience" of grace, so firmly stressed in the *Explanatory Notes.* The "four volumes" mentioned in the "Model Deed" contained either forty-three or forty-four sermons, depending on whether or not one counts "Wandering Thoughts" (it was not in the first edition of the "four volumes" [1760] but appeared in subsequent editions [before 1763]). All this suggests that Wesley was clearly interested in coherent doctrinal norms but was equally clear in his aversion to having such norms defined too narrowly or in too juridical a form. Thus, he was content with exegetical "notes" (eager to borrow heavily from others), plus a sampling of sermons (he would have dismissed all haggling over the *number* of "standard sermons"!)—and, of course, the Wesley hymns (Charles' and his own). These non-confessional norms served his people well for the better part of two full centuries.

Wesley's refusal to define "doctrinal standards" too narrowly was a matter of principle: it was in no way the sign of an indecisive mind. Such a notion makes no sense when one considers how confident his own theological self-understanding was (as reflected in his controversial writings), and in his arbitrary decisions as an editor. Take a single example from several hundred: in *A Christian Library* (vol. 31), he felt free to make some fairly drastic revisions of the *Westminster Shorter Catechism* and thus on his own authority to "correct" what was a semi-sacrosanct text! Then, too, there were his equally drastic revisions of the Book of Common Prayer, with his brusque self-justification for simply having omitted a large fraction of the Psalter, characterizing the excluded Psalms as "not fit for the mouths of a Christian congregation." No, Wesley's refusal to provide the Methodist people with a confession for subscription was the conviction of a man who knew his own mind on every vexed question of Christian doctrine, but who had decided that the reduction of doctrine to any particular form of words was to misunderstand the very nature of doctrinal statements.

WESLEY'S THEOLOGICAL METHOD

But does this mean, then, that Wesley was an indifferentist? *Me genoito!* [Absolutely not!] His working concepts of doctrinal authority were carefully worked out; they were complex and dynamically balanced. When challenged for his authority, on any question, his first appeal was to the Holy Bible, always in the sense of Article VI in the XXXIX Articles—to which he had subscribed but which he was prepared to quote inexactly. Even so, he was well aware that Scripture alone had rarely settled any controverted point of doctrine. He and his critics had repeatedly come to impasses in their games of prooftexting—often with the same texts! Thus, though never as a substitute or corrective, he would also appeal to "the primitive church" and to the Christian tradition at large as competent, complementary witnesses to "the meaning" of this Scripture or that. Even in such appeals, he was carefully selective. For example, he claimed the right to reject the damnatory clauses in the so-called "Athanasian Creed"; he was prepared to defend Montanus *and Pelagius* against their detractors. He insisted that "private judgment" was the keystone of the Protestant Reformation.

But Scripture and tradition would not suffice without the good offices (positive and negative) of critical reason. Thus, he insisted on logical coherence and as an authorized referee in any contest between contrary propositions or arguments. And yet, this was never enough. It was, as he knew for himself, the vital Christian experience of the assurance of one's sins forgiven that clinched the matter.

Thus, we can see in Wesley a distinctive theological *method*, with Scripture as its pre-eminent norm but interfaced with tradition, reason, and Christian experience as dynamic and interactive aids in the interpretation of the Word of God in Scripture. Such a method takes it for granted that faith is human *re*-action to an antecedent action of the Holy Spirit's prevenience, aimed at convicting our consciences and opening our eyes and ears to God's address to us in Scripture. This means that our "knowledge of God and of the things of God" is more nearly a response of trusting faith in God in Christ as Grace Incarnate than it is a mental assent to dogmatic formulations however true. This helps explain Wesley's studied deprecations of "orthodoxy," "theological opinions," "speculative divinity" and the like. It illumines his preoccupation with soteriology and his distinctive notion of grace, in all its modes, as the divine constant in every stage of the "order of salvation" (from repentance and just-ification, to regeneration, sanctification—on to glory). And it justified Wesley's willingness, given honest consensus on essen-tial Christian doctrine, to allow for wide variations in theological formulation and thus for Christians "to think and let think." This was less a mood of doctrinal compromise than it was a construc-tive alternative to the barren extremes of "dogmatism," on the one side, and "indifferentism," on the other.

Wesley's theological pluralism was evangelical in substance (firm and clear in its Christocentric focus) and irenic in its temper ("catholic spirit"). It measured all doctrinal statements by their biblical base and warrants. He loved to summon his readers "to the letter and the testimony," understood as "the oracles of God." But this reliance on Scripture as *the* fount of revelation was never meant to preclude a concomitant appeal to the insights of wise and saintly Christians in other ages. And it never gave license to "enthusiasm" or to irrational arguments. Finally, since the devils are at least as clear in their theological assents as believers are, real Christians are called beyond "orthodoxy" to authentic experi-ence—viz., the inner witness of the Holy Spirit that *we* are God's beloved children, and joint-heirs with Christ. It is this settled sense of personal assurance that is "heart-religion": the turning of our hearts from the form to the power of religion. Christian experience adds nothing to the substance of Christian truth; its distinctive role is to energize the heart so as to enable the believer to speak and do the truth in love.

This complex method, with its fourfold reference, is a good

deal more sophisticated than it appears, and could be more fruitful for contemporary theologizing than has yet been realized. It preserves the primacy of Scripture, it profits from the wisdom of tradition, it accepts the disciplines of critical reason, and its stress on the Christian experience of grace gives it existential force.

EXPERIENCE: WESLEY'S AMENDMENT TO THE ANGLICAN TRIAD

The Edwardian reformers (Cranmer and Harpsfield in particular) had placed the Church of England under the authority of Scripture but they had then refocused its use more largely in the liturgy (so that "the Christian folk could be immersed in Scripture as they prayed!"). The Scripture is equally the baseline of Anglican doctrinal essays, especially those born of controversy. One has only to notice the differences in method and intention in, say, Richard Hooker's *Laws of Ecclesiastical Polity* (1594 *et. seq.*) to see how far Anglicanism stood apart from continental Protestantism. In Hooker, Scripture, tradition, and reason are carefully balanced off in a vision of natural law, "whose seat is the bosom of God, whose voice is the harmony of the world" (E.P.,I, XVI, 8). There is no contradiction between reason's discoveries of natural law and faith's discoveries of revelation (cf. E.P. III, ix, 2). Bishops John Bramhall and Simon Patrick had mastered "Christian Antiquity" and had put it to good use. Thomas Tenison (Archbishop of Canterbury when the brothers Wesley were born) had defined "the Protestant theological method" as the conjoint "use of Scripture, tradition and reason" and had defended this against the Socinians (who had, as Tenison believed, downscaled tradition and ended up with nothing better than a tepid biblical rationalism). Even after Wesley, Francis Paget (Hooker's best editor) could claim, quite plausibly, that "the distinctive strength of Anglicanism rests on its equal loyalty to the unconflicting rights of reason, Scripture and tradition." This, then, was the tradition within which Wesley took his stand; before the judgment bar of "Scripture, right reason and Christian Antiquity" (*Works*, Preface, vol. 1, 1771).

It was Wesley's special genius that he conceived of adding "experience" to the traditional Anglican triad, and thereby adding vitality without altering the substance. What he did was to apply the familiar distinction between *fides quae creditur* and *fides qua creditur* (from a theoretical faith to an existential one) so as to insist on "heart religion" in place of all nominal Christian orthodoxy (cf. "The Almost Christian"). He had found support for this in Cranmer's wry comment (in *Homilies*, IV), about the devils who *assent* to every tenet of orthodoxy, "and yet they be but devils still." It was this added emphasis on "experience" that led Gerald Cragg (in his *Reason and Authority in the 18th Century*) to entitle his chapter on Wesley, "The Authority of Revitalized Faith." Wesley would have amended that to read "The Authority of Vital Faith."

With this "fourth dimension," one might say, Wesley was trying to incorporate the notion of *conversion* into the Anglican tradition—to make room in it for his own conversions and those of others. It is not irrelevant that in his report of the so-called "Aldersgate experience" of May 24th, 1738, he takes us back to his very first conversion (to "seriousness" and self-dedication in 1725); thence on to his grand mystical illumination in 1727. After "Aldersgate" and after his ambivalent encounters with the Moravians in Herrnhut, the *Journal* recounts his rediscovery of a vital doctrine of justification by faith *in his own tradition*, in November of 1738. But this had then been followed by a lapse into the depths of religious anxiety (in January 1739). The process then reached its climax in the spring of 1739 with the "discovery" of his true and life-long vocation as an evangelist and spiritual director.

The success of Methodism as a religious society within the Church of England bolstered his sense of freedom to amend Anglican customs without rejecting the Anglican heritage. He quietly ignored the possibility that, in the process of reforming the national church, he was opening a way for his "societies" eventually to "separate" and go it alone as "sects" trying to become "churches" on their own. Over against the Anglican tradition of the church as *corpus mixtum*, Wesley demanded more of his societies, as disciplined communities of true believers. Against the Anglican reliance on church as ministrant of the means of grace, Wesley opposed the doctrine of justification by faith *alone* (and argued, mistakenly, that this doctrine was a novelty in Anglicanism!). To the Anglican tradition of baptismal regeneration he added conversion and "new birth" as a Gospel requisite. To the Anglican contentment with the Book of Common Prayer as a complete blueprint, Wesley added a medley of "irregularities": field-preaching, extempore prayer, itinerancy, class meetings and the like. To the Anglican tradition of the "natural" alliance between church and state, he opposed the concept of church as a *voluntary association*. The effect of such changes was to put the question of authority into a new context: to relate it more nearly to the individual's conscience, to small group consensus, and also to link it practically with the ideal of "accountable discipleship," (to use an apt phrase of David Watson's).[1] The practical effect of this was to make every Methodist man and woman his/her own theologian. He nowhere gave his people an actual paradigm for their theologizing; somehow, he hoped that they would adopt his ways of reflection as their own. The truth is, however, that his bare texts, unannotated, did not suffice to make true "Wesleyans" out of those who have continued to bear his name and who honor him as patriarch. This is why the editors of the new edition of his *Works* hope that more ample annotations will help both "Wesleyans" and non-Wesleyans in the "discovery" of the richness and sophistication of his special sort of "folk-theology."

THE CORE OF THE WESLEYAN QUADRILATERAL

Even that cheerful thought may be thwarted, however, so long as the phrase "the Wesleyan quadrilateral" is taken too literally. It was intended as a metaphor for a four-element syndrome, including the fourfold guidelines of authority in Wesley's theological method. In such a quaternity, Holy Scripture is clearly unique. But this in turn is illuminated by the collective Christian wisdom of other ages and cultures between the Apostolic Age and our own. It also allows for the rescue of the Gospel from obscurantism by means of the disciplines of critical reason. But always, biblical revelation must be received in the heart by faith: this is the requirement of "experience." Wesley's theology was eclectic and pluralistic (and I confess my bafflement at the hostility aroused in some minds by such innocent adjectives). Even so, it was a coherent, stable, whole, deriving its fruitfulness from its single, soteriological focus in the Christian evangel of *Jesus Christ*—"who for us men *and for our salvation* came down from heaven and was made *man!*"

When I first began reading Wesley's entire corpus with some care (after many years as a credentialed professor of the "history of Christian thought"), I was puzzled by the score or more brief

---

[1][David Lowes Watson, *Accountable Discipleship* (Nashville: Discipleship Resources, 1984); also *The Early Methodist Class Meeting: Its Origins and Significance* (Nashville: Discipleship Resources, 1985).]

summations of "the Gospel" that Wesley sprinkles almost casually along the way—never twice in the same form of words (which suggests that, before Coleridge or Wittgenstein, Wesley had come upon the secret that language [and the language of religion in particular] is, by its nature, "incomplete"). Little by little, it dawned on me that Wesley's purpose in these summaries was to refocus the entire range of his theological reflection upon the crux of the matter: which is to say, *salvation*. For example:

> "Let us prophesy according to the analogy of faith"—St. Peter expresses it, "as the oracles of God"; according to the general temper of them, according to that grand scheme of doctrine which is delivered therein touching original sin, justification by faith and present, inward salvation. There is a wonderful analogy between all these, and a close and intimate connexion between the chief heads of that faith "which was once for all delivered to the saints." [*Explanatory Notes*, on Romans 12:6, on "the analogy of faith"].

He is eager for theological dialogue, but his real concern is with

> the most essential parts of real experimental religion: its initial rise in the soul, that goes on to faith in our Lord Jesus Christ, which issues in regeneration, is attended with peace and joy in the Holy Ghost, thence to our wrestlings with flesh and blood, and finally to perfect love.[2]

All Wesleyans are familiar with his metaphors of "porch," "door" and "room" of "true religion" [*The Principles of a Methodist*, in *JWW* VIII:472–74]. Similar encapsulations of the *ordo salutis* abound, some in obvious places but some in unexpected places— as, for example, in the "Preface" to the *Explanatory Notes Upon the Old Testament* (the vast bulk of which was simply lifted from others):

> [In your reading of the Scriptures] have a constant eye to the analogy of the faith, [which is to say], the connexion and harmony there is between those grand fundamental doctrines of

[2][Outler has condensed these words of Wesley from a longer passage. See "A Second Letter to the Author of the Enthusiasm of the Methodists and Papists Compar'd" in *WJWB* 11:381.]

original sin, justification by faith, the new birth, inward and outward holiness.

As an Anglican priest, he will assume a shared faith with "A Gentleman of Bristol" (Jan. 6, 1758) in

the principles of the Church of England as being confirmed by our Liturgy, Articles and Homilies—and so also by the whole tenor of Scripture [notice this catch phrase; it is a favorite, repeated in many different contexts].

In another place, he summarized the essential Gospel in yet another set of theses:
1. That without holiness no man shall see the Lord:
2. That this holiness is the work of God, who worketh in us both to will and to do;
3. That he doeth it of his own good pleasure, merely for the merits of Christ;
4. That holiness is having the mind that was in Christ, enabling us to walk as He walked;
5. That no man can be thus sanctified till he be justified;
6. That we are justified by faith alone.[3]

This comes in a sermon; this particular form of words is never used again.

The obvious methodological question posed by summaries like this is whether such variant expressions oversimplify or distort "the *essence* of the Christian Gospel." For Wesley, it was enough to point to its soteriological core in evangelical terms. As far as the full range of theological opinions is concerned, he is more relaxed—even to the point of tolerating the "overbeliefs" of the Roman Catholics and also the Reformed doctrines of election and predestination. It is this skillful balancing of the essentials off from the adiaphora that allows Wesley to escape both the rigidities of dogmatism *and* the flabbiness of indifferentism.

THE APPEAL TO SCRIPTURE

In the new edition of *Wesley's Works*, we have tried to alert even the casual reader to the extent to which Wesley was, as he claimed he was, *homo unius libri*. To an extent that I had not

[3]["The General Spread of the Gospel," ¶13.]

realized before I wore out the first of two concordances we used in tracing down Wesley's Scripture citations (quotations, paraphrases, allusions, echoes) the Bible was truly his second language. His rhetoric throughout is a tissue woven from the biblical texts and paraphrases and his own crisp Augustan prose ("plain truth for plain people"). His appeal to Scripture goes far deeper than the use of texts in support of his own views. His larger concern was to let each part of Scripture be pondered in the light of the whole, obscure texts in the light of the more lucid ones—and all of them, always, in the spirit of prayer, *coram Deo*. Scripture is not merely God's address to the believer—it is inspired by the Holy Spirit who in turn inspires the believer's understanding. The Bible is to be read *literally*, save where such a reading leads to an absurdity or to an impugnation of God's goodness. Scriptural commands are not to be construed legalistically; they are to be seen also as "covered promises." Even allegory is occasionally resorted to (as with the image of "The Wilderness State"). The Apocrypha may be used for edification, though not for sermon texts. Wesley was capable of partisan prooftexting; and yet also felt free to alter the *Textus Receptus* by appeal to older MSS; and he had no qualms in nuancing some Greek words arbitrarily (as with *paroxusmos* in Acts 15:39), where he insists that only Barnabas lost *his* temper, but never St. Paul. The clearest impression that remains after all the tedium of tracing Wesley's biblical sources is of a man very much at home in the Bible and quietly confident of his understanding of its "general tenor."

THE APPEAL TO TRADITION

There is another sense, however, in which the notion of Wesley as the man of "one book only" is patently absurd. He read voraciously and in all genres. He had a special fondness for the Fathers of the early centuries. He thought that the Greek theologians had understood the Gospel more profoundly and therapeutically than their Latin counterparts. He came at the Fathers with an Anglican bias (he had been at Oxford in the twilight of a great age of patristic scholarship), in the tradition of Richard Field, Henry Hammond and Simon Patrick. He was not in the least intimidated by learned detractors of patristic wisdom (like Jean Daille and Conyers Middleton).

What Wesley learned most from the Eastern Fathers was the

rich notion of the Christian life as a participation in the divine (i.e., salvation as the restoration of the ruined image of God in the human soul). The stage for his Aldersgate experience had been set by the Scripture with which he began that day: 2 Peter 1:4 (cf. Wesley's paraphrase: *ta megista hemin timia epangelmata dedōretai, hina genesthe theias koinōnoi phuseōs,* and the crucial phrase, "partakers of the divine *phusis*").[4] It was in this sense of "participation" in the divine life that Wesley had already understood the mysteries of grace and free will, of prevenient grace as the Holy Spirit's constant initiative, of "perfection" as a process rather than a completed act. There is much Anselmian language in Wesley ("acquittal," "imputation"), but there is even more that stresses the notion of healing (*therapeia psuches* "healing of souls"). He was neither "Augustinian" (indeed, he has some tart comments about the great bishop), nor "Pelagian" (he actually doubted that *Pelagius* had been a "Pelagian")—and he could interpret *dikaiosune* not only as the "imputation" of Christ's righteousness to the repentant believer but also its "impartation" as well.

From the Latin traditions, he seems to have learned most from men like William of St. Thierry—who had taught that *love* is the highest form of *knowledge*—and from the Victorines (Ruprecht of Deutz, Hugh, *et al.*) with their bold notion that God had used the Adamic Fall to bring about a greater total good than if Adam had not sinned (*O felix culpa!*).

All of this is a way of saying that, for Wesley, the Christian tradition was more than a curiosity or a source for illustrative material. It was a living spring of Christian insight. Reading Wesley against his sources amounts to an eccentric excursion through the length and breadth of the history of Christian thought. And because a lively sense of "tradition" has now come to be a prerequisite in ecumenical dialogue (cf. J. J. Pelikan's essay, *The Vindication of Tradition*), it is all the more important for Wesleyans (and others), to discover how much he had learned from the Christian past and thus also to learn for ourselves the importance of being truly at home in that past.

THE APPEAL TO REASON

But Wesley was no antiquarian. We know of his inborn tendency to require a reason for everything from his father's well-

[4]*JWJ* I:472.

known complaint to Susanna about his personal habits. He never discounted his university training in logic nor his life-long interest in contemporary science and culture. He lived in the perilous transition from an earlier theocentric rationalism that sought to reconcile religion and science (as in John Ray's *Wisdom of God in Creation*—the prototype for Wesley's *Survey of the Wisdom of God in Creation*) to the Enlightenment's outright rejection of supernaturalism (as in the deists and David Hume). To be a theologian in eighteenth-century Britain was to struggle with deism and secularism (cf. Joseph Butler, William Paley, *et. al.*). Wesley's acknowledgment of rationality as normative was both principled and pragmatic. He took logical order as a paradigm for the order of being itself (as any good Ramist[5] would, or later, the Kantians). He remained a disciple of Locke and Aldrich all his days. But his vivid sense of mystery kept him aware of reason's limitations (as in "The Case of Reason Impartially Considered"). Richard Brantley (in *Locke, Wesley and the Method of English Romanticism*, 1984) has analyzed Locke's influence on Wesley. But no one, to my knowledge, has provided a comparable study of Wesley and Malebranche, or the Cambridge Platonists, or John Norris, or Bishop Berkeley, *et. al.*

Wesley's understanding of reason led him to a religious epistemology that hinges, crucially, on his view of intuition as a "'spiritual sensorium'" in the human mind that constitutes what is most distinctively human, viz., our capacity for God. This is part of God's creative design and it points to the chief inlet of the Holy Spirit into the human soul and spirit. A dissertation was accepted recently by Rome's Angelicum University on *The Perceptibility of Grace in John Wesley* (by Daniel Joseph Luby—a layman!). It is a superb probing of the importance, for Wesley, of "immediate perception" [of spiritual reality]. Such unexpected developments remind us of how much we also need a full-fledged monograph on "*rationality* in the Wesleyan spirit." Even so, "our knowledge of God and of the things of God" does not come from intuition, inference, or deduction alone. Always it is a prevenient and unmerited *gift* and must, therefore, be experienced as an inward change of heart and head in which the mind's intuitions of the

---

[5][For Wesley's assimilation of Ramist influences see *The Encyclopedia of Philosophy* VII:66–67].

truth are *realized* in the heart (as when *Christus pro nobis* becomes *Christus pro me*).

Here a careful distinction is needed. The "experience of grace" is indeed deeply inward, but it is not a merely subjective "religious affection." It is an objective encounter (within "the heart," to be sure) of something not ourselves and not our own (something truly transcendent). It is an inward assurance of an objective reality, viz., God's unmerited favor and pardoning mercy, an awareness of the Spirit's prevenient action in mediating the grace of our Lord Jesus Christ to the believer. It is, therefore, the experience of a *given*—a divine action that can only be reacted to, in trusting faith or in prideful resistance. It is this stress upon the sheer givenness of spiritual insight and of divine grace that distinguishes Wesley from Pelagius—and for that matter, from Arminius and Episcopius. Had he known of Kant (his younger contemporary!) Wesley would have agreed with at least the first two paragraphs of his first *Critique of Practical Reason* (1788):

> There can be no doubt that all our knowledge begins with experience. . . . In the order of time, therefore, we have no knowledge antecedent to experience and with experience all our knowledge begins.
>
> But though all our knowledge begins with experience, it does *not* follow that it arises *out of experience*.

When, therefore, zealous and pious souls conclude that the intensity or inwardness of their own feelings is the measure of truth (and when they invoke Wesley's "strangely warmed heart" as a witness to such a correlation) nothing but pious sentimentality can ensue and, with it, a sort of narcissism that readily turns into an anti-intellectualism. The verb forms in the familiar phrase, "I felt my heart strangely warmed" give us an underdeveloped clue. "I felt" is in the *active* voice; "strangely warmed" is *passive*.

In this light, one may read with profit another of Wesley's "summaries," this one of the gist of Christian experience at its best:

> It is hard to find words . . . indeed there are none that will adequately express [and he was serious in his conviction that religious language is apophatic and, therefore, also polysemous] what the children of God experience. But perhaps one might say (desiring any who are taught of God to soften or strengthen the

expression) that "the testimony of the Spirit" is an inward expression *on the soul,* whereby the Spirit of God directly witnesses to my spirit that *I* am a child of God, that Jesus Christ hath loved *me* and given Himself for *me*—and that all my sins are blotted out and that I, even I, am reconciled to God ["The Witness of the Spirit," I.i.7].

Dr. Sugden's comment on this passage, invoking the authority of W. B. Pope, takes Wesley to task for this emphasis on the *objectivity* of the Spirit's activity and of the human role as wholly reactive. This reminds us of how, in the history of Methodist theologizing, Wesley's heroic efforts to save us from subjectivity and sentimentality have so often gone so largely for naught.

THE PAST AND FUTURE OF THE
WESLEYAN QUADRILATERAL

Wesley's theological method was distinctive, and maybe unique (for one cannot identify any of his disciples who adopted it as a whole or in his theological spirit). Adam Clarke, Richard Watson, W. B. Pope, and others grasped much of the substance of the patriarch's teaching, but they were bent on remaking him into a *biblicist* (Clarke) or a *systematic* theologian (Watson and Pope). Indeed, Watson went so far as to entitle his own exposition of Wesleyan theology in the Calvinist fashion, *Theological Institutes.*

All Wesleyans have agreed on the primacy of Scripture and then differed (not always helpfully) in their hermeneutical perspectives. This seems to me to have come from a neglect of Wesley's own hermeneutical focus on "the analogy of faith"; I cannot cite a single essay by a Wesleyan exegete or theologian in which the *analogia fidei* is a governing notion. In the nineteenth century, Wesley's reliance on the Christian tradition as a whole (and especially the Fathers) was quietly jettisoned (even by Methodist historians, like Sheldon and Cell). His confidence in reason, *within its proper limits,* has given way to an emotive anti-intellectualism or else its opposite, e.g., an overconfidence in reason (as in Bowne and Brightman). His focus on "experience"— *as a soteriological category*—has been turned into a variety of empiricisms, bolstered by a pragmatic appeal to "practical results."

The term "quadrilateral" does not occur in the Wesley corpus—and more than once, I have regretted having coined it for contemporary use, since it has been so widely misconstrued. But if we are to accept our responsibility for seeking *intellecta* [concepts, ideas] for our faith, in any other fashion than a "theological system" or, alternatively, a juridical statement of "doctrinal standards," then this method of a conjoint recourse to the fourfold guidelines of Scripture, tradition, reason, and experience, may hold more promise for an evangelical and ecumenical future than we have realized as yet—by comparison, for example, with biblic*ism*, or traditional*ism*, or, rational*ism*, or empiric*ism*. It is far more valid than the reduction of Christian authority to the dyad of "Scripture" and "experience" (so common in Methodist ranks today). The "quadrilateral" requires of a theologian no more than what he or she might reasonably be held accountable for, which is to say, a familiarity with Scripture that is both critical and faithful; plus, an acquaintance with the wisdom of the Christian past; plus, a taste for logical analysis as something more than a debater's weapon; plus, a vital, inward faith that is upheld by the assurance of grace and its prospective triumphs, *in this life.*

The epoch that looms before us, whether we like it or no, is a postliberal age, in which the dogmatisms of the pre-Enlightenment orthodoxies and the confident dogmas of "liberalism" (e.g., "progress" and "human perfectibility") will come to seem increasingly outmoded. It is, predictably, a time of troubles for the whole world, with no assured future for our plundered planet or for a humanity addicted to self-defeating strategies masked with the illusions of good intentions. The still-divided fragments of the Christian community are more interested in honest doctrinal consensus than ever before. But this is also to say that it is a time when the study of Wesley has a distinctive contribution to make.

Neither Wesley's theology nor his methods are simple panaceas. They are not like the TV dinners that can be reheated and served up quickly for immediate use. They call for imaginative updating in the new world cultural contexts (the sort of thing that John XXIII spoke of as *aggiornamento*—care in preserving the kernel, imagination in renovating the medium). Wesley's vision of Christian existence has to be reconceived and transvalued so that it can be as relevant in the experience of the late twentieth century as it was to alienated English men and women in 1740! This requires that it must be refocused in ways neither doctrinaire on the one hand, nor trendy on the other. Wesley avoided such barren polarizations and so, one thinks, we may also—if our theologians, like his, are as deeply immersed in Scripture (at home in its imagery and mystery), as truly respectful of the Christian wisdom of past ages, as honestly open to the disciplines of critical reason, as eagerly alert to the fire and flame of grace.

Wesley's complex way of theologizing has the ecumenical advantage of making fruitful linkages with other doctrinal traditions without threatening to supplant any of them and without fear of forfeiting its own identity. There are, however, at least two prior conditions for such linkages: that Wesley be rescued from the stereotypes in which his professed disciples have cocooned him, and that we recover for ourselves the rich manifold of *tradition* from which he drew so freely and creatively. These conditions can be best met by learning more and more from Wesley himself (the whole Wesley, including "the later Mr. Wesley" as reflected in *A Christian Library* and *The Arminian Magazine*) and yet also learning more and more, and on our own, from the rich manifold of Christian traditions from which Wesley learned so much.

This is a daunting challenge and I freely confess that it is more of a task that I have myself been able to bring off to my own satisfaction. But I can testify, with great gratitude, that my communing with Wesley and his sources has been immensely enriching, in my theological concerns and in my own growth in grace. It is, therefore, with full assurance that I commend such explorations, not only to those who bear the Wesleyan insignia, but to all others who may care to extend their acquaintance with a rare man of God.

Towards a Re-Appraisal of John Wesley as a Theologian

———†———

[1961] Outler's Presidential Address to the American
Theological Society became one of his first published
presentations of the case for a re-examination of Wesley
and the inherited assumptions about him. Outler offers
fascinating glimpses of the politics, burdens, and surprises
of the research required to provide a critical text of
Wesley's works.

John Wesley has a secure niche in church history, as a great evangelist and organizer. His stature as a theologian is much more doubtful. Methodists have tended to stress his warm heart and his zeal—prized virtues among us! Non-Methodists have had scant stimulus to look behind this stereotype.

It may be mere gallantry, then, for me to argue in this august company that:

1. Wesley was a major *theologian*.
2. His methodology and motifs are still significant for contemporary theology.
3. He has rarely been fairly and fully read, whether by his champions or detractors.
4. This is partly due to the fact that there is no proper (critical) edition of his writings.

I do not expect these propositions to appear self-evidently true. Indeed, I have come to be persuaded of them somewhat latterly, and this in the course of an assignment that has turned out far differently than I had expected.

When the program of A LIBRARY OF PROTESTANT THOUGHT was being shaped up, I proposed a volume of Wesley's specifically theological writings, in a critical text and with proper footnotes—to provide students with some primary source material that is not easily accessible and that consequently goes unread. The idea was coolly received at first, and several counter-proposals were suggested. Why not, said one, put John and Charles together in one volume along with John Fletcher? Or again, put Wesley in a volume along with Whitefield, Venn, Romaine and Simeon. Yet another scheme would have combined Wesley, Zinzendorf and Francke. In the end, it was voted that John Wesley should have a volume of his own—but then, as so often happens, the proposer was handed the job.

It seemed a manageable assignment until I got into it. Partly because of my patristics training and party because of the reservations earlier expressed, I wanted to do the sort of job on Wesley one would do on Origen or Augustine. The obvious place to begin was with the texts of the various items I wanted to consider for inclusion. It was not till then that I discovered that save for the Curnock edition of the Journal, the Telford edition of the Letters, and the Sugden edition of the Standard Sermons, no serious critical editing had been done on the Wesley corpus since the Jackson edition of 1829–31. What was more, the Jackson edition was neither comprehensive nor critical—and its attention to context and background was negligible. Yet this is the text which has been reprinted throughout the last 130 years without revision—this is the text of the Zondervan reprint, despite the publisher's blurb about a new edition. Having got that far, it seemed obvious that the Jackson edition should be revised by collating it with the available Wesley manuscripts. It was, you see, "common knowledge" that these manuscripts had been collected and preserved by our British Methodist brethren. So, off I put to England—to be told by the archivist at Epworth House that *no* manuscripts of the theological treatises were known to exist. Further rummaging about proved him to be only slightly wrong. I did find holograph copies of six unpublished sermons, one of the published sermons, unpublished fragments of *The Journal* and background notes for his *Notes Upon the New Testament*. Incidentally, I stumbled onto something else, too: the holograph of Wesley's account of his love affair with Sophie Hopkey prepared for his mother on the first anniversary of Sophie's elopement; and a secretary's copy of Wesley's account of his affair with Grace Murray. Curnock had seen both manuscripts, but collation showed that he had published bowdlerized versions of them with no indication as to the places where his Wesleyan piety and Victorian taste dictated omissions. These minor additions to the materials for a biography helped to make Wesley a more believable and complex person than his published *Journals* display—but they add nothing significant to his theological writings, so cannot be included in the *LPT* volume.

The next best thing to do was to collate the Jackson text with the pre-Jackson editions of the items I wanted—only to find here that Wesley had had very bad luck with his printers, had usually been too busy to correct his proofs, and had allowed the printers to discard the manuscripts after the first printing. One way and another—with more help from the Wesleyana collections in the States and Canada—I have finally got a fairly reliable text, collated against Wesley's handwritten annotations in his set of the Pine edition of 1770, which is now in the library of Richmond College.

As a relief from this picayunish work, I compiled a list of the books that Wesley cited and started to plow through them in the

British Museum and the Dr. Williams Library. At Oxford, John Bodley's librarian (himself a Canon of Christ Church) helped me explore the libraries of Christ Church and Lincoln, and check on what was there in Wesley's day. I "discovered" what everybody else may already have known: that even if Hanoverian Oxford was in a slump, the deposits of Fell and Aldrich at Christ Church were very impressive, especially in patristics. Remembering that Wesley at Oxford was an obsessive-compulsive neurotic, driven to improve each shining hour, I began to see something of the pattern of his "sources." He was a voracious reader but not always careful or docile. He soaked up selective impressions and then stocked them for subsequent use. But it soon became plain that his controlling interest was *theological.*

The portrait that was emerging in this study was both familiar and unfamiliar—and I began to realize that the tradition of Wesley biography, formed by the first biographers (Whitehead, Moore, and Tyerman) had never been seriously challenged. It was from them that the notion derived that Wesley's theology was a subordinate interest to his really important business: managing the Revival and founding the Methodist church. Alexander Knox is almost the only exception to this general view. In a letter to Hannah More, Knox (tutor to Jebb, tutor to Keble) asserted that Wesley's interest was primarily theological—and unique in what Knox called his synthesis of Augustine and Chrysostom![1] The more I have read, the clearer is my conviction that Knox had the better of it over Wesley's Methodist biographers.

Wesley's theology has been understood—or misunderstood—in a wide variety of ways. Cell discovered the Calvinist in him; Piette identified his catholic emphases but misidentified them as Roman; Cannon's Wesley resembles a mid-nineteenth-century American Methodist, Hildebrandt's a Lutheran pietist; in Dillenberger and Welch's *Protestant Christianity* he gets lost amongst the eighteenth-century evangelicals; Lee makes him out a forerunner of nineteenth-century liberalism; Knox[2] finds him amongst the enthusiasts, Rupp amongst the Puritans; Otto Nall represents the majority view in seeing him as a theological indifferentist whose

[1][See *Remains of Alexander Knox, Esq.* 4 Vols. (London: Duncan and Malcolm, 1844) 3:152–53; 4:482–83.]
[2][Ronald Knox, Roman Catholic author of *Enthusiasm: A Chapter in the History of Religion, With Special Reference to the XVII and XVIII Centuries* (New York: Oxford University Press, 1950.)

favorite motto was "Think and Let Think." There is, of course, a core of fact in each of these images but none of them displays the man in sufficient depth.

I have no hope of succeeding where better men have failed, but in the course of what began as a minor editorial chore a new image of Wesley as a theologian has taken shape in my mind, which makes more sense to me than the others. In such cases one must always suspect that sort of academic vanity that makes like Jack Horner with hypotheses in place of plums. It is vain to disavow vanity. But it has occurred to me that an equally competent monograph on Philoxenus of Mabbogh or Matthew of Acquasparta would earn more praise in *Academia* than anything I might write about John Wesley.

Wesley was no theological titan, no system builder, no theologian's theologian. Christian eggheads have never loved him—nor was he fond of us. His speculative powers were limited, partly from disuse. By design and intent he was a folk theologian. The substance of his thought was gained from reading and conference, but its form was shaped by the exigencies of an incessant popular ministry. Unlike the typical evangelist, however, Wesley's popular ministry was consistently directed by his basic theological convictions. For half a century he was in one controversy after another—and all of them theological. In each of them his stand was defined by what he took to be the essence of "genuine Christianity": "justification by faith and holiness of heart, together with a life consistent with the same." Practical questions were decided by theological norms and theological questions judged by their import for experimental Christianity. As preacher, author, and publisher, Wesley's chief concern was with what nowadays we call "theology for the laity." His constant aim was "plain words for plain people." For those of us who do not fear or despise *hoi polloi* [the masses], Wesley is worth considering as a theologian-evangelist, doubly and equally concerned for Christian truth and its actual manifestation in uncommon living by common people. We are all uneasy, albeit in varying measure, with popular Christianity. But is there not a vital office in the Christian community for the folk theologian whose intellectual competence is high, if not actually first-rate, who formulates the Christian message so that plain people may believe and live it understandingly? Wesley chose this office and served it with distinction.

His "folk theology" was a unique fusion of many traditions

controlled by his intention to undercut or bypass the classical disjunctions between Roman and Protestant extremes. He believed in faith *and* good works, Scripture *and* tradition, revelation *and* reason, sovereign grace *and* human freedom, particularism *and* universal redemption, the witness of the Spirit *and* an ordered polity, repentance *and* the expectation of perfection, the priesthood of all believers *and* an authorized representative ministry. This is to say, of course, that John Wesley was an eclectic, as is any theologian worth his salt. The real question about eclecticism is the principle of eclection and the elements of the fusion. In Wesley's case the principle can be called *evangelical catholicism*. The elements are chosen from almost every band in the theological spectrum. He began with a wide acquaintance with the kaleidoscope of seventeenth-century English theology and borrowed freely (1) from the Puritans: their doctrine of the Christian life; (2) from the Nonjurors: their emphasis upon liturgy as the main factor in Christian continuity; (3) from the Caroline divines (Taylor, Beveridge, Tillotson, Horneck, *et. al.*); (4) even from the Latitudinarians (Stillingfleet, Tillotson, Burnet, *et. al.*) with their preference for "comprehension" over "toleration." Early on, he took a flyer with William Law, Michael Molinos, and the French Quietists. At Oxford he began the lifelong study of patristics, with a special interest in the Fathers of the Desert. He modeled the Holy Club on fourth-century monastic patterns as he had learned them from Macarius the Egyptian—naturally unaware that in the Macarian corpus he was reading a composite of Alexandrine and Cappadocian ascetical theology. Ephraem Syrus guided his interest in hymnody and liturgy. He carried with him to Georgia (as part of one of the strangest libraries a missionary ever had!) the two folio volumes of Beveridge's *Synodikon*—an immense collection of Eastern canons and liturgies—and he not only studied this with his "select company," but also used his Savannah parishioners as guinea pigs in some strange liturgical experiments based on this material. The response he got was an accusation that he was neither proper Anglican, Roman, nor Dissenter—a malicious charge but one not as far off the mark as has been thought.

When Wesley landed at Deal, February 1, 1738, the substance of his theology was already in his head. It still had to pass from head to heart, be shaped in the forge of controversy and justified at the bar of history. But very little new *doctrine* was thereafter added or lost. In his last days aboard the *Samuel* he undertook a retrospective appraisal of his theological development and wrote out the results in a very interesting memorandum.

Not that this mattered very much at the time—for Wesley was a sadly discredited man, pathetically uncertain of his future. For a dozen years since his conversion of 1725 he had toiled himself, and dragged others along with him, on the ascetic way that Marcarius had taught him would lead to "freedom from anxiety" (*apátheia*) and "full salvation" (*teleiosis*). In the Holy Club and in Georgia he was, in his own eyes, a *proestos* of the sort described in Macarius as the leader of a monastic company. His fantastic plans had miscarried, wildly. It is hard to see "a practical genius" in the John Wesley of those first thirty-five years. At the same time he had begun to react violently against "the Quietists," for there is a great gulf fixed between Marcarius and Molinos, and Wesley instinctively preferred the Eastern notion of *synelthesis* and *synergeia* [cooperation] to either the Roman or the Protestant forms of "stillness."

And yet, in less than two years, this compulsive little man, with his strange talent for charming a few and offending many, had become the acknowledged leader of a highly successful religious movement that was to grow under his hand through the succeeding half-century. How does one account for this remarkable change?

Lord Macaulay's schoolboy knows the answer: "Aldersgate." This has been the dramatic focus of Wesley mythology ever since Whitehead and Moore wrote their first biographies. It seems a pity to demythologize it now. Yet neither the schoolboys nor the scholars have noticed the paucity of Wesley's own references to Aldersgate nor the many other decisive events he cites, nor yet other and earlier passages (e.g., in the Georgia *Journals*) which recount similar moments of exaltation and ecstasy. But, most important of all, there is the evidence that after Aldersgate he continued to be troubled with just those symptoms of spiritual unsettlement which real faith was supposed to remove. It was after Aldersgate and at Herrnhut that the Moravians, who had taught him the difference between the faith of a servant and the faith of a son, fenced him from the Lord's table as *homo perturbatus*.

This is not to deny that Aldersgate was a pivotal event in Wesley's career. It was a real conversion: from belief to faith, from hoping to having. Yet it was only *one* in a series of events stretching from the first miscarriage of the Georgia mission to the half-unexpected success of his first essays at field preaching. It was this last, more than Aldersgate, that settled Wesley's heart and vocation. Peter Böhler had counseled him to "preach faith until you have it and then because you have it you will preach it"; that is, preach the doctrine of justification by faith (which Wesley had always believed) until he had the personal assurance of it so that his preaching could be "testimony." But what actually happened was that Wesley "preached faith" until *others* had it— and it was *their* faith that confirmed *his* and launched him on his evangelical mission. After the Revival gets under way, the echoes of inner turmoil fade out of Wesley's writings almost altogether, displaced by a Macarian *apatheia* (unanxiousness), which is rarely shaken, whether in tumult or triumph.

Success brought controversy and the necessity of drawing the line between doctrinal essentials and *adiaphora* [things indifferent]—where he *was* willing to "think and let think." The first rift came with the Moravians, to whom he was closely bound and deeply indebted. But it began to be increasingly plain that their emphasis upon "stillness," their contempt for "the means of grace," and their phobia against "works righteousness" amounted to antinomianism. Here Wesley drew a sharp and rigid line—for antinomianism was, in his eyes, as dreadful a heresy as justification by works. Justification by the faith-that-works-through-love is the bedrock on which everything rests in Wesley's theology. One of his very first publications (1739) is an abridgment of the first four Edwardean *Homilies*. He digested thirty-six quarto pages into twelve duodecimo pages—with few visible seams— and entitled the tract "The Doctrine of Salvation, Faith, and Good Works, Extracted from the Homilies of the Church of England." This tract must be understood as Wesley's own theological manifesto. It defined a position from which he never wavered: the fusion of soteriology and ethics. "Our faith in Christ comes first," he says, "but thereafter must be nourished with good works," for faith is in order to righteousness, as justification by faith quite literally implies.

The Moravians took this as a denial of the first article of the Reformation. In retort, Wesley spoke of their "foolish solifidianism," "the German stillness," and addressed an astonishing epistle to the Moravian leaders, reviewing the controversy and reaffirming his *synergism* (Eastern style, that is). This was all painful and sad—but the doctrinal issue was clear: faith generates a process of growth and discipline aimed at spiritual and moral perfection. The Moravians were right in identifying this as catholic teaching but mistaken in tagging it "popery." It was, instead, the tradition of Cranmer and Taylor, of Gregory of Nyssa, Chrysostom and the authors of the so-called "Spiritual Homilies of Macarius."

His next great doctrinal struggle was with the Calvinists and it was over predestination. Wesley had no quarrel with the Calvinist doctrine of God's sovereignty. On this point he said, "We stand not a hair breadth's from Calvinism." He was a grateful heir to the English Puritans and the new England revivalists, notably Jonathan Edwards. But when George Whitefield began in 1739 "to preach the decrees," Wesley was drawn into yet another painful struggle within his own familiar company. Certainly at first he had no special objection to the doctrine of predestination when taught and held as "an opinion" (that is, as one way among others of confessing God's sovereign grace). But the Calvinists made it an essential. Whereupon Wesley opposed it as invalid, on three grounds: (1) all the varied versions of predestination, when developed, turn out to be "double," with a strict entail of "irrespective reprobation." To Wesley, this impugned the goodness of God, which could not be rehabilitated by an appeal to "the secret providence of God." (2) The decrees may comfort the elect but they tend to inhibit the sinner's hunger and thirst for righteousness—and so add to the gravitational pull of antinomianism; (3) *predestination* confuses the *temporal* dimensions of the *ordo salutis*. It seeks to preserve God's initiative by placing it in the past; and insures against the future by ignoring its radical uncertainty. Wesley had learned (again mostly from the Easterners) that Jesus Christ is *the* Elect Man in whom all God's children are elected, that the Holy Spirit is the active Agent of election, that the living present is the "time" of election, that election may be and normally is renewed moment by moment but it also may lapse and be regained—but never without the risk of waning faith or new rebellion. Predestination, in Wesley's eyes, was either an indifferent or else an actually bad way to interpret the essential truth of God's sovereignty and freedom to act in and for his creatures. In 1740 he published a sermon entitled "Free Grace"; in 1770 he issued a minute condemning Calvinism as "poison to faith." This, incidentally, confirmed the schism between the Wesleyan Methodists and the Calvinist evangelicals (largely associated with the Countess of Huntingdon). In 1752 and in 1774 he wrote two very interesting essays, *Predestination Calmly*

Considered and *Thoughts Upon Necessity*. All of this got him tagged with the pejorative label "Arminian."

This brings us to a very complicated problem that I have not yet unraveled to my full satisfaction: Wesley's relation to Arminius.[3] *If* he read Arminius *himself* before 1740, I do not know the evidence to prove it. He did read him after 1742, and when in 1778 he established a house organ to counteract the Calvinist propaganda, he called it *The Arminian Magazine*. But in his little tract "What Is An Arminian?" the answer boils down to any Christian who denies irrespective reprobation and affirms some version of the doctrine of universal redemption. But this is clearly not a specific connection with Arminius himself. My guess is that Wesley agreed with the thesis of Peter Heylyn's *Historia Quinquarticularis* that Arminius was a Protestant specimen of a genus of Christian teachers whose tradition runs unbroken back to ancient times. I would not want to belaud Heylyn as a historian, but it is worth noting that in Arminius' own library (as Bangs has shown) the largest fraction is composed of patristic items. Obviously, Wesley agreed with Arminius against Gomarus and the Canons of Dort—and for a time, at least, he worked with the Amyraldean distinction between conditional and *un*conditional election.

It was a dangerous thing for Wesley to give umbrage to the Calvinists, for it ensured their settled distaste for him; and in the two centuries since, they have given him a bad press by repeating in scorn what some Methodists assert with misplaced pride: Wesley's proper posture was on horseback, or a stump, not in the library chair; his genius was not in his head but in his heart.

A third collision occurred early in the Revival with the administration of the established Church. Ironically enough, it was Joseph Butler (a great theologian) who first threatened Wesley with an interdiction for preaching without a local license; and it was Edmond Gibson (a great canonist) who refused to interdict him, even in the face of worse provocation than Butler had to bear. The eighteenth-century Church of England was a church in the doldrums, thwarted in almost every effort to rise to the challenge of its time and to set its house in order. The foremost obvious reasons for its predicament were: (1) its Erastian submission to the civil power; (2) its unpreparedness for the social

[3][Outler later unraveled this problem. See "John Wesley as Theologian—Then and Now" below, 55–74.]

upheavals that kept unsettling the Restoration Settlement; (3) the suspension of Convocation; (4) the untoward results of the Acts of Toleration—whereby the Church of England simply ceased to be *the* Church of England and of all English Christians.

In such a situation, where the *ministerium ordinarium* was hindered in its function, Wesley conceived of himself as a *minister extraordinarius,* commissioned by the Holy Spirit for a special mission in and for the Church. He would have welcomed specific authorization for this project, but, even without it, he felt warranted because he understood his ordination at Oxford as an extraparochial license. He believed he was following the precedents of men like John Gilpin and the sequestered ministers of the Commonwealth. Thus warranted, he proceeded to employ lay preachers as his "curates," responsible to the Church. He made a sharp distinction between "preacher" and "minister"—and imposed it on his preachers with or without their agreement. His "ordinations" of 1784 were, essentially, a futile attempt to delegate *his* vicarial authority to American surrogates. He was dismayed when the American Methodists struck out on their own path without much more than lip service to their British "father-in-God."

The point to this digression is that Wesley's troubles with his fellow Anglicans were more deeply theological than political or practical. Wesley's ministry *was* irregular; Wesley's personality *was* a nuisance; but history plainly shows that irregularities and nuisances are not unusual or insoluble problems for Anglicans. Wesley's real offense was his doctrine and his discipline. His doctrine was denounced as "enthusiasm"; his discipline was deplored as fanaticism. Wesley's main response is to be found in his *Earnest Appeal to Men of Reason and Religion.* I am inclined to think that this is the most important single essay that he ever wrote. In it he defends his mission and message first against the Deists, then against the Latitudinarians, and finally against those Tory churchmen with whom, as a congenital conservative, he had the most natural ties. The skeleton of his argument is simpler than its detail and nuances. He poses as a question whether anyone will deny that England desperately needs a revival of religion. The Methodist movement is such a revival; its teachings are the plain, old doctrines of the Henrician reformers, the ancient Fathers, and the apostles; its discipline is the effort to apply the gospel in practice with utter seriousness. Methodists (this is an ironic twist, for Wesley disliked the term "Methodists" and turned it on his tormentors to mean "ideal Christian") are immune to the doubts of the rationalists, for thinkers insensitive to the data of revelation cannot reason to valid conclusions on any question touching revelation, including the question of whether there *is* such a thing or not. If rationalists want to be rational about religion, they must take it seriously (i.e., become Methodists). Those of real religious concern ought to make common cause with the Methodists or, at the very least, not hinder them. The chief business of the Revival is the ordering of Christian life to its full potential, assuming that human beings have God-given powers to respond to God in faith, to grow in grace, and to attain whatever *telos* God has in store for humanity. The Methodists take the gospel seriously and rely on God's promises of full salvation with a lively expectation. This is *not* "enthusiasm"—for that, rightly defined, is the presumption that makes inner feeling the *judge* of Scripture, tradition, and reason. Wesley is as brusque with real "enthusiasts" as are those critics of his who charge *him* with enthusiasm. Religious truth is given in experience but not created by experience.

Wesley's doctrine of "experience" or "assurance" (not quite but nearly synonymous terms) is actually a doctrine of religious knowledge. It can be shown, I think, that his mentors here, other than the Fathers, are Berkeley (the *New Theory of Vision*), John Norris (the *Oxford* Platonist) and Malebranche. He was an idealist, but of a rather special sort—significantly distinct from the Hegelian Lotzean tradition. As omnipotent and constant Creator, God has utterly free access to every creature and every creaturely process. Human awareness of God is not of God's being *"there,"* but of God's always having been *"here."* It is therefore, a sort of primitive knowledge, as is our knowledge of self and of the elemental categories of thought: immediate, indemonstrable, undeniable. It is, in this respect, analogous with sensation, for sense experience as such is immediate, incommunicable, and immune from doubt. Doubt and error begin, in both cases, with interpretation and practical judgment—and are as prolific as any skeptic would assert. But the aboriginal power of vision remains— and with it the capacity of being aware of God. The Scriptures provide infallible testimony, which the Holy Spirit may then transform into inward self-understanding and authentic faith. This experience of the transformation of belief into trust is "present," "immediate"—as palpable in its order as the sight of color or the smell of food. But it is not an epiphany nor does it yield magical knowledge or dispositive power. It is rather like the confidence that a child gains when he "experiences" the "buoyancy" of water—and starts swimming. The "experience" of buoyancy is neither an inference nor merely a confirmed hypothesis. It is an operative reality, as prerequisite to action as action is prerequisite to judgment. The Christian's "assurance" of God's justifying, reconciling love is of this order. It can be lost, it can be corrupted; it can be regained and refined. It can even be matured, so that as the faithful grow into the habit of trusting God's love they can also come to trust their own intentions to love God above all else and all else in God. *This* is "perfection," the true *skopos* [goal] and *telos* [end] of the Christian life.

This brings us, finally, to the notorious and vexed question of Wesley and perfection—his most distinctive and misunderstood teaching. On this score he has been badly pummeled by those who took it for granted that what he meant by perfection, possible in *this* life, was what Aquinas and the Westminster divines had insisted was "reserved for the state of glory only." His indignant denial that he taught a notion of "sinless perfection" was taken to prove that he was simply unwilling to stand by the implications of his own premises. Wesley never qualified his claim that "perfection" was his most nearly distinctive doctrine. But he was lamentably unsuccessful in explaining it to those who already knew what it meant. I think that I now can show that at least a good deal of the cross talk came from the fact that Wesley's critics were denying the Latin tradition of *perfectus est* [made perfect," i.e., static or completed perfection] while Wesley was affirming a somewhat impressionistic version of the Eastern tradition of *teleosis* [becoming perfect]. I do not pretend that Wesley mastered the niceties of the Christian Platonists—but he did pick up some of their leading notions and adapt them to his evangelical enterprise. He explicitly tells us that his notion of the ideal Christian (*The Character of a Methodist*) was modeled on Clement's portrait of the Christian Gnostic in the *Miscellanies*, VII. He took Clement's distinction of the vertical levels of *pistis* and *gnosis* and altered it to be a horizontal line of genetic development with decisive *phases*. Faith is the threshold of the Christian life and establishes the basis for "the rise and progress of religion in the human soul." The notion of *gnosis* is decerebrated and made equivalent to *agape*. The fullness of love is the fullness of salvation and the essence of sanctification. As he had learned from the Eastern ascetics, the interim between justification and sanctification is a rocky path demanding a true *askesis* [spiritual discipline] in order to advance to the *telos* in which faith and love are fused. But this is a process extended through time, and if at any given moment your conscious intentions are wholehearted, you are in and for that moment, *teleios* [perfect].

The goal of the Christian discipline is freedom from the tyranny of evil and the achievement of a Christian *apatheia*—not apathy, but unanxious striving. Dropping off the speculative gantry of these ideas, Wesley shaped them into a message that the goal *of* life is attainable *in* life—though obviously by the same sort of unmerited gift from God that bestirred justifying faith. But if the goal of life is attainable, it should then be sought and "expected" (in the quite literal sense of *expectare*)—and this by every serious Christian. "Perfection," "holiness," "sanctification," "full salvation" are simply so many terms to denote one thing—loving God above all else and all else in God, so far as one's *conscious* will and *deliberate* acts are concerned. The antonym to "perfection," in Wesley's mind, was "idolatry": the conscious preference of some *creature* to the Creator. Wesley knew, as well as anybody else, that our *sarx* [flesh] is with us for life, at enmity with both *nous* [mind] and *pneuma* [spirit]. The counterbalance to his doctrine of perfection is his doctrine of sin in believers—which recognizes that growth in grace entails the uncovering of hitherto unwitting sins and entanglements—and that each such "discovery" precipitates a crisis. One either repents and so maintains his loyalty to God—that is, his "perfection"—or else he ratifies with his conscious will his hitherto indeliberate defect—and so lapses from his "perfection." Wesley's critics assumed that a doctrine of earthly perfection was "soft" on sin. Wesley retorted that the deniers of *his* kind of perfection credited sin with a greater power than the grace of God, at least so long as the soul was in the body.

Normally, Wesley thought that the gift of full salvation was given in the *articulis mortis* [at the point of death]. Then, if ever, a person faces the radical question of his or her supreme loyalty in utter seriousness. This notion helps to explain Wesley's lifelong interest in the *ars moriendi* [art of dying] and his diligent collection of "good deaths." There is, however, no theoretical hindrance to its occurrence before death—which only is to say that it would seem *possible* for a Christian to love God above all else as far as conscious volition in the matter was concerned. But what is so received may also be cast away, and what is cast away may also be recovered. The decisive function of Wesley's doctrine of perfection was its stimulus to valid Christian aspiration and its reminder that faith is perfected in love. *Teleiosis* does not mean "fulfilled and finished." It means "up to par thus far."

What happened to Wesley's doctrine of perfection is a sad story. Friends and foes alike too easily heard the Latin connotation of *perfectus est* and had little feeling for the Eastern monastic background from which Wesley had drawn his ideas. In our time, it has come to be child's play to shatter both pretensions to and expectations of "righteousness." But the iconoclasts have discovered that a forensic and putative righteousness is not really rousing good news to those who are quite literally sick of the dichotomy between soteriology and ethics that has come to be in vogue. Wesley's real concern with "perfection" was that it held soteriology and ethics together in vital balance and so signified the fullness and integrity of the Christian life. Where shall we look today for this kind of balance in contemporary theology?

All I can say about Wesley's doctrine of grace—without elaboration—is that he thought of grace as the divine energy in and for persons (thus prevenient and cooperating as well as saving). Grace is sacramental (*i.e.,* always mediated in and through the creature) but not sacerdotal (*i.e.,* never at human disposal).

I've left no time to speak in detail of his notions of the church and the ministry, his political philosophy (violently Tory) or his economic views—which were more medieval than modern. I make nothing of his genius for organization nor his unintended contribution of another denomination to the Protestant *potpourri.* It is enough, here and now, to contend that, quite apart from his place in ecclesiastical history, John Wesley deserves a theological reappraisal of his place in the history of Christian thought and of his relevance for contemporary theology. As matters now stand, he is not really accessible to scholarly study and will not be until there is a properly edited edition of his works. But would this be of serious use and value to any but the Methodists—who have managed comfortably without one now for quite a spell?

In some ways Wesley was a pathetic figure. The movement he founded had already altered the course he had set for it even before he died. In America, especially, Wesley has been invoked oftener than he has been read and usually has been read with a low-church anti-intellectualist bias that celebrates his warm heart and worn saddlebags, unconcerned with his theology. But this very pathos could rescue the study of Wesley from the genetic fallacy that haunts most denominational histories. It is more important, I have come to believe, to study Wesley's theology in the light of his antecedents than his successors. Such a study would, I think, exhibit a theological method and temper of uncommon relevance for contemporary theology in the new epoch before us—a method that takes the business of "lay theology" seriously and practices it successfully; that is ecumenical in the crucial sense of being both evangelical and catholic; that appropriates more of the patristic tradition and orthodox ethos than any other version of Protestant Christianity; that offers something like a third way in many of the two-valued disjunctions that plague modern Christianity (liberalism vs. neo-orthodoxy; Protestant vs. Catholic; those that praise God and denigrate humanity vs. those who praise humanity and patronize God; the breast-beaters vs. the tub-thumpers; the eggheads vs. the hucksters). Wesley's theology is no panacea for all our ills and dangers. But the intentions of his theology and its basic method deserve to be reconsidered as a fruitful resource—amongst many others, of course—for ecumenical theologizing, today and tomorrow.

John Wesley as Theologian— Then and Now

——†——

[1974] Outler responded to the call for a critical text of Wesley by editing an anthology for the Library of Protestant Theology. Then followed more than two decades of meticulous editing of Wesley's sermons for the Wesley Works Editorial Project. Throughout that time Outler wrote numerous essays exploring Wesley's continuing relevance as a theologian. In this essay, he focuses on Wesley's gift as a "synthesizer," with significance both for his own time and for the "faltering liberal tradition" of Outler's time.

It is small wonder that when, in 1777, an obscure Irishman named James Kershaw took to prophesying "that all the Methodists are to go over to America in the belly of a whale," John Wesley promptly pronounced him "stark, staring mad."[1] But even the daft Kershaw would not have been far off the mark if only he could have foreseen how, in due course, swarms of *American Methodists* would be transported to England, not in the belly of a whale but in a modern equivalent—the intercontinental jet. Thus it is that we are here tonight, a small but eager swarm, gathered with English and Irish and European Methodists—and other Christians—on a very special occasion: the first regional conference (of this particular sort) of the World Methodist Historical Society. We are happy to be here, we are thankful for the vision and thoughtfulness of the planning and labor that have made our meeting possible and we are grateful, as ever, for the unfailing hospitality of our English hosts. We are also joined in the earnest hope that this conference is a favorable omen for an expanded program and outreach of the Society in its concern to strengthen and support the enterprise of serious historical inquiry amongst Methodist people in general and their scholars in particular. For my own part, I count it an honor—and a very real personal pleasure—to have a share in the occasion and to have this assignment from the Program Committee to offer you a summary of some of my own probings into Wesley's theological formation and to assess his theological contributions—then and now.

One begins, of course, with one's general attitude toward Wesley and the question as to what sort of demands he makes upon his interpreters and assessors. Here, one of the first great lessons I have learned from him is that, just as he himself "dared call no man Rabbi,"[2] neither does he demand any such thing of us, in anything resembling an uncritical acceptance of *all* his views and attitudes, on the grounds of his *ex officio* authority as our

[1]See his letters to Christopher Hopper, Feb. 1, 1777, Joseph Benson, Feb. 15, 1777, and Thomas Wride, July 8, 1785, *JWL* VI:252, 254; VII:279.
[2]Cf. First Preface, *A Christian Library* (1749–1755), I, ix, ¶ 10. See also *JWW* XIV:222, and "Obedience to Parents," II.3.

father in the faith. His own life-long endeavor was not to find some master to follow, but rather to keep learning, from many masters, where the line should fall between the basic core of essential Christian belief and that wide spectrum of allowable (and arguable) opinions purporting to interpret that basic core. *Mutatis mutandis* [with due alteration of details], we may ourselves feel free to follow his example in this and to seek for a defensible boundary between Wesley's "opinions," about which we, and others, may confidently "think and let think,"[3] and those truly basic insights of his that remain as options and resources for us and others in our strugglings for a truly contemporary *and* ecumenical theology for ourselves. Something like this, I suggest, is both our opportunity and obligation—even if we must also expect a lively disagreement among us, and between us and the non-Methodists, as to what is "core" and what is "opinion," and why.

The longer I have lived and worked with him, the easier I feel in this freedom to follow his own eclectic principle—and all the more as I see the great closed systems of Christian doctrine that have competed in the past now in one degree of disintegration or another. Thus, even if ever there was good warrant for the hero cult in which Wesley was the cult hero, that warrant need bind us no longer. In my own case it has happened that, with no weakening of my loyalty to his best insights, I feel no need to defend such particular failings (in my eyes) as his peculiar triumphalisms and rationalizations regarding the Methodist movements,[4] his debater's way of ignoring the best intentions of his critics, his petulance in "delivering his soul" when frustrated. Even when we do actually imitate him in such lapses, we have no right of appeal to his example as an excuse.

Or again, one may take him, as I have, as a major theological mentor and guide, and still feel free to dissent from or to qualify some of his substantive theological views. For example, there is his biblical literalism and scattershot exegesis, which belong to his time but not to ours—and we may dissent here without rejecting

[3]See "On the Trinity," ¶2; "On the Death of Mr. Whitefield," III.1; "The Wedding Garment," Sec. 14; "The Nature of Enthusiasm," ¶36; *JWJ* VI:133–34 and VII, 389; *JWL* VI:383 and VII:190.

[4]Cf. "The Causes of the Inefficacy of Christianity," ¶18; "Some Account of the Work of God in North America," I.8; "On Laying the Foundation of the New Chapel, Near the City-Road, London," I.4, II.11.

his valid stress upon the primacy of Scripture as the source of the Christian revelation. Again, there is his Christology (which strikes me as inadequate) and his theory of the Atonement (which strikes me as blinkered). It seems to me that such opinions might very well be "updated" without weakening his vital emphasis upon a *Christocentric soteriology* as "core." A different perspective than his is now possible on such matters as his Tory politics and his proto-Marxist denunciations of surplus accumulation,[5] not to speak of his anti-Roman and anti-Semitic prejudices (which he shared with "all right-thinking Englishmen" of his day). Without *understanding* all these (and much else, of course) there is no historical understanding of Wesley. But they no longer confront us with decisions that need be based on the question of loyalty or disloyalty.

Obviously, the main reason why we need not defend him in such matters is that his abiding significance rests elsewhere, on secure foundations that seem to me, at least, to support the judgment to which I have come (after a very different initial thesis), viz., that Wesley is *the* major Anglican theologian in the entire eighteenth century and also one of our major resources for twentieth-century theology. A dozen years of probing his mind and his sources have convinced me that his theological importance—then and now—turns around on at least three crucial foci.

First, he was a clear-headed *synthesizer* of a rich, multifaceted tradition—that very rare sort of eclectic who actually understood the options he had to choose between. Second, he was an effective *communicator* whom the common people heard gladly and responded to with fervor and effect. Third, under the desperate pressures of his age, he discovered a way of "third alternative theologizing" that amounts to *a special method* all its own. It is this particular method that I have come to regard as crucial for any really fruitful interpretation of Wesley as theologian. This particular mind-set took shape in Epworth and Charterhouse, but it acquired its distinctive character at Oxford—where he received a very solid education despite all the university's shortcomings, about which he was so vocal. At Oxford, he soaked up the good essence of classical culture as well as the traditions of central Anglicanism. All his life thereafter, Wesley would go on dropping

---

[5]Cf. "On Riches," ¶4; "The Causes of the Inefficacy of Christianity," ¶12; "On Worldly Folly," I.4; "The Danger of Increasing Riches," I.1, 16.

Greek and Latin tags as casually as breathing and would go on spending out of the theological capital bequeathed him from his Anglican heritage (including the Anglican Puritans!). It was at Oxford that his native love of learning became a lifelong habit— together with a passion for sharing his learning that never slackened. He professed to be *homo unius libri*[6]—and we must understand his intention here. But the phrase itself is wildly misleading. The fact is that he read omnivorously and turned all of it to use in any project that came to hand.[7] Most popularizers depend on garbled gleanings from a limited repertory of secondary sources. Wesley was a popularizer whose explorations of the primary source material pass easy belief. Other evangelists could match him at Scripture proof-texting, but none was so deeply concerned as he with the interactions between theology and contemporary culture—and with the theological formation of his people. There were not many vital issues stirring the world of his day that he ignored or about which he had no confident opinion. With Ray, Huygens, Buddeus, Hervey and others, he surveyed "the wisdom of God in creation" as a curious exercise in "natural theology."[8] In these explorations he was unaccountably impressed by the weird notions of John Hutchinson and not so strangely repelled by the theories of Sir Isaac Newton.[9] He cites "the

[6]Cf. his Preface to *Sermons on Several Occasions*, ¶5, and the sermon "On God's Vineyard," I.1; "A Plain Account of Christian Perfection," ¶10 (*JWW* XI:373); and his letter to John Newton, May 14, 1765 (*JWL* IV:299).

[7]He was a shameless borrower, he had a genius for abridgment, and the range of his sources is incredible. For example, the evangelist who denounced the English theatre as "sapping the foundation of all religion" (letter to the Mayor and Corporation of Bristol, Dec. 20, 1764, in *JWL* IV:279) had already read and stored up a strange repertory of Restoration dramas. One instance may serve for half a dozen: in 1726 or 1727 he had read Thomas Otway's *The Orphan; Or, the Unhappy Marriage*. In 1759 he quotes from it, to rather good effect but without acknowledgment, in his sermon on "Original Sin"!

[8]Cf. his *Survey of the Wisdom of God in the Creation: or a Compendium of Natural Philosophy*. Five vols.; 3d ed., enlarged (1777).

[9]Cf. his *skepticism* about Newton in the *Survey, ibid.*, IV:44, 46, and III:328. By V:237, however, he had decided that "Dr. Rogers has overturned the very foundation of this fashionable hypothesis [of Newton's]"! See John Rogers (M.D.), *A Dissertation on the Knowledge of the Ancients, in Astronomy and Optical Instruments; on the Physical Causes of the Earth's Diurnal and Annual Motions; on the Distances of the Planets from the Sun, and its Magnitude*. London, 1755.

common supposition as to the plurality of worlds"[10] as casually as one of us might nowadays mention the DNA genetic code. All of which is to say that he was an *evangelist-with-a-difference:* a scholar of sorts who found his way into the hearts of the masses without condescension, and yet also without dampening his own unflagging intellectual curiosity.

There was no single tradition that he found acceptable, no particular theological "school" that he ever cared to join. This meant groping his own way through the blood-and-ink-stained tangles of two centuries of controversy that most of us have forgotten or never knew. This background is his constant—and generally unconscious—frame of reference. Most of his crucial theological statements are mere iceberg tips of submerged hulks of congealed conflict. All the decisive presuppositions in his mind are products of this turbulent past—which is one reason why he is so easily misinterpreted when read in terms of the later developments of Wesleyan theology.

The oldest and most tortured of these inherited struggles was political: the desperate issue as to the true locus of legitimate power in the civil state, in the economic community and in the church. This contest had convulsed England since before the Reformation and it helps explain Wesley's deep, instinctive fear of popular sovereignty. A lifelong Tory (who nevertheless denied divine right absolutism), he had to live and work, for four decades, under a "Whig supremacy" that he abhorred.[11] Thus it was easy for him to reject politics as a direct means to any of his own distinctive ends (moral or ecclesial). He was, at heart, an a-political creature, subservient to neither the church nor the state, and yet not concerned to subvert them either. This gave him more freedom than most of his contemporaries from political distractions in the exercise of his evangelistic mission.

It was a time when the mind and soul of the nation were being severely shaken by the bold challenges of a new secularism and the faltering defenses of the old traditions. It was an age of

---

[10]"The New Creation," ¶8. Cf. Wesley's quotation from Louis Dutens, *Inquiry* (1769), in the *Survey, ibid.*, V, 114: "the notion of the Plurality of Worlds [has become familiar] thanks to the elegant work of Mr. [Bernard] de Fontenelle." See also Harold Nicolson, *The Age of Reason* (1700–1789), (London: Constable & Co., 1960), 31.

[11]Cf. Basil Williams, *The Whig Supremacy, 1714–1760,* in The Oxford History of England (Oxford: Clarendon, 1952).

conflict: between an old idealism and a new empiricism, the residues of Christian "Platonism" (Cudworth, Norris) and an emergent naturalism (Newton, Locke). Instinctively, Wesley rejected these polarizations and conceived of a third alternative of his own—in which he rejected the notion of innate ideas, thus opting for empiricism as a theory for our knowledge of *finites* (nature), even as he also insisted on *direct intuition* in our "knowledge" of infinites ("God and the things of God"). This is a project worth much more probing than we have time for here, because it has something rather special to say to us *now*, when the old incantations about the omnicompetence of science have begun to lose their magic spell.[12]

On yet another front, Wesley was caught between the devotees of "tradition" versus the partisans of "modernity." The traditionalists looked back to an idyllic past from which the current world had visibly declined. The modernists took hope from the knowledge explosion of the seventeenth and eighteenth centuries and its promises of progress.[13] Wesley was a conservative at heart and yet also open to the future. Thus he found it possible to welcome all valid "progress," *provided always* that we acknowledge the overarching order of Divine Providence as its source and boundary.[14]

Wesley's England was a wretched contrast between the newly rich and the newly poor, with the growing miseries of the urban ghettoes added onto the ancient inequities of the feudal past. And yet this same Hanoverian England was, overall, more prosperous than any preceding century—and much more stable

[12]See, for example, "The Princeton Galaxy" in *Intellectual Digest*, III:10 (June, 1973), 25–32. This disenchantment with the omnicompetence of science and technology is the common theme in books as diverse as Carlos Castaneda's *Journey to Ixtlan* (New York: Simon & Schuster, 1972), Theodore Roszak's *Where the Wasteland Ends* (Garden City, N.Y.: Doubleday, 1972) and William Burrough's *Exterminator* (New York City, 1973)— and in much of the ecology mystique, generally. What religion stands to gain from it all is still uncertain but that a new kind of epistemology is in the making is clear enough—and Wesley's possible contribution to the process may be worth more than has yet been realized.

[13]See, e.g., George Hakewill, *An Apologie of the power and Providence of God in the Government of the World. . . 1627*, and Joseph Glanvill, *Plus Ultra: or the Progress and Advancement of Knowledge Since the Days of Aristotle . . .* London, 1668.

[14]Cf. "Of Former Times" (1787).

politically. Halévy's famous thesis is, therefore, a compound error. In the first place, it ignores the fact that England had already *had* its real revolution (viz., the transfer of civil power from Crown to Parliament in the successive revolutions of 1688–89 and 1714). In the second place, Halévy—and Thompson!—presuppose that the discontents of the eighties and nineties could ever have been mobilized into successful rebellion, and this seems to me absurd. But, most of all, this notion of Wesley as a savior of the standing order presupposes his own fervent commitment to that order— and this, too, is absurd. Wesley *was* opposed to "rebellion," in any and all its forms. He did denounce "Wilkes and Liberty"; he did condemn the American patriots and the French Jacobins; and he did speak well of "King and country"—all out of his lasting horror of anarchy based on his memories of the Civil War and the Commonwealth. At the same time, he was also a vigorous, constant critic of the *status quo,* and even more: an active agent of social change. I could not name another Englishman of his century (not Paine nor Price nor Cobbett) who so heartily identified himself with the English poor or whose identification was more heartily accepted by them.[15] His sympathies were all on their side; and no one before Marx spoke more unsparingly of the social evils of surplus accumulation.

I would suggest, therefore, that Wesley was also a *revolution-ary-with-a-difference,* just as we have noted in his role as evangelist. The effect of his movement was to provide a new experience for thousands of faceless men and women—experiences of worth before God, of new dignity and status in intensive small groups, together with unaccustomed leadership roles, etc. This helped to create a new kind of political creature, not to be found in France before or after their Revolution: a sizable group that was immune to revolt and yet vigorously committed to humane causes both at home and abroad.[16] John Wilkes had finally drawn his sword to

[15]Cf. Wesley's letter to Brian Bury Collins, June 14, 1780 (*JWL* VII:23–24): ". . . the choicest of London society: I mean the poor." E. P. Thompson, *The Making of the English Working Class* (New York: Pantheon, 1968), 41, claims that "Primitive Methodism was a religion *of* the poor; orthodox Wesleyanism remained as it had commenced, a religion *for* the poor." With regard to Wesley himself, this statement is simply untrue.

[16]For an interesting, albeit somewhat superficial, exploration of this development, see Bernard Semmel, *The Methodist Revolution* (New York: Basic Books, 1973). For a distempered contention that Methodism helped

defend the Bank of England from the mob he had earlier helped to raise. Wesley would have stood down the same mob on principle, but he could scarcely have cared less for the Bank of England as such.

On the doctrinal side, English Christianity had suffered a protracted and agonizing polarization between the self-styled Puritans and those they had managed to mislabel as "Arminian." This struggle had raged, off and on, from the days of William Whitaker and Peter Baro, the "Lambeth Articles" (1595) and the Hampton Court Conference (1604).[17] It swirled around a cluster of irreconcilable claims as to the terms of one's justification before God and the human role in the mysteries of our salvation. In its

prevent the revolution England should have had, see E. P. Thompson, *op. cit., passim.*

[17]By the last decade of the sixteenth century, the Puritans felt strong enough to try for a decisive commitment of the Church of England to an explicitly Calvinist standard of doctrine. In 1595, Whitaker prepared nine "articles," *ad mentem Calvini* [according to the mind of Calvin], which were approved by Archbishop Whitgift and others in a conference at Lambeth Palace in November of 1595 (cf. *COC* III:523–24). These "Lambeth Articles" affirm double predestination and reprobation (with "a certain number of the predestinate which can neither be augmented or diminished"), irresistible grace, perseverance, etc. Queen Elizabeth declined to approve them (as having been produced without royal permission) and at the Hampton Court Conference (1604), they were rejected once again by James I (influenced by his new bishop of London, Richard Bancroft). This was an omen of a protracted struggle that would run for a full century, enlisting most Anglican theologians on one side or the other. The important point here is that Anglican anti-Calvinism clearly antedates the influence of Arminius and the Synod of Dort (cf. Carl Bangs, *Arminius: A Study in the Dutch Reformation* [New York and Nashville: Abingdon, 1971], 207–10). Indeed, Arminius was more influenced by Peter Baro (cf. Bangs, 208) than the other way round. Later, there *were* avowed disciples of Arminius in England (cf. Owen Chadwick, "Arminians in England," in *Religion in Life*, 29:4 [Autumn, 1960]: 548–55), but the label "Arminianism" as a blanket term for Anglican synergism was a victory for the Puritan propaganda and has caused endless confusion ever since. Its roots are *catholic* whereas Arminius' reaction to Dutch hyper-Calvinism was scarcely affected by the concurrent conflicts in the Roman Catholic Church over grace and free will. Of the crucial names in that struggle (Baius, Lessius, Bañes, Molina, and Bellarmine) only Bellarmine appears in Bangs' Index (pp. 369–76) but with no suggestion that Arminius had actually *read* him. In England, however, Bellarmine was widely read and every Anglican apologist worth his salt had to have a go at him.

longer background were the old, perduring traditions of English nominalism and Erasmian Christianity. But there were fresher and still bitter memories on both sides: the Laudian repressions, the anarchies of the Commonwealth,[18] the brutalities of the Restoration, the decline of "Old Dissent" and the rise of latitudinarian moralism. The "Arminians"[19] saw antinomianism as the normal consequence of the Calvinist syndrome of "election," "irresistible grace," and "final perseverance."[20] For the Puritans, on the other hand, the great enemy was *synergism*, in any form.[21]

Wesley had grown up with a gospel of moral rectitude and then had been converted (in 1725) to the "holy living" tradition of Jeremy Taylor, William Law, Thomas à Kempis, and the Eastern fathers (Macarius, Gregory of Nyssa, Ephraem Syrus, *et al.*). His landmark statement of this tradition may be seen in the sermon on "The Circumcision of the Heart" (1732–33). Then, in 1738, under the guidance of Peter Böhler and others, he was converted yet once again—this time to the "grand article of justification by faith alone." This provided a new foundation for his preaching and for the evangelical theology of his first four volumes of *Sermons on Several Occasions* (1746–60). The foundation, that is, not the *whole* of his Christian understanding. Among the generality of "Evangelicals," the *true* doctrine of justification presupposed "election," "irresistible grace" and "perseverance" as premises—but there was never a moment in Wesley's life when he was even partially persuaded on any one of these points. His main agreements with the Calvinists were on the primacy of Scripture and "original sin"; thus far he would go and no further. Thus, he was forced here again to seek a third alternative, at the cost of being misunderstood and denounced by evangelicals and latitudinarians, on opposite sides.[22] Instead, he reached back to the nominalists'

[18]Cf. Christopher Hill, *The World Turned Upside Down* (New York: Viking, 1972), chaps. 6–10.

[19]Called, instead, "the *old* English Protestants" by Peter Heylyn in his *Historia Quinquarticularis* (London, 1681), Part III, xxii, 631.

[20]In the *Oxford English Dictionary*, the first citations of "antinomianism" coincide with this period.

[21]Cf. Richard Hill, *Logica Wesleiensis: or, the Farrago Double-Distilled* . . . (1773), and Augustus Toplady, *An Old Fox Tarr'd and Feather'd: By an Hanoverian*. . . (2d ed.; 1775).

[22]For critiques from this latter quarter, cf. the six letters from "John Smith" in Henry Moore's *Life of John Wesley*, II:473–576, and also Josiah Tucker's *A Brief History of the Principles of Methodism* (4th ed., 1777).

distinction between God's sovereignty in creation (*potentia absoluta*) and God's accommodations to human freedom (*potentia ordinata*).[23] He reached back still further, to the medieval tradition of *in se est*,[24] and then tried to *fuse* the Protestant article on justification by faith (imputed righteousness) with the Catholic insistence on the impartation of actual righteousness in *the process* of Christian maturation (from regeneration to sanctification).

One of the shibboleths in the controversy was the phrase, "the imputation of Christ's righteousness." This harked back to Trent's scholastic distinctions as to the four "causes" of justification[25] and to Bellarmine's defense of Trent in his *De Justificatione*.[26] All Protestants denounced Bellarmine *pro forma*, but the Puritans went much further, drawing a sharp line between the imputation of Christ's righteousness to sinful man as the *"formal"* cause of his justification and any other way of speaking of it—for example, as "meritorious cause." This was not merely a quibble, either. At stake were radically different notions of the inward

[23]Cf. "Thoughts on God's Sovereignty," *JWW* X:361–63. See Heiko A. Oberman, *HMT* (Cambridge, Mass.: Harvard University Press, 1963), 30–37.

[24]Cf. Oberman, *HMT* 129–45. See also "Methodism's Theological Heritage: A Study in Perspective" [reprinted below, 191–211]. Cf. "Working Out Our Own Salvation," III.6–7; "The Signs of the Times," II.10; "The General Spread of the Gospel," ¶9; "The Imperfections of Human Knowledge," ¶1; "On Schism," ¶21. For a sample of Luther's consistent rejection of this *in se est* tradition, cf. *Table Talk* in *Works* (1967), 54:392.

[25]Schaff, *COC* II:94–95: "Of this Justification the causes are these: the *final* cause indeed is the glory of God and of Jesus Christ, and the life everlasting; while the efficient cause is a merciful God who washes and sanctifies gratuitously, signing, and anointing with the Holy Spirit of promise, who is the pledge of our inheritance; but the meritorious cause is his most beloved only-begotten, our Lord Jesus Christ, who, when we were enemies . . . merited justification for us by his most holy Passion . . . and made satisfaction for us unto God the Father; the *instrumental* cause is the sacrament of baptism, . . . lastly, the sole *formal* cause is the justice of God, not that whereby he himself is just, but that whereby he maketh us just, whereby we . . . are renewed in the spirit of our mind, and we are not only reputed, but are truly called, and are just, receiving justice within us, each one according to his own measure, which the Holy Ghost distributes to every one as he wills, and according to each one's proper disposition and co-operation."

[26]Cf. James Brodrick, S.J., *Robert Bellarmine, 1542–1621* (London, 1950), Vol. II, chap. XIX, 1–69, "The Controversy About Grace." See also Bellarmine's *Controversies* . . . , III (1596), Parts V–VII.

springs of the Christian life, its psychological motivations and ethical goals. The imputationists denounced those who stressed holy living as advocates of works righteousness (and, therefore, as papists). In turn, *they* were accused of antinomianism. The result was a protracted, excited debate that had pitted really great theologians like Davenant and Downham against Jeremy Taylor and William Beveridge, men like Richard Baxter against men like John Bunyan—with dozens in the supporting casts on either side. Then comes Wesley, who is finally forced to a decision of his own. His report of this decision and how he came by it (in his *Journal* for November 12, 1738) is so casual as to be actually misleading:

> In the following week [after a theological crisis precipitated by his discovery of Jonathan Edwards' *Faithful Narrative* . . .], I began more narrowly to inquire what *the* doctrine of the Church of England *is* concerning the much-controverted point of just-ification by faith; and the sum of what I found in the Homilies, I extracted and printed for the use of others.[27]

What you would never guess from this entry is that there was no *consensus* as to "*the* doctrine of the Church of England" on justification, and never had been. Something else not often enough noticed here is that it was neither Böhler, nor Aldersgate, nor Hernnhut that settled the question for Wesley, but rather his own Homilies and the Articles!

We can, therefore, take three of Wesley's sermons—"The Circumcision of the Heart" (1732–33), "Justification by Faith" (1746) and "The Lord Our Righteousness" (1765)—as landmarks in a progression of thought toward a doctrine that (1) redefined repentance as *self-knowledge* (of our radical need of divine grace) and, therefore, not a meritorious *work;* that (2) denied all human merit, and affirmed Christ's atoning death as the *meritorious* (not formal) *cause* of our justification; that (3) distinguished between voluntary sins (sin properly so-called) and our involuntary shortfallings ("wandering thoughts," "sin in believers," etc.); and then, that (4) stressed "holiness of heart and life" as the agenda and goal of the Christian life. This allowed him to speak of justification as *pardon* and yet also of "real *and* relative" changes in

---

[27]*JWJ* II:101 (italics added). Cf. "The Doctrine of Salvation, Faith and Good Works, Extracted from the Homilies of the Church of England" (1738) in *JWO*, 123.

the believer's heart and life.[28] Justification is God's work *for* us (for Christ's sake); sanctification is God's work *in* us (through the Holy Spirit). In justification we "*gain* God's favour"; and yet we must seek also to "*retain* it" through obedience and love.[29]

Wesley claimed, in all sincerity, that he differed not a hair's breadth from Calvin on justification[30]—and on this score, he was right, in a way. But he also taught, as *essential*, a doctrine of Christian perfection that scandalized the Calvinists—as well as the moralists, for different reasons! His crucial text here was Galatians 5:6 (the faith that *works* by love"—i.e., *fides formata!*) and his two key notions were God's unmerited mercy in our justification and our *active* participation in "working out our salvation."[31] He died without ever understanding why the other evangelicals held him at arm's length despite his pathetic pleas for alliance with all evangelicals.[32] And yet it was precisely Wesley's attempt to integrate the Protestant *theologia crucis* with the catholic *theologia gloriae* that gives his doctrine of the Christian life its special richness.

This constant emphasis on the mysterious interaction of God and humanity in our salvation shows up in Wesley's unwearied repetition of one aphorism after another about faith and its fruits. He was a eudaemonist: it was self-evident to him that all our truly human aspirations are oriented toward happiness.[33] But human hunger for happiness can be sated only by holiness; thus, one of Wesley's favorite pairings is "happy *and* holy."[34] When, however, he comes to specify the *essence* of holiness, it is so simple that it

[28]Cf. his sermon on "Justification by Faith," II.5, and "The Scripture Way of Salvation," I.3.

[29]Cf. his open letter "to Several Preachers and Friends," July 10, 1771 (*JWL* V:263–67), and also the letter to Adam Clarke, Nov. 26, 1790 (*JWL* VIII:249).

[30]Cf. his letter to John Newton, May 14, 1765 (*JWL* IV:298).

[31]Cf. "The Great Privilege of Those That Are Born of God," I.6–10, II.9.

[32]Cf. his claims in "The Lord Our Righteousness," II.6–20.

[33]"The best end which any creature can pursue is happiness in God," in "The Righteousness of Faith," II.9; see also "The Unity of the Divine Being," ¶9, 10.

[34]Cf. *JWL* I:16, 92, 114, 218; *JWJ* I:447; II, 89–90; *JWW* IX:235, 436; and sermons "The General Spread of the Gospel," ¶27; "On Perfection," II.13; "Spiritual Worship," III.6, 7; "The Important Question," III.6; "An Israelite Indeed," I.2; "The Discoveries of Faith," ¶6; "The Unity of the Divine Being," ¶9, 16, 21; "The Wedding Garment," ¶19.

seems downright simplistic, until you see him working it out across the range of its combinations. Holiness is the love of God and of humanity—the *perfect* love of God and of our neighbor reigning over *all* other loves and interests.[35] And it comes down, finally, to this—"that we love God because *he* first loved us"—and in the power of God's love, we can learn to love our neighbors, grace-fully.[36]

Is this a doctrinal hodgepodge or actually a higher synthesis—this blending of a Protestant doctrine of justification (*minus* "election," "irresistible grace" and "perseverance"!) and a catholic doctrine of sanctification (*minus* the apparatus of priestcraft!)—this wedding of the theologies of the Cross and of glory? Seen one way, this is a question to leave to the historical theologians (let *them* read Downham and Sherlock on this point, if they've nothing more urgent to do!). But it also may very well be that the theological enterprise in our time has come back round to the point where these questions about "justification" and "sanctification" are newly relevant and urgent (how *are* we to interpret humanity's need for reconciliation and wholeness—and *God's* provisions for them?). And if this be so, then Wesley's "third-alternative" way has more bearing on *our* problems than most of our other options.

Ours, they tell us, is a world come of age (which, of course, was David Hume's point two centuries before Dietrich Bonhoeffer). And we can see for ourselves that it is a world coming apart at the seams. Just as obviously, the confidence that Rousseau and Feuerbach and Teilhard have encouraged us to cling to—as to what the human potential and prospects really are—has come to be newly doubtful. Their utopian visions, and ours, have turned out to be tragically illusory. They (and we?) reckoned without the reality of a radical human flaw—partly because we were able to deny the older myths of "the Fall" and "original sin," partly because technology has promised us so much and has also delivered so much. And yet it becomes plainer by the day that, in

[35]Out of more than two dozen similar statements, cf. *JWW* VIII:4, 474; "The Important Question," III.2; "Of Former Times," ¶11, 22; and his letter to Mary Bishop, February 4, 1776 (*JWL* VI:205–06).

[36]Cf. the Preface to *A Christian Library*, ¶7, I:viii (*JWW* XIV:222). See also, "The Unity of the Divine Being," ¶16: "In two words, true religion is gratitude and benevolence: Gratitude to our Creator and supreme Benefactor, and benevolence to our fellow-creatures."

the face of the rising tides of *anomie* and antinomianism throughout Western society and all its cultural spin-offs, none of the older
traditions—neither the liberal nor the fundamentalist traditions—
can any longer suffice, and not even the newer excitements of
pentecostalism either. The hungers of the human heart still cry out
for something like Wesley's gospel of God's unmerited love *and*
the Christian disciplines of love and joy!

Everywhere there is a fresh hunger for *living* faith (in
something or other), for spiritual excitement in place of conventional religion. A stifling disenchantment spreads across the
world—and with it, a welcome for almost anything that promises
truly enhanced meanings for human life. This is what the drug
scene is all about; this is what the counterculture and the
encounter culture have been trying to tell us. For the generality of
nominal Christians—and also the vaster masses of humankind—
Christianity is either Dullsville or just another "interest group."
Wesley's particular methods of generating excitement might not
work today—although Professor Oden has pointed out some
striking parallels between Wesley's "societies" and modern therapy groups.[37] And yet Wesley's concern for heart religion, his
emphasis upon worship as a vivid sense of God's awe-full
presence and strengthening love, his stress on small-group
mutuality, his splendid indifference to pomp and circumstance—
all these still resonate in our hearts today. Wesley would have
fewer misgivings than most of us about unconventional happen-
ings in church or out. What would appall him is the flatness of
what passes, for so many, as "church work."[38]

On yet another frontier the liberal tradition is faltering for its
basic confidence in human perfectibility and the rule of reason is
being sharply challenged by such men as Roszak, Castaneda and
Perelman. The old Cartesian prescription for "clear and distinct
ideas" is more and more boldly challenged. Perelman's *The New
Rhetoric*[39] may serve as a sign-event for this new mentality—with
its thesis that humanly significant truth simply does not come in

[37]Thomas C. Oden, *The Intensive Group Experience; The New Pietism*
(Philadelphia: Westminster, 1972), 56–88.
[38]Cf. "Thoughts Upon Methodism," in *JWW* XIII:258: "I am not
afraid that the people called Methodists should ever cease to exist either
in Europe or America. But I am afraid lest they should exist only as a dead
sect, having the form of religion without the power."
[39]Notre Dame, Indiana, 1969.

closed systems but rather in bursts of insights and through the alchemies of persuasion. But Wesley was never content with the linear visions of Newton and Locke, and he may still have something to teach us about *the language of feeling* in the processes of personal transformations and self-realization.[40]

Our age, like Wesley's, is fascinated by fresh visions of a new humanity. It is now a blasphemy to deny that men, women or youth—of whatever sort or condition—are all equal in their human dignity and rights and this is so despite the blasphemers that remain amongst us. We have finally *seen* the secular vision of the gospels according to Marx and to Freud: a human community liberated by human effort from injustice and illusion. Wesley would have rejected these secularisms out of hand and would have insisted—as many of us have ceased to do—that human blindness to the human flaw can only lead a self-deceived humanity to an uncomprehended doom. This means, however, that *his* "good news" in this *new* scene might also be newly relevant: the Scripture's revelation of God's unmerited grace through Christ's redemptive love in the sacral community of the Holy Spirit, the gospel of God's righteous rule in human hearts as our only hopeful alternative to catastrophe.

But any such renewal of our awareness of the human predicament raises yet another major current issue—one that slices across the boundaries of denominational theology. If the human plight, at bottom, is radical and utterly serious, then what are the conceivable terms of any authentic reconciliation between God and humankind? The stark antitheses of the Reformation on this point are no longer live options—if only because their forensic presuppositions no longer fit the human condition as we know it now. Still more recent stereotypes (nineteenth-century liberalism, "neo-orthodoxy," "existentialism," etc.) are also disintegrating before our eyes. And now that the Roman Catholics have joined us in the ecumenical forum, we have to deal once more with the ghosts of Bellarmine and Newman, and this is altogether fitting. The old chasms between Protestants and Catholics may not have been bridged but they do not follow the same old fault lines as before. The old "either/ors"—between the

---

[40]Cf. his letter to Samuel Furley, May 21, 1762 (*JWL* IV:181): ". . . in spite of all my logic, I cannot so prove any one point in the whole compass of philosophy or divinity as not to leave room for strong objections."

Protestant emphasis upon God's sheer gratuity in our justification or the catholic insistence on actual righteousness in our "sanctification"[41]—call for new "both/ands." The Protestant fear of moralism, in an increasingly a-moral society, is increasingly unrealistic. The catholic dread of antinomianism is still warranted, but its traditional safeguards were never less effectual.

To much of this, Wesley seems to have little to say, *directly*. And yet, on the central issue—of divine grace and human consciousness—his basic insights are still as pertinent as any I know, in the whole history of Christian thought or in the new frontiers of psychotherapy. Behind all his dated (and disposable) "opinions" lies a total view of the Christian life, comprehensive and realistic: of God above all else and all else in God; of the human plight running deeper than any human cure for it (hence the need for a "new creature in Christ"); of Christ's love as God's love, redeeming our true humanity; of the Holy Spirit as God's inspiring presence in all "expanded consciousness" (a synonym for "religious experience"?). Besides, Wesley had a remarkably practical rule for judging *extraordinary* gifts of the Spirit (ecstasies, miracles, etc.).[42] It strikes me as still applicable, even in these days of new charisms and claims. No profession of an "extraordinary gift" (tongues or whatever) is to be rejected out of hand, as if we knew what the Spirit should or should not do. He was a cool hand himself, but Wesley had no disdain, on principle, for ecstasies and mind-blowings. What he *did* insist on was that such gifts are *never* ends in themselves, that *all* of them must always be *normed* (and judged) by the Spirit's "*ordinary*" gifts [love, joy, peace, patience, kindness, etc., etc.].[43] Like faith, all spiritual gifts are in order to *love*, which is the measure of *all* that is claimed to be from God, since God *is* love.

We've time for only one more point, out of a dozen that might be made. It concerns Wesley as "communicator." The fact is

[41]Cf. *Lumen Gentium*, chap. V. [In *The Documents of Vatican II* (New York: America Press, 1966). Cf. the Protestant response to *Lumen Gentium*, written by Outler himself, 102–6.]

[42]Cf. 1 Cor. 12:28b—and see his letter to Dr. Warburton, bishop of Gloucester, Nov. 26, 1762 (JWL IV:340), for Wesley's "list" of them: (1) exorcism; (2) glossalalia; (3) handling serpents; (4) immunity to poisons; (5) spiritual healing; (6) discernment of spirits, etc.

[43]Cf. Gal. 5:22: "love, joy, peace, long-suffering, gentleness, goodness, faith, meekness, temperance. . . ."

undeniable. He did get through to the unlikeliest audiences—this mincing don who quoted Jesus and Horace to Kingswood miners, touching off hysterics and yet also changed lives in a ratio that seems nearly random. This reality still leaves me bemused, after all my years with him. The other day, though, one of my "media" friends was commenting on the notorious failures of preachers in their use of the obvious potentialities of "electronic mass communication." His thesis was that the days of extended verbal utterance are long gone. Nowadays, said he, all of us have spots before our eyes: "radio" spots, TV "spots," "short inputs"—in news briefs and advertisements. The result is that most of us are already so overloaded with disparate and discordant "information" that what we need most of all, is less new "input" and more new *perspectives.*

All our homiletical traditions, however, are oriented the other way round. They assume that our audiences come equipped with basic Christian perspectives and that what they need most is focus and motivation. "New formulations for the old truths": this was the slogan in my seminary days. But, clearly, this is a condition contrary to fact, nowadays. It is the Christian perspective in general that is lacking, in the churches and out—and there are few who will stay to hear it expounded in any fullness (not even in our classrooms). Moreover, the electronic media could not provide protracted exposure for us, even if they wanted to. The "hot-gospellers" are exceptions; their "show-biz" is quite different.[44] But it flashed through my mind, as this man was talking, that *this* was the function of those "short sketches" that Wesley sprinkled so liberally throughout his sermons and letters: short summaries of his gospel or of his special way of putting it.[45] And this is why he could oversimplify without embarrassment and rely on metaphors in place of argument.[46]

For my own part, I realize that I'm too set in the old ways to

[44]Cf. James Morris, *The Preachers* (New York: St. Martin's Press, 1973).

[45]Cf., e.g., "Heavenly Treasure in Earthen Vessels," I.3, and "The Wedding Garment," ¶6; also his letter to George Downing, April 6, 1761 JWL IV:146) and his open letter "To Various Clergymen," April 9, 1764 (JWL IV:237).

[46]As in the famous simile about the "porch," the "door" and the "room" of religion; cf. his letter to Thomas Church, June 17, 1746 (JWL II:268).

learn to do this sort of thing very well. I mistrust aphorisms, for I've seen them degraded into slogans all too easily. And whenever a theological formulation of mine comes out too clear and simple, there is a reflex uneasiness that something's been overlooked. But I do believe that there's a lesson somewhere here in Wesley that a new generation of preachers might very well learn to translate into their own "new rhetoric," with "rules" that might run something like this:

1. The people must be "*made*" to hear the *whole* Gospel (and this means pithy, arresting, summative language).
2. Our aim must be reaction (the "direct pitch" for *action*— what Wesley called "application");[47]
3. Actions must be aimed at sustained responses (e.g. reinforcements by significant interest groups);
4. Persuasion must be based on *nuances* of competence and authority, not their flaunting!

Preaching like this might very well turn the church around—and Wesley would be the first to ask, "Why not?"

I know, as well as you, that any such advertisement of Wesley's relevance as a contemporary theologian is largely fatuous in our present situation. For one thing, it implies a challenge to Methodist theologians and preachers alike to take him seriously—precisely *as a theologian!*—and we are tragically unprepared for anything like this. We have, by now, a nearly irreversible tradition of "anti-intellectualism" in Methodism which neither nourishes nor cherishes theology as top priority. Moreover (or, rather, consequently!), we have no developed, ecumenical tradition of Wesley-studies at all comparable to what is already commonplace in the case of Luther, Calvin, St. Thomas, *et. al.* Most of our Methodist theological professors have been trained in ecumenical centers (which is altogether right and proper) but with often little or no acquaintance with Wesley himself as a resource for ecumenical theologizing. The result is that *Wesleyan theologians* are rare enough to be listed as "an endangered species." And, speaking generally, Wesley has still to be "discovered" by the non-Methodists as an ecumenical resource for them—save for bare glimmers of recognition from Orthodox like Georges Florovsky, Catholics like Michael Hurley, Pentecostalists like Richard DuPlessis, Lutherans like Martin Schmidt, and Anglicans like

[47]See his letter to Joseph Taylor, Feb. 14, 1787 (JWL VII:369).

Garth Lean. Even so, the day will come—or at least should be prepared for—when Wesley's embracing vision of God's grace transforming human nature into its full potential, of the Cross of Christ and the glory beyond, of "holiness" as *the* Christian life style will find its rightful place in the kind of Christianity that can survive the catastrophes that almost surely lie ahead.

Wesley died with a hymn on his lips; its text was Isaac Watts' "I'll Praise My Maker While I've Breath." You can call it a pious gesture, if you like—for there is no doubt that Elizabeth Ritchie's account of Wesley's death is a highly self-conscious example of the *ars moriendi* tradition that Wesley had taught his people for so long. But there was also something more: it was a closing statement as to what the breath of life is for—and what it had been for, for him, over the span of seven incredible decades. We *have* been made (*all* of us) for fellowship with God. God has made us so that *all* our lives may be protracted acts of praise and blessing. This is not only our chief end but our true enjoyment. Wesley had been a wayfaring, joyful witness to this bedrock reality: it was the *cantus firmus* of all his experience and reflection.[48] Thus it was a last reiteration, at the very end, of his earliest vision of "holy living and holy dying":

> I'll praise my Maker while I've breath,
> And when my voice is lost in death,
> Praise shall employ my *nobler* powers.
> My days of praise shall *ne'er* be past,
> While life *and* thought *and* being last—
> Or immortality endures!

---

[48]"To make our daily employment a sacrifice to God: to buy and sell, to eat and drink, all to his glory," in "Sermon on Our Lord's Sermon on the Mount IV," III.4.

The Place of Wesley in the Christian Tradition

———†———

[1976] This essay was delivered in 1974 at an international gathering of scholars at Drew University to launch and commemorate publication of the Oxford Edition of the Works of John Wesley. Outler delves into historical sources both familiar and obscure to support his thesis that Wesley was "the most important Anglican theologian of the eighteenth century." One may need to read the essay with something like *The Oxford Dictionary of the Christian Church* at hand.

To write synoptically of John Wesley's place in the Christian Tradition in a single essay is a bit intimidating. A lifetime's study of the history of Christian thought has resulted in no better than a smattering acquaintance with "the Christian tradition," viewed as a *historiographical* problem. A decade with Faith & Order's Theological Study Commission on Tradition and Traditions (1952–1963) prompted a good deal of pondering about this tradition, as a *theological* problem. A dozen years spent with Wesley, now in my old age, has opened up an exciting horizon of inquiry as to his place in and import for the Christian tradition— now and tomorrow. But inevitably, the limits of this essay will force me to broad generalizations without their full evidence and arguments. To the offended or the skeptical, I can only plead that there's a lot more where this came from. The rest of you, who prefer summaries to a full script, ought to be thankful for what you are not about to receive!

Until our own times, certainly, Wesley's "place" was clearly established (albeit with contrary evaluations): he was the founder of Methodism. For Methodist triumphalists this was enough— one thinks of Tyerman's sincere paean: "Methodism is the greatest fact in the history of the church."[1] What *this* needed was an adequate etiology, and Wesley met that need. To the radicals amongst Methodism's despisers (e.g., E. P. Thompson) it was enough to fix on Wesley the blame for Methodism's failures to support the revolutionary aims of "the English working class."[2] Secular historians (Halévy, Robertson, Semmel) have recognized Wesley's historical influence without probing deeply into the *theological* basis for it (although Semmel is something of an exception here—and his book is likely to stand as a landmark in Wesley studies for just this reason).[3]

---

[1]Cf. Luke Tyerman, *The Life and Times of the Rev. John Wesley* (New York: Harper, 1872), I:1.

[2]*The Making of the English Working Class* (New York: Pantheon, 1964), 41–46, 53–54, 362–64.

[3]Bernard Semmel, *The Methodist Revolution* (New York: Basic Books, Inc., 1973; London: Heinemann Educational Books, 1974).

Non-Methodists (with a few exceptions) have found Wesley easy enough to ignore or else to assess in terms of their own several traditions. Hildebrandt measured him by the yardstick of Luther; Piette recognized the catholic elements of his doctrine but scarcely understood his Protestantism; Professor Schmidt has seen him as a crossbreed of Puritanism and Pietism.[4] No major Calvinist historian (to my knowledge) has studied him in depth—unless you reckon Horton Davies as a "Calvinist"—but there have been Methodist scholars concerned to stress the "Puritan" elements in Wesley's faith and thought (Cell, Newton, Monk). Anglicans, generally, have been content to leave him to the Methodists. Alexander Knox, Robert Southey (and Canon Overton) considered him an offbeat Anglican—and, in our time, there have been specialized studies by men like Ronald Knox (quondam Anglican), V. H. H. Green, and Garth Lean. But none of these regarded Wesley as a significant Anglican *theologian*—and none attempted the unpacking of the huge jumble of his sources as a way of explaining his resultant theological position. Roman Catholics, by and large (with a few happy exceptions like Fr. Hurley), have felt no need to go behind Wesley's outspoken anti-Romanism to notice similarities and differences in his doctrines of justification as compared with the *early debates* on this subject at Trent (Seripando, Pole, Sanfelice)[5] or with Bellarmine in the later *De Auxiliis* controversy. No Roman whom I know has yet noticed (in print) the remarkable resonances between Wesley's teachings on "holiness of heart and life" and those remarkable chapters in *Lumen Gentium*, IV and V.

My own interest in Wesley has less to do with his stature and function as Methodism's cult hero than with what I have come to regard as his significant achievements *as a theologian*—in his special historical situation. He has gone unnoticed by historical theologians, generally, partly because he was not a theologian's theologian, partly because he belonged to no single school and founded none. Wesley's lack of epigones needs further analysis, but not here and now. The historical theologian is bound to view mass evangelists and popularizers with suspicion, as being

---

[4]"The English heritage and the German contribution formed in John Wesley a true and authentic alliance." Martin Schmidt, *John Wesley: A Theological Biography* (London, 1962), I:309.

[5]Cf. Hubert Jedin, *A History of the Council of Trent* (London, 1958), Vol. II, ch. v, 166–96.

derivative or simplistic. "Landmark theologians" are more readily identified by their genius for, say, metaphysics (St. Augustine, St. Thomas) or hermeneutics (Luther) or system-building (Calvin). But Wesley was a *folk*-theologian—with no academic base (such as Luther had or the Halle pietists), no political base (Calvin and Knox) and no intention of founding a new denomination, even if one did emerge (over his dead body!).

On the other hand, we don't have many mass evangelists of record with anything like Wesley's immersion in classical culture, his eager openness to "modern" science and social change, his awareness of the entire Christian tradition as a living resource—and even fewer with his ecclesial vision of a sacramental community as the nurturing environment of Christian experience. One thinks of Richard Baxter, Charles Simeon, St. John Bosco as possible analogs—each comparable in some respects but not in all.

Thus a resultant thesis has been forming in my mind in answer to this nagging puzzle—"How best to characterize this man?"—that *John Wesley was the most important Anglican theologian of the eighteenth century because of his distinctive, composite answer to the age-old question as to "the nature of the Christian life"*: its origins, growth, imperatives, social impact, final end. Over five decades in a revival that he directed solo, less by foresight than shrewd reaction, his constant problematic was soteriology—amongst people who had few incentives to be comforted by verbal or abstract answers. Everything creative in his theologizing (including his sources and his way with them) has this practical concern as its warrant. This explains his hermeneutics (*sola scriptura*), his appeals to tradition, his impulse to controversy, his tenuous alliances with other evangelicals, his gallant "appeals to men of reason and religion," etc.

This root question as to the nature of Christian existence had first been defined for him at Epworth—largely in his theological tutorials with his mother (continued by correspondence from Oxford). It had been redefined in his ambivalent experiences in the Holy Club; it had been brought into focus in his confrontations with the Moravians and Salzburgers in Georgia; it had turned into an agonizing groping for faith with Peter Böhler. The agony had been resolved—dramatically and for a time—at Aldersgate, but the larger problem continued to press upon him throughout the unfolding drama of the Revival and his further theological reflections. He denied that he ever changed his theological position after 1738, partly because his basic intentions had never changed. But the nuances and equilibria of the position *did* change and these changes are the only clues I have found to explain his otherwise incredible eclecticism, e.g., that theological medley in *The Christian Library*, those strange exhumations in *The Arminian Magazine*.

Within the terms of this hypothesis, one can set the succession of Wesley's theological stages in a credible perspective and, even more importantly, comprehend, at least in part, the dynamics of the Wesleyan syndrome (repentance, justification-regeneration-sanctification), the Wesleyan aversion to antinomianism ("speculative" and "practical"),[6] the Wesleyan doctrine of grace, the Wesleyan wedding of the evangelical principle with the catholic substance of Christianity. In short, it was Wesley's distinctive undertaking to integrate "faith alone" with "holy living" in an authentic dialectic.

Everyone knows that the antithesis of "faith alone" and "holy living" was the most tortured issue in classical Protestantism—and between Wittenberg, Geneva, and Rome. These two disparate visions had set Luther and Calvin as fiercely against the Täufer as the papists.[7] It was this polarization (as Professor Allison has argued in *The Rise of Moralism*[8]—an important if also biased study) that had produced two rival traditions in Anglican theology and two centuries of stubborn controversy. Bishop McAdoo has analyzed this same phenomenon rather differently and in a much more richly nuanced argument (in *The Spirit of Anglicanism*).[9] *Mutatis mutandis*, the live issue at the heart of the tumultuous controversies in the Roman Catholic Church—in Jansenism and in the *De Auxiliis* battle—was not a speculative issue but the question as to what it means to become and be a Christian. This is one of the reasons why Vatican II was a landmark, since it created a new climate in which to probe the ancient problems of "grace and free will." The fourth world synod of Catholic bishops in Rome focused on the theme "The Evangelization of the Modern

---

[6]On this point, cf. Semmel, *op. cit.*, ch. II, "The Battle Against 'Speculative' Antinomianism," 23ff., and ch. III, "Confrontation with 'Practical' Antinomianism," 56ff.

[7]Cf. John S. Oyer, *Lutheran Reformers Against Anabaptists* (The Hague, 1964), 212, 234.

[8]New York: Seabury, 1966.

[9]New York: Scribner's, 1965.

World." If you set this against Bangkok, Lausanne, and Jerusalem it becomes obvious that Christian evangelism and nurture is truly an ecumenical horizon.

It was Wesley—heir to the Protestant agony but rooted in an older, richer tradition of Scripture *and* tradition—who recognized more clearly than any other theologian of his time that the old Reformation polarities had ceased to define the Christian future (which is the score on which he surpasses Butler, whose mind was far more powerful). Thus—in the swirlings of the Revival and in reaction to its anomalies—Wesley conceived his theological vocation as the message of "faith alone" *and* "holy living," affirmed together in negation of all polarizations. It is in terms of his success and failure in *this* attempt—and in whatever sense we can say that this attempt is still relevant to us—that we may speak of Wesley's "place" in the Christian tradition.

Almost from the beginning, of course, there were shrewd observers who realized that Wesley was into a theological juggling act that might well come to no good end. In 1742, the bright young vicar of All Saints, Bristol (Josiah Tucker), commented on the instabilities he perceived in Wesley's teachings and the confusions they were creating.[10] From September 1745 to March 1748, a friendly critic signing himself "John Smith" (almost certainly *not* a bishop) tried to help Wesley see that his doctrine of "palpable inspiration" was incompatible with his avowed catholic views of grace, the means of grace, and the meaning of sacramental community. Wesley politely rejected their counsel[11]—he really never learned much from critics—and argued instead that there was already proof enough that "faith alone" *and* "holy living" could actually be held together, and were being held together—in the experience of the Methodist Christians! In this same early period Wesley broke with Whitefield because of his one-sided stress on *sola fide*—and then with William Law for precisely the opposite emphasis. Wesley turned on the Establishment—symbolized for him by Bull, Tillotson, *et al.*—accusing them of placing moral resolution ("works") ahead of "faith alone." He forfeited the B.D. degree (that, as Fellow of Lincoln, he was morally

---

[10] *A Brief History of the Principles of Methodism* (Oxford, 1742).

[11] See *The Principles of a Methodist. Occasioned by a late Pamphlet entitled, "A Brief History of the Principles of Methodism"* (Bristol, 1742). For the "Smith-Wesley" correspondence *in extenso*, see Henry Moore, *Life of the Rev. John Wesley* (London: Kershaw, 1825), II:473–576.

obligated to take) because of a "supposition speech" that is, clearly, one of the worst sermons he ever wrote: the Latin is elegant but the spirit is uncharitable, hypocritical, and reckless.[12]

As the Revival wore on it was the Calvinist remnant in the Church of England that offered Wesley his sternest challenge. Moreover, the battle lines between them were defined by the old distinction between the "causes" of justification—"formal" versus "meritorious." The debate on this point runs back at least to Frith and Gardiner, Cartwright and Hooker, Whitaker and Baro, Davenant and Thomas Jackson, *et al.* Finally, in 1765, Wesley took his stand (in "The Lord Our Righteousness")—affirming Christ's death as the *meritorious* cause of our justification, denying it as *formal* cause. Five years later, he shattered the uneasy truce with a theological "minute" on justification in and for his annual Conference. My first impression of this "minute" was that it was carelessly drafted (it *is* lacking in nuance!). More lately, however, I've come to believe that Wesley *meant* to provoke the Calvinists— as indeed he did. Subsequently, he was willing to mitigate his offense but not to retract his offending views. Otherwise, he would not have published Fletcher's "vindication"[13] when it might so easily have been suppressed—nor unleashed Walter Sellon and Thomas Olivers on the predestinarians.[14] It is simply untrue that Wesley ever abandoned the *sola fide*—but it is likewise undeniable that, after 1770, his stress was on "holy living" in opposition to its distortions (as he saw them) by the other evangelicals. It is no

[12]"Hypocrisy at Oxford," Isa. 1:21, June 27, 1741. Thomas Jackson published the English text of this sermon under the title, "The True Christianity Defended," in *JWW* VII:452-62. The Latin text—in Wesley's holograph—is in the Morley Collection, Wesley College, Bristol.

[13]"A Vindication of the Rev. Mr. Wesley's Last Minutes: occasioned by a circular, printed letter, inviting principled persons, both clergy and laity . . . to oppose them in a body. . . ." Signed "J. F[letcher]. July 29, 1771." [This was sponsored and edited by Wesley himself.]

[14]Cf. Walter Sellon, "A Defence of God's Sovereignty . . . "; "Arguments Against General Reprobation Considered"; "An Answer to Aspasio Vindicated"; "Sermons on I Tim. 4:14 and Titus 3:5," in *Works* (London, 1814), 2 vols. See also Thomas Olivers, "A Defence of Methodism: Delivered . . . in a public debate . . . held in London . . . 1785, on the following question, Have the Methodists done most good or evil?" (Leeds, 1818); "A full defence of Rev. John Wesley, in answer to several personal reflections cast on that gentleman by the Rev. Caleb Evans. . . ." (London, 1776); "A full refutation of the doctrine of unconditional perseverance: in a discourse on Hebrews" (London, 1790).

accident that his first great sermon ("The Circumcision of the Heart," 1732–33) and his last great one ("The Wedding Garment," 1790) bracketed a lifelong plea: for the love of God above all else and the love of all else in God.

The "interim" between this "beginning" and "end" defies simple narration, for it involves an elaborate analysis of Wesley's sources and his use of them. On this score he is downright unhelpful, largely (one supposes) because he saw no need for documentation (save from Scripture) for his particular readers. What is required, therefore (and what has yet to be done adequately, by my lights at least), is a reading of Wesley against what Wesley himself read, with a view to some sort of form-critical history of his sources and editorial procedures—as in his sermons, the *Journal*, *The Christian Library*, and *The Arminian Magazine*, etc. This is a job that I've begun but not finished (and now may never)—and space is too limited here for more than some core samplings from an incomplete exploration. Even this, however, will illustrate what I mean by trying to place Wesley in his own times, on his own terms—within a critical historiographical perspective.

One place to begin is with the underestimated fact that both his parents were converts to Anglicanism after their careful upbringings in Nonconformity. There is a stereotype of Samuel, Sr., as "self-seeking"—of which it is enough to say that either he was superlatively inept in his self-seeking or else was sadly self-deceived. He *was* inept—*and* eccentric *and* a born loser—but his prime motives were stubbornly principled, and those principles were Tory Anglicanism, buttressed by that horror of further anarchy from Nonconformity that had triggered his first conversion. How else explain his quixotic defense of Henry Sacheverell, *or* Bishop Atterbury, *or* his reckless attacks upon the Dissenters? Susanna Annesley's Anglican conversion was more reflective but no less painful—the youngest daughter of Nonconformity's great patriarch, moving from Dissent to its other verge. John Wesley was bred up—in this climate of unrewarded virtue—to a theological position not fairly labeled "Arminian" or "Laudian" and certainly not "latitudinarian." It was, instead, what Peter Heylyn had already described and defended as "the old English Protestantism"—older than Dort and Arminius, older than Henry VIII.[15]

[15]Cf. his *Historia Quinquarticularis* (London, 1681), Part III, ch. xxii, 631.

The elder Wesleys understood this as a gospel of moral rectitude (the prevailing Anglican view at the time) and John imbibed it, even as he was learning the craft of preaching from his father (including a code of abbreviations). From Susanna he had learned the essence of will-mysticism (Castañiza-Scupoli and Scougal).[16] From both Susanna and Samuel, Sr., he had come by his lifelong aversion to predestination.

At Charterhouse and Christ Church he experienced a basic reorientation (what I'd call a "conversion," as does *Webster's Dictionary*)—to the tradition of Christian humanism, twin-rooted as it was in the classics and the Scriptures. His later disparagements of his formal education need to be weighed against the obvious fact that it bore him a lifetime harvest of information, insights and a characteristic rhetoric (his comments about "plain words for plain people" to the contrary notwithstanding).

In 1725, he was converted yet again—this time to the existential import of the "holy living" traditions of his childhood and adolescence (this, plainly, is what he is trying to tell us in paragraph two of the successive editions of his *Plain Account of Christian Perfection*).[17] If a man is entitled to but one conversion in his lifetime (as the pietists insist), *this* wasn't it. But its burden ("holy living") became as profound an element in his continuing Christian concerns as *sola fide* did after 1738. Incidentally, Wesley claimed later that, at this stage of his Christian development, he had never heard of the *sola fide*,[18] but this is hyperbole, to say the

---

[16]Cf. Juan de Castañiza [i.e., Lorenzo Scupoli], *Spiritual Conflict*, tr. by Robert Reade and revised by Richard Lucas (London, 1698); and Henry Scougal, *The Life of God in the Soul of Man; or the Nature and Excellency of the Christian Religion*, etc. (1677); 6th ed. with a preface by Gilburt Burnet (London, 1733).

[17]*A Plain Account of Christian Perfection, as Believed and Taught by The Reverend Mr. John Wesley, from the Year 1725, to the Year 1777*, in JWW XI:366–448. (Six editions were printed between 1766–1789).

[18]For example, cf. "Remarks on Mr. Hill's Review" (JWW X:403): ". . . I did not see clearly that we are saved by faith till the year 1738." Also his letter to William Law, in JWL I:239–42, dated May 14, 1738, where Wesley sharply criticizes his old mentor for not having "advised" him of "this living, justifying faith in the blood of Jesus." In his "Farther Appeal . . . " (JWW VIII:111). Wesley says he was ordained deacon in 1725 and "during all that time I was utterly ignorant of justification and confounded by sanctification. . . ." In one of his last sermons, "On the Wedding Garment," ¶ 18 (JWW VII:317), he says, "Only about fifty years

least. We know that, later, he alludes to almost every issue in the great debates that had been triggered by Dort and TULIP, to the antinomianism of John Saltmarsh and Tobias Crisp (solifidianism run wild), to Bull, Baxter and Bunyan. We also know that he turned to Cranmer (in 1738) for validation of his "new" theology and that in 1744 he had his preachers read Baxter's *Aphorisms on Justification* (1640)—a scarce item even then, since Baxter had already disowned it.[19] Did Wesley learn *all* this *after* Aldersgate? Of course not; not even poor lectures at Oxford could have failed to orient him toward this notorious past. And even in his own time there were men like John Guyse (1680–1761) and Philip Doddridge (1702–1751). What Wesley meant was that, until his confrontations by the Moravians and Salzburgers, he had never been challenged by *sola fide* as a personal demand for decision. The aftermath of this confrontation—Peter Böhler, Aldersgate, Herrnhut, Jonathan Edwards' *Faithful Narrative of a Surprising Work of God in New England* (published in 1736, but not read by Wesley until October of 1738)—makes clear, good sense, and it adds up to a twin conclusion: 1738 was Wesley's theological *annus mirabilis* (miraculous year) and Aldersgate was the dramatic moment in that year when he reversed the priorities between *sola fide* and holy living, never to reverse them again.

It is, however, gravely misleading to suppose that Aldersgate settled Wesley's *mind* or stabilized his subsequent reflections. He was, by instinct, a reactor—and the unfoldings of an unscripted religious movement kept him in much more of a theological turmoil than he ever confessed to—although its signs are abundant, once noticed. The Moravians realized this quickly and fenced him from their communion as *homo perturbatus*.[20] Then there are those brief apertures into his recurring religious despair—as recorded, for example, in the *Journal* for January 4, 1739, or in that letter to Charles, June 27, 1766.[21] More important was his quiet abandonment of his early equation of justification with assurance that drove so many people into hysterical despair.[22]

ago [i.e., 1738–40] I had a clearer view than before of justification by faith—and in this time, from that very hour, I never varied. . . ."
[19]And had not authorized its second (last) printing in 1649.
[20]Cf. Daniel Benham, ed., *Memoirs of James Hutton* (London, 1856), 40.
[21]Cf. *JWJ* II:125, and *JWL* V:14–16. See also *JWO* 80–82.
[22]Cf. Bernard G. Holland, " 'A Species of Madness': The Effect of

Then there was the epidemic (at Colne, and elsewhere, in the sixties) of profession of *entire* sanctification as a "second blessing"—Wesley's acceptance of these "facts" and the adjustments in his theoretical accountings for them. Finally, there were the changes forced on him in his struggles with the Moravians and the Calvinists.

One way to comment on these various deviations from the trajectory that had been set for him at Aldersgate is that, although Wesley had finally got the *sola fide* in its proper and prime place in the mystery of salvation, he was simply unwilling to abandon his holy living motif or assimilate it to *sola fide*, as the Calvinists had done:

> We need [Beza had said] not use the slightest labour to determine whether this one or that [justification or sanctification] precedes in order, since we never receive the one without the other.[23]

This meant, in effect, that Wesley rejected each of the classical Protestant formulations of *sola fide*, since none of them allowed for his doctrine of perfection and the expectation of being perfected in love in this life.[24] In their place he developed a soteriology based in part on classical Augustinian foundations (Christology, original sin, etc.) but that evangelized the Christian ethic and moralized the Christian evangel, that linked justification with regeneration, that affirmed both the imputation and impartation of righteousness, that repudiated both human self-assertion and passivity. He turned out "rules" by the dozen—but also with warnings that even the most scrupulous rule-keeping will get you only to the state of being an "almost Christian." He developed intensive small group nurture and therapy for Christian maturation (as Professor Oden has so shrewdly noticed).[25] But all of these were elements in his larger project: to describe and promote the Christian life as rooted in faith and fruiting in love.

John Wesley's Early Preaching," in *Wesley Historical Society Proceedings,* Vol. XXXIX, Part 3 (October, 1973), 77–85, and especially 81–85.

[23]Cf. William Forbes, *Considerationes Modestae et Pacificae* (1658), in *A Library of Anglo-Catholic Theology* (1850), I:173.

[24]Cf. "The Large Minutes," 1766, p. 54.

[25]Thomas C. Oden, *The Intensive Group Experience: The New Pietism* (Philadelphia: Westminster, 1972), 56–88.

He intimates as much, in a tantalizing report of his activities for the week of November 12–18, 1738:

> Sunday, November 12—I preached at the Castle (Oxford). In the following week I began more narrowly to inquire what the doctrine of the Church of England is concerning the much-controverted point of justification by faith; and the sum of what I found in the Homilies I extracted and printed for the use of others.[26]

This is a strange understatement. The obvious reference here is to the Homilies and the Articles, and to a resultant pamphlet (Wesley's first theological charter), *The Doctrine of Salvation, Faith and Good Works According to the Church of England* (1738). But this agenda by itself would not have busied Wesley for a full week. The Homilies and Articles had complex backgrounds and then there were the debates that followed. There was the further fact that Wesley knew (as everyone else knew) that *the* doctrine of the Church of England on "this much-controverted" point had never reached consensus.

The Homilies—at least those decisive for Wesley—meant Cranmer, and back of Cranmer there was Martin Bucer (with his doctrine of *iustitia duplex* [twofold righteousness] and his conciliatory formulae in *The Regensburg Book* [1541]), with Gropper and Contarini. Also back of Cranmer was Melanchthon (and his *causa concurrens*)—plus the not so incidental fact that Cranmer's father-in-law was Andreas Osiander. Still further back was the fountainhead of Christian humanism in England: Erasmus; and back of him, the free-will traditions of English nominalism (*facere quod in se est*[27] [to do what is in oneself]) plus the "holy living" mysticisms of Richard Rolle and Juliana of Norwich.

The Articles were the Anglican bastion for the *sola fide* Tradition and had been construed by the Calvinists as an official

---

[26]*JWJ* II:101.

[27]Cf. Wesley's *Oxford Diary*, V, [vi]: "Q? How steer between Scrupulousity, as to particular instances of Self Denial, and Self-indulgence? A. Fac quod in te est, & Deus aderit bonae tuae Voluntati (do what is in yourself and God will assist your good will)." Cf. also the sermons, "On Working Out Our Own Salvation," III. 6–7 (*JWW*, VI:512–13); "The Signs of the Times," II.10 (*JWW* VI:311); "The General Spread of the Gospel," ¶ 9 (*JWW*, VI:280); "The Imperfections of Human Knowledge," ¶ 1 (*JWW*, VI:337); "On Schism," ¶ 21 (*JWW*, VI:410).

sanction for their famous "five points": TULIP. But Wesley knew that this predestinarian interpretation of the Articles had in fact been declined by the majority of Anglican divines in the seven decades following the collapse of the Puritan Commonwealth. He had, therefore, an interesting exercise: working his way back through this thicket (from Edwards to Juliana) and then deciding to abridge Cranmer's matchless rhetoric and use it as piling for his own position. Here, then, was an Anglican who was prepared to surrender the Anglican cause against the Puritans and Dissenters on many counts (prelacy, vestments, a settled clergy dependent on secular support, etc.). He was also on the threshold of taking up the Täufer tradition of field preaching and intensive small group discipline.[28] Even "the world is my parish" bit was an old Täufer motto.[29] And yet he was still a staunch and self-conscious Anglican, determined to graft his evangelical message onto its Anglican rootstock. He rejected popery but went still further— rejecting sacerdotalism even as he sought to develop a complex doctrine of *sacramental grace* consonant with Hooker's *Laws of Ecclesiastical Polity*, V. He would presently wear out his welcome at St. Mary's, Oxford, but would continue accepting his Lincoln stipend without any *quid pro quo*. He would denounce the Establishment and nearly all its works, pass sweeping judgments against its priesthood and universities, give the bishops of Exeter and Gloucester the back of his hand—and still hold his Methodist people within the Church of England even after their separation was virtually predetermined. One might guess that there was a tacit agreement amongst the English bishops (or was it just their weakness?) to avoid a shootout with the Methodists (apart from local troubles, etc.). Thus the Methodist mission still continued largely in and for the Church of England—as Richard Graves recognizes, satirically, in his *Spiritual Quixote:*

[28]For a reference to field preaching and "Corner Preachers," cf. Oyer, *op. cit.*, 128. Wesley never admits this lineage but the plaques on Hanham Mount make it clear enough. They read (1) "Out of the Wood Came Light"; (2) "Dedicated to the Field Preachers, 1658–1739"; (3) "From 1658–1684 persecuted Bristol Baptist preachers preached in Hanham Woods to the people of this neighbourhood. The preachers often swam the flooded Avon and risked imprisonment and death for their faith." Whitefield and Wesley were following in their train!
[29]Cf. Franklin Littell, "The Anabaptist Theology of Missions," in *The Mennonite Quarterly Review*, XXI:1 (January 1947): 12.

> Our modern itinerant reformers are acting in defiance of
> human laws, without any apparent necessity of any divine
> commission. They are planting the gospel in a Christian coun-
> try.[30]

Much has been made of Luther's "preface" to the Romans as
the stimulus for Wesley's heartwarming at Aldersgate. Less has
been made of Wesley's subsequent strictures on Luther's *Commentary on Galatians*[31] and on his deficient doctrine of sanctification.

> Who has wrote more ably than Martin Luther on justification
> by faith alone? And who was more ignorant of the doctrine of
> sanctification, or more confused in his conceptions of it?[32]

Where Luther and Wesley are furthest apart is on the double point
of invincible concupiscence and "sin in believers"; this is further
correlated with their differences as to an expectation of Christian
perfection in this life.

As for Wesley and Calvin, there was the repeated claim
(sincere, I think) that, on the point of justification, Wesley stood
no further than a hair's breadth from the Genevois.[33] And there is
no doubt that Wesley came close to the Calvinist hard line on
point T of TULIP: "total depravity and original sin." But he never
seriously considered any of the other four points. Prevenience
always seemed to him a more fruitful notion than election;
universal redemption was a clear choice over limited atonement;
he could never understand how *grace* could be irresistible or
perseverance final. There was even a therapeutic side to his
doctrine of God's lost image in sinful man so that the possibility of
its restoration (*therapeia psuches*) remained, even in his fallen state.
Instead of sin being rooted in the passions, Wesley saw it
stemming from the will: it was defined, therefore, as "a violation
of a known law of God."[34] The noisy gong between Wesley and

[30]*The Spiritual Quixote: Or, the Summer's Ramble of Mr. Geoffry
Wildgoose* (1773) [Barbauld Edition, London, 1820], I:55.
[31]Cf. *JWJ* II:467.
[32]"On God's Vineyard," I.5 (*JWW* VII:204).
[33]Cf. "Minutes of the Second Annual Conference, Bristol, Thursday
August 1, 1745," Question 22f. in *JWO* 151–52. See also Wesley's letter to
John Newton, May 14, 1765 (*JWL* IV:298).
[34]Cf. "On Perfection," II.9; III.9 (*JWW* VI:417, 423); see also Wesley's
letter to John Hosmer, June 7, 1761 (*JWL* IV:155).

the Calvinists was the doctrine of predestination, but the deeper issue between them was the seemingly fine point of Christ's atoning death being either the *formal* or the *meritorious* cause of justifying faith. Trent had distinguished five "causes of justification":

1. Final cause: the glory of God
2. Efficient cause: God's gratuitous mercy
3. Meritorious cause: Christ's passion and death
4. Instrumental cause: baptism
5. Formal cause: the conferred justice of God.[35]

The Puritans, following William Perkins' lead,[36] promptly misconstrued Trent's fifth point as meaning the infusion of an *inherent human righteousness*—which, of course, was "works righteousness"! In opposition, therefore, they insisted that Christ's death was the *formal* cause of our justification—from which the TULIP syndrome followed as a logical consequence, since formal causes are efficacious by definition and it is self-evident that Christ's death is not efficacious *in all.*

The Anglican reply (and it had to be cautious, lest it appear to agree with Trent!) was that justification's *formal* cause is God's covenanting mercy to all who believe. But this allows the affirmation of Christ's death as *meritorious* cause (cf. Trent's point three!). After a quarter century of preaching the *sola fide* in a way that included imputation and impartation, relative and real changes, justification *and* regeneration, etc., Wesley felt constrained to formulate this position, as we mentioned, in "The Lord Our Righteousness."

This (and that 1770 "minute") meant that Wesley's last two decades were caught up in a constant polemic carried to the point of tedium and overkill. Its tone is reflected in the title of Wesley's house organ that he forged as his prime weapon in the war: *The Arminian Magazine* (1778). This title represents a defiant acceptance of a pejorative label that the Calvinists had pinned on him (like "Methodist" back at Oxford)—an epithet they hurled at most of their opponents. Laud was an "Arminian," but so, too, were Hales and Montague and even Baxter! Thus, Wesley became an

[35][See n.25 in "John Wesley as Theologian—Then and Now" above, 65.]

[36]Cf. William Perkins, *A Golden Chaine, or The Description of theologie; Containing the Order of the Causes of Salvation and Damnation, According to God's Word.* . . . London, 1591.

"Arminian"—chiefly in the sense that he had never been a Calvinist! But he might also have been called a "Baxterian" (with as much or little precision) and, in any case, his "Arminianism" was not learned from Arminius himself, certainly not in his formative years. Arminius does not appear in *The Christian Library*,[37] where Wesley parades most of his theological favorites. In *The Arminian Magazine* we have Peter Bertius' funeral sermon,[38] and a pro-Remonstrant history of Dort[39]—and that is all.

What we do find in this polemical arsenal is a fantastic panel of ancient witnesses to the old debates of which we have been speaking, some of them so obscure, *to us*, that one wonders wherever Wesley could have found them. There are, for example, Thomas Goad, Samuel Hoard, John Plaifere, Laurence Womock, *et al.* (from the English side), and Sebastian Castellio from the Continent—all advocates of free will and "holy living." I offer you Plaifere and Castellio as two samples from a dozen: they are representative and have been ignored (as far as I know) by Wesley scholars. If I'm mistaken on this point, a friendly correction would be welcome.

John Plaifere is so obscure that he fails to show in the *Dictionary of National Biography*—and has only one entry in the *British Museum Catalogue* and the McAlpin Collection.[40] But this one item, *Appello Evangelium* (1651), turns out to be a very interesting essay—all the more so when you consider its appearance at the zenith of Puritan power. It argues for "the *true* doctrine of divine predestination concorded with the *orthodox* doctrine of God's free grace and man's free will"—and is self-consciously Erasmian. What is even more unexpected (and significant) is that when Wesley—a ruthless abridger—comes to a long quotation in Plaifere on *justification* (from a century-old volume entitled *A Necessary Doctrine and Erudition for Any Christian Man* [1543]), he leaves *that* particular passage almost intact. Some of you will recognize, of course, that this *Necessary Doctrine . . .* is the so-called "King's Book" (of Henry VIII) and that one of the chief

---

[37]Although we have Sir Henry Wotton's biography (with a character sketch of Arminius) in XV:342ff.

[38]Cf. Vol. I (1778), 9–17.

[39]*Ibid.*, 17–28; 49–58; 97–107; 145–54.

[40]*Appello Evangelium* [*An Appeal to the Gospel*] *for the true doctrine of the Divine Predestination, concorded with the orthodox doctrine of God's free-grace, and man's free-will. . . .* London, 1651.

drafters of the article on justification was probably Stephen Gardiner—a staunchly *Catholic* bishop supporting a stubbornly *Catholic* king in a hot dispute with the pope (a frequent occurrence in medieval Europe). Plaifere's quotation appears in *The Arminian Magazine* in Volume I, pp. 545–49; in the Lacey edition of *The King's Book* (1932) the same passage runs from pp. 147–51—and argues for a view of justification recognizably similar to that of Cardinal Pole's at Trent.[41] What are we supposed to make of all this?

Maybe even stranger is Wesley's 100-page-plus selection (in volumes IV [1781] and V [1782]) of Sebastian Castellio's "Dialogues on Predestination, Election and Free Will" (1st edition, 1578). Castellio [Chateîllon] may be familiar to you as an elegant Latinist, translator of Scripture and à Kempis, a famous raconteur of Bible stories and an ardent advocate of religious toleration. But only Buisson has attempted a substantive discussion of these theological dialogues—and not very perceptively, either. Wesley seems to have discovered them in a volume published in Frankfurt in 1696 in which *four* dialogues (#IV. *De fide*) were bound together with a translation of the *De Imitatione Christi*—from monkish to Ciceronian Latin (*"è latino in latinum"*). Wesley wanted this text of à Kempis for his scholars at the Kingswood School. But he must also have noticed an "address to the reader" in it by none other than Faustus Socinus! He may or may not have known that Castellio's *Dialogues* had been denounced by Sir Francis Knollys to Lord Burleigh and the Earl of Leicester and then suppressed by Queen Elizabeth.[42] This is why I find his introduction so intriguing:

> Numberless treatises have been written, in this and the last age, on the subject of Predestination: but I have not seen any that is written with more good sense and good humour, than Castellio's *Dialogues*, wrote above two hundred years ago. Yet I know not that they have ever appeared in our tongue. I believe, therefore, the putting them into an *English* dress will give pleasure to every impartial reader.[43]

[41]Cf. Jedin, *op. cit.*, II:172, 181, 189.
[42]Cf. Ferdinand Buisson, *Sébastien Castellion: sa vie et son oeuvre (1515–1563)* (Nieuwkoop: B. de Graff, 1964), Appendice cxviii, II:498.
[43]*The Arminian Magazine*, IV:vi. Cf. also JWW XIV:289.

What were readers to make of Castellio, or we, of Wesley's interest, or of Wesley's as the only English translation printed? What this shows is that Wesley had an immense bibliography under review (rarely the famous titles, either—or the ones that have come down to us as "famous"). He had analyzed these old controversies with skill and shrewdness and had chosen his options in accordance with a self-chosen image he was willing for the world to see (if any would take the trouble to notice his unadvertised clues). It is the image of an Anglican folk-theologian, a mass-evangelist, a small-group therapist, whose message was *faith working by love leading to holiness*. This central vision is clear and its exposition is far more richly nuanced than any of his interpreters (as far as I know them) have seemed yet to realize. What is more, after checking the roster of Wesley's colleagues in the history of Christian thought, I find very few of them (saving always the handful of speculative geniuses) who have surpassed or even matched his grasp of theology as a *scientia practica*.

Over the course of Christian thought about the mystery of salvation—to venture a glittering generality that covers a multitude of analytic sins—one may see two great contrasting perspectives. They have always been in unstable tension and when either has succeeded in obscuring the other, the results have been debilitating. One has been more largely associated with what we have come to call Latin Christianity; the other is more characteristically Eastern and Greek. The code words, in Latin Christianity, have been "pardon," "acquittal," "remission," "final glory," etc.; in Greek Christianity: "forgiveness," "reconciliation," "*participation*," "perfection." Latin Christianity has been dominated by forensic images, metaphors from the law courts (Roman and medieval); Greek Christianity has been fascinated by visions of ontological "participation in God": *metousia theou*. One stresses the Cross; the other points to the Cross but also past it, to the glory beyond. No theologian worth the label has ever denied either of these emphases outright—but the historian who cannot see and feel the radical differences in tonality between the two traditions (without explaining them away by references to politics, etc.) is strangely insensitive. And yet, one of the capital features of our own new ecumenical age—tragically crippled as we are in the present moment with a near total collapse of practical statesmanship in the movement—is the mutual interaction of Western and Eastern theologies and theologians and the consequence for our newer views and experiences of Christian spirituality. This means, at the very least, that any Protestant theologian who, by intention and partial achievement, has grasped the vital unity of both Pardon *and* Participation motifs is at least as relevant for our times as most other spokesmen for more disjunctive systems—and more relevant than our current fashion-mongers of the so-called "new theologies." Wesley, in my judgment, grasped this vital unity firmly, and this is what gives him his distinctive "place"— then and now.

For classical Protestantism—to put no finer point on it—has been dominated by the forensic-pardon theme of "rightwising," in conscious contrast to all forgiveness-participation themes. Roman Catholicism has maintained the participation theme but has linked it with theories of sacramental action and a sacerdotal control of the means of grace that marks it off from the patristic traditions of Irenaeus, Gregory of Nyssa, Maximus the Confessor, *et al.*

Wesley inherited the participation-motif from Castañiza-Scupoli, de Renty, Gregory Lopez—even William Law—before he discovered its primal sources in the Johannine Gospel and its patristic interpreters (under the stimulus of the patristic revival in Oxford that he joined in). Thus, "holy living" as a vision of Christian existence was his earliest orientation. But there is a flaw in any such orientation unless it is balanced off by a firm emphasis on *sola fide* (*sola Dei Gloria!*)—and this became the burden of Wesley's bitter complaint against "the mystics"[44] *before* Aldersgate, and frequently thereafter.[45]

But *sola fide* has its own inbuilt extremism—Wesley denounced it as "solifidianism."[46] This, in Lutheranism, tended toward a dominance in the church by exegetes and "dogmaticians" or else a move toward inwardness (pietism)—and, in both, to one sort or another of political quietism (*cuius regio*, and all that). In the Reformed tradition, stress on the *sola fide* tended to translate sovereign grace into sovereign fiat (election) and to envisage theocracy as a political ideal (the divine right of the elect to rule!).

Wesley sought—and I think found—a third alternative to these polarities in his concept of faith alone, working by love,

[44]Tuesday, January 24, 1738, *JWJ* I:420. Cf. also his letter to his brother Samuel, November 23, 1736 (*JWL* I:207).
[45]Cf. *JWJ* III:18, 241. See also *JWL* V:341; VI:44.
[46]Cf. *JWJ* II:174; "Predestination Calmly Considered," *JWW* X:266f.; also *JWW* XIV:231.

aimed at holy living: pardon *in order* to participation! Salvation, he tirelessly proclaimed, is by grace, through faith, unto those good works which God has prepared that we should walk in them— acting out our love of God in love to neighbor and all creation (cf. Eph. 2:8–10). Does this faith nullify the moral Law? *Mē genoitō!* [Certainly not! cf. Gal. 2:17b; Rom. 6:15b.] Much rather, we *establish* the law by faith.[47] Moreover, faith is not an end in itself and therefore not an ultimate concern, not even in Tillich's sense. Faith is in order to love, as love is in order to blessedness, which is God's original design for human creatures. The holy life (love as a pure intention) is the happy life; no other is or can be, now or ever. Thus, justification and sanctification are God's gifts received and shared by faith, hope and love (these three and none by itself alone). Wesley believed this and taught it—and this serves to place him in the Christian tradition more firmly and significantly than his undeniably great role as "founder of Methodism."

We may speak of the contemporary relevance of this message and mission only in a postscript. The situation is something like this, in my view. The issues of the sixteenth to eighteenth centuries are now no longer current, in their historic modalities, save in the case of our still-living ancestors whom we call "fundamentalists." The controversies between Lutherans and Reformed, between the Anglicans and the Romans and the Täufer are simply passé, as far as the horizons of contemporary theology may be scanned. And yet the concerns that were advanced and defended in those controversies are still with us and require new problematic formulations in authentically ecumenical terms. The old ensigns—*sola fide, sola scriptura,* "holy church," "holy tradition" (all "either/or")—are no longer rallying points for future theologizing. But still there is no assuagement for the pain and emptiness and hunger of the human heart for a meaningful life and a meaningful death—and there can be none apart from God's sovereign grace gracefully received (what else was *sola fide* all about, really?) or apart from "holy living" (God's grace enabling human love to flower and fruit in happiness, personal and communal). The old disjunction between "evangelical" and "catholic" is no longer a fruitful polarity and the only conceivable

[47]Cf. Sermons XXXIV, "The Original, Nature, Property, and Use of the Law," XXXV, "The Law Established Through Faith, I," and XXXVI, "The Law Established Through Faith, II" (*JWW* V:433–66).

Christian future is for a church truly catholic, truly evangelical and truly reformed. John Wesley—as an evangelist with a catholic spirit, a reformer with a heroic vision of the Christian life created by faith matured in love, a theologian who lived in and thought out of the Scripture and Christian tradition and who brought all his judgments to the bar of experience and reason—*this* Wesley offers a treasure to the church of tomorrow that will leave it the poorer if ignored.

The irony, of course, is that this thesis (right or wrong) is not readily verifiable, since Wesley is not really accessible, for want of proper, critical editions and competent studies from across the entire spectrum of ecumenical scholarship. The rescue of Wesley from his Methodist cocoon and his neglect by non-Methodists was part of the original vision of the Oxford Edition of *Wesley Works*. In my own view, it is still the project's chief warrant and best hope.

John Wesley's Interests in the Early Fathers of the Church

———┼———

[1983] Outler urges a critical interpretation of Wesley which reaches beyond the eighteenth-century context. His own research indicates that the echoes of early and Eastern Christian spirituality are "more pronounced" in Wesley than in any other theologian of his century. Outler sees Wesley's distinctive appropriation of the Patristic tradition as a primary source of his Spirit-centered view of grace. All this provides further evidence for Outler's thesis that Wesley was a competent folk-theologian who understood the complexity and depth of the Christian tradition.

It has been John Wesley's misfortune to be judged by stereotypes generated by his followers, and by still other stereotypes generated by his critics. Even in the rare cases where the Wesley *corpus* itself has been read with some care, the lack of adequate critical editions has allowed good scholars (Lindström, Deschner, Piette, Schmidt and even Frank Baker) to interpret Wesley in his eighteenth-century situation, and its nineteenth-century aftermath, and to leave the immense range of his earlier sources largely unexplored. The result is that Wesley has yet to be studied in any great breadth and depth in the light of those sources and their shaping influences on his thought. It is the aim of the Oxford edition of *Wesley's Works* to redress this imbalance and to develop new patterns in Wesley studies.

All about us lie the results of interpretation by stereotype. Always and invariable, in Methodist circles, and in other traditions deriving from nineteenth-century Methodism, there is the Wesley hero cult: the haloed image of the founding father. The founding of Methodism was what God raised him up for and, in Methodist eyes, this was to a very noble purpose, since Methodism, from the mid-1700s until recently, was one of the really spectacular success stories in all of church history. This was eagerly explained, in Methodist folklore, by John Wesley's charisma as an evangelist, by Charles Wesley's lyric gifts as hymnist, by the providential favor of the Holy Spirit and not least, of course, by Methodist gumption.

But Methodism's success story has not been universally applauded. To the Anglicans, it has seemed largely an annoyance—a motley of presumptuous schismatics with unfounded claims to their ministerial orders and deplorable tastes in liturgy, architecture, and ethos. To the Lutherans and Calvinists, Methodists have appeared as synergists and "enthusiasts" content with lamentable low standards of theological education, given to emotional and pragmatic sanctions in their evangelical zeal. And, whatever faults could be charged against the Methodists were quite easily traceable to the Wesleys, and John in particular. Admittedly, there has always been enough in Wesley's oversimplifications to provide ample prooftexting for most of these critical reservations and, therefore, to warrant the neglect that his early critics had decided was the proper punishment for such ecclesiastical upstarts. So it was that Wesley studies were turned inward, by Methodists, for Methodists, or, quite exceptionally, by non-Methodists, yet with Methodists as their primary audience. More Methodists, until lately, have read Piette and Todd than Roman Catholics; more Methodists have read Schmidt than have the Lutherans; and more Methodists have read Luther and Calvin than Lutherans and Calvinists have ever read Wesley. One could safely give prizes to all the Anglicans who have read Wesley despite the fact that he thought he was one of them.

It would, therefore, be only a perpetuation of the Wesley hero cult for me to suggest that Wesley deserves a fresh look as the founder of Methodism. This has not been part of my own crusade toward altering the focus of Wesley studies. My concern is the reexamination of Wesley's thought in the context of his eighteenth-century ambience and his backgrounds, reaching back into the tangle of the seventeenth-century controversies and their antecedents. And I have steadily assumed that it is in this perspective that his relevance for contemporary discussions of ecumenical theology would become most evident.

It would be far beyond the mark to claim that Wesley ever was a theologian's theologian or that he deserves a ranking with the major figures in the history of Christian thought. My suggestion is rather different: it is simply that Wesley ranks high with the folk-theologians who have blessed the church from time to time and that this role has not been sufficiently realized, that his theological competence and his special gifts for finding fruitful alternatives to barren polarities have been underestimated by devotees and critics alike. He belongs, as I have come to see it, in an interesting group of significant figures in English theology whose neglect has left the rest of us somewhat the poorer than we know: like-minded predecessors such as Richard Baxter, John Goodwin, Joseph Meade and successors such as, say, Horace Bushnell.

By "folk-theologian," I mean one whose special gifts are in the communication of the gospel with literally marvelous powers (i.e., powers not easily explained) of outreach and ingathering, of upbuilding and nurturing, of the folk (viz., the unlearned masses, the humble and poor, nominal Christians who are candidates for conversion to "heart-religion") and for lives transformed by grace to Christian service. It is clear that it was in this role that Wesley understood himself. In the Preface to Volume I of *Sermons on Several Occasions,* he actually belabors this point:

> Nothing appears here (in these sermons) in an elaborate, elegant or oratorical dress . . . for I now write, as I generally speak, *ad populum*—to the bulk of mankind—to those who neither relish nor understand the *art* of speaking; but who, notwithstanding, are competent judges of those truths which are necessary to present and future happiness. . . .
>
> I design plain truth for plain people. Therefore, of set purpose, I abstain from all nice and philosophical speculations, from all perplexed and intricate reasonings, and, as far as possible, from even the show of learning. . . .
>
> Nay, my design is . . . to forget all that I have ever read in my life. I mean: to speak in the general as if I have never read an author, ancient or modern (always excepting the inspired). . . .

The measure of folk theologians—from St. Chrysostom to Billy Graham—is threefold: 1) their grasp of the gospel itself (the *fides historica*) in its fullness and integrity; 2) their competence as theologians, viz., in their understanding of how perplexed and intricate the reasonings really are that lie back of all apparently "plain truths"; and 3) their determination to make their message their medium—rather than counting so heavily on the media. Judged by these norms, St. Chrysostom rates toward the top of any such scale (as did St. Augustine in his *Sermons*), and Luther, and Horace Bushnell. Our modern popularizers, as a tribe, rate toward the bottom and have given a bad name to this particular genre as a whole. My point, a conclusion from two decades of living with him and trying to reconstruct the elaborate apparatus that he has so deftly concealed from his readers, is that he is a better folk-theologian than has yet been realized and that John Wesley's folk-theology is much more of a resource for contemporary theology, ethics—and ecumenics—than has yet been discovered by others.

This larger thesis, and the program that it entails, runs far beyond the limits of this evening's session. But we shall review a single "slice" of it to illustrate Wesley's grasp of the Christian tradition in general and of the patristic epoch in particular.

In the eighteenth century and before (Jacques-Bénigne Bossuet), the Roman Catholic Church had already developed a two-source theory of its *magisterium:* Scripture and tradition—

with a tilt toward tradition as the final arbiter in disputed questions. The sixteenth-century Reformers had returned to a single-source theory of doctrinal authority (*sola scriptura*) and had rejected tradition out of hand as "filthy stinking puddles of man-made wisdom." Anglicans, following Erasmus and Cranmer, and after their bruising collisions with the Puritans, had opted for a complex norm of "Scripture, Reason and Christian Antiquity." One sees this in Hooker, Hammond, Beveridge, and in the great patrologists of the late seventeenth and early eighteenth centuries: Wake, Fell, Grabe (and the Nonjurors, like Nelson and Deacon). A bonus from this was their conservation of a strong sense of tradition that did not have to be placed over, or even over against, Scripture as the *prime* source of what they spoke of as "Standing Revelation." Wesley expanded this triad to a quadrilateral by adding Christian experience. By this he meant, quite specifically and exclusively, the experience of the inward assurance of God's favor and grace, in justification and pardon, in the Christian's progress along the *ordo salutis*. Not experience in general, not feeling as such, or in itself; only the sense of pardon and of being led of the Spirit into the faith active in loving works (Galatians 5:6; his favorite text).

In the Methodist traditions after his death, this fourfold compound of doctrinal authority disintegrated. The rationalists of the Enlightenment discounted tradition, experience and even Scripture, save where it squared with their reading of right reason. Romantics and pietists discounted tradition and reason, except for the purpose of polemics, and turned to experience as their touchstone for Christian truth, including the truths of Scripture. They boldly appealed to Wesley himself for this privatizing move away from objective standards of doctrine and morality. They could do this, of course, only by ignoring the most distinctive element in his theology (concealed from them by his chosen habits of simplifying complex issues.) And yet, one cannot point to another theologian in the eighteenth century with a stronger sense of tradition, in a very broad sense, or whose popular theology was more heavily influenced by what he had learned from his Christian ancestors, both immediate and remote.

In his Preface to the self-edited *Works* of 1771–1774, he had quite self-consciously submitted his writings to the threefold norms of "Scripture, Reason and Christian Antiquity." In 1789, in *Farther Thoughts on Separation from the Church*, he reaffirmed a lifelong predilection:

> From a child, I was taught to love and reverence the Scriptures as the oracles of God: and, next to these, to esteem the primitive Fathers, the writers of the three [to five] first centuries.

John Wesley had learned first about the Fathers from his own father's *Advice to a young Clergyman:*

> Most of the Fathers [of the fourth century] are well worth reading, but especially St. Athanasius, and above all, St. Basil. If I were to preach in Greek, St. Chrysostom would be my master.

Samuel Wesley, Sr., also recommends DuPin as a good historian and also "the first Councils, which our church receives, as she does the Fathers, as Witnesses of the Faith and Exemplars in practice. . . . By the writings of these three or four first centuries, you will be sufficiently armed against the novel opinions of the Papists, Sectaries and Hereticks. . . ." Wesley was further influenced by the Nonjurors, such as Robert Nelson, for whom the patristic writers were both inspiration and normative sources.[1]

His years at Oxford had followed one of its most notable epochs of patristic study and it was one of the members of the Holy Club, John Clayton, who was a competent patrologist and who enlisted the whole Club in the diligent study of the Fathers, from Ignatius to Athanasius. Wesley's Oxford education, which later he would unfairly disparage, had introduced him to the five different "worlds" he would continue to live in, concurrently, throughout his whole career: Scripture, the classics, the early church Fathers, the Reformation, and the new world of science (John Ray, William Derham, Isaac Newton, and the discoverers of electricity!).

I wish there were time to review the range and quality of Wesley's acquaintance with these separate worlds in some detail, and especially the world of the Fathers, to which we now turn. Certainly, if you want to ask detailed questions, I should be delighted, for I have been grubbing about in these footnotes for twenty years now and the sense of Wesley's crucial indebtedness to these people has grown over the years, along with some sense of having learned to think at least some of his thoughts after him. Indeed, the thesis I would propose on this point is this: John

---

[1] See William Beveridge's *Synodikon* and John Wesley's use of it; see also *JWJ* I:37).

Wesley's reflection of early and Eastern motifs of Christian spirituality—1) a therapeutic view of the *ordo salutis* as contrasted with any forensic one; 2) the *telos* of human life in God; 3) the person and primal agency of the Holy Spirit in Christian existence; 4) prevenient grace; 5) the concordance of grace and free will; 6) the inspiration of Scripture and its pneumatological interpretation; 7) salvation as the restoration of the image of God in humanity; 8) ascesis and discipline in Christian living and, above all; 9) the distinctions between the "moments" of justification and sanctification and, therefore, a doctrine of open-ended perfection in this life—such reflections are more pronounced in Wesley than in any other theologian in his century and they provide his theology with its most distinctive traits. A corollary of this is that the general absence of an awareness of this patristic tradition in the minds of his contemporaries, and those of us since then, is a partial explanation as to why his theology was so readily and so sadly misunderstood even by those who bore his name and professed to revere his authority.

"Christian Antiquity" was no antiquarian interest of Wesley's. He was a quite conscious primitivist, convinced that the early church fathers, especially before the disastrous alliance of state and church under Constantine, were closer in time and spiritual insight to the apostles and hence, to pure Spiritual Christianity. And since one of his most earnest aims was the restoration of apostolic Christianity in Great Britain, both the apostolic church and the church of the early church fathers were vivid models for him in the program of the Revival. He was very much aware of some interesting parallels too: Apostolic and ante-Nicene Christianity was a minority and illicit religion; the early Christians were in the world but not of it, as he wished the Methodists to be; their conceptions of the nature and role of theology were more exegetical and paranetic [morally instructive] than speculative, as he desired his own theologizing to be. Thus follows his interest in Beveridge and Cave, and later, Mosheim; and so, also, his interest in an extensive, if not fully expert, patristic scholarship.

Wesley's leadership in the Revival had scarcely become visible to the public at large before the coherence and integrity of his doctrines came into question from discerning critics. In 1742, Joseph Tucker, then Vicar of All Saints, Bristol, afterward Canon of Gloucester, and probably at the behest of Bishop Joseph Butler, published a critique of the nascent movement, charging Wesley with wanting to have his doctrine of salvation both ways: justification by faith alone and also "sinless perfection." Wesley, in 1742, responded with two tracts: 1) *The Character of a Methodist* and 2) *The Principles of a Methodist.* They deserve to be read as a sample of his spirit and style of controversy and yet also because of his almost impudent definition of "Methodist" as "Christian," and his reaching back to Clement of Alexandria's picture of the perfect Christian in the Seventh Book of *Stromateis.* The chief difference was that Clement had conceived perfection on a vertical scale of ascent, whereas Wesley turned this notion on its side, into a more nearly lateral scale of extent.

In 1749, he began to collect *A Christian Library.* These were presented in fifty volumes between 1749 and 1755. This was by far his most ambitious single publishing venture, and we can easily understand why it fell so far short of his hopes for it, as a popular resource for his Methodist people. They have never been all that interested in "choice pieces of divinity" either then or now. It is chiefly valuable to us as a mirror to his doctrinal interests and a demonstration of his immense acquaintance with the whole repertory of patristic, Puritan, and Anglican literature. In the very first volume, he confronted the Methodists with extracts from, "The Epistles of the Apostolic Fathers: St. Clement, St. Ignatius and St. Polycarp." In a preface to these extracts, he stressed the direct connection of these men to "what Christ and his Apostles taught," and concludes, "Consequently, we are to look on their writings, though not of equal authority with Holy Scripture (because neither were the authors called in so extraordinary a way to the writing them, nor indued with so large a portion of the blessed Spirit) yet as worthy of a much greater respect than any composures which have been made since." He dates "St. Clement's Epistle to the Corinthians" as "a little before the Jewish War broke out, which ended in the destruction of Jerusalem"; this was the learned opinion in his day. He also includes an abridgment of *The Homilies of Macarius,* which he had read in the great Pritius edition of 1698. He also knew Macarius in an anonymous English translation of 1721. He found a sympathetic soul in St. Ignatius; he knew but seems not to have been much influenced by Justin, except in his notion of the salvation of conscientious "heathen." Johann Ernst Grabe's great edition of St. Irenaeus had been done at Christ Church just two decades before and it seems clear that Wesley's conception of the *ordo salutis* is deeply influenced by the Irenaean doctrine. Clement of Alexandria was a favorite; Origen is cited seven times with obvious sensitivity. He knew Tertullian well enough to quote a couple of obscure passages; he knew St. Cyprian in the magnificent new edition of Dean Fell, but he has a reference to Cyprian that none of us has yet found. It is a simile illustrating eternity, in which a small bird comes every thousand years to pluck a single grain of sand from an immense heap of sand and when the whole heap has been removed, one day of eternity will have passed. John Wesley had this illustration from his father, but, if the original is in Cyprian, I have not found it. If any of you could give me even a clue, that would be cause for joyful celebration!

The *Homilies* of Macarius present a special case. As noted above, Wesley knew, and greatly admired, Macarius the Egyptian. In his extracts of those Homilies and in his highly favorable references to Ephraem Syrus, we see the same vision of Christian existence that he also had come to have, viz., the progressive surrender of the human will to God, always freely out of love, the prevenient action of the Holy Spirit in all human reactivity, the changes rung on the theme of impartation and participation in God's grace *metousia theou* (the overflow of the super-abundance of divine goodness). Here is a special doctrine of synergism: the notion of the immanent presence of the Holy Spirit in the human spirit which does not cancel or preempt human deliberation. *Metousia theou* is a doctrine of two concurrent energies in human behavior. The divine is the active role; the human is the reactive. But the grace of the Holy Spirit is resistible and sin attaches to those human reactions that are deliberate resistances and not to the entirety of all human appetition or affect. This distinction between "sin, properly so-called," as a deliberate violation of known laws of God, as contrasted with either the Lutheran *simul justus et peccator* or with any fatuous doctrines of "sinless perfection" (William Cudworth or James Relly), lies at the very heart of Wesley's doctrine of Christian perfection. In 1954, Werner Jaeger, protégé of Ulrich von Wilamowitz-Moellendorff, the greatest classicist of our century and himself the editor of the works of Gregory of Nyssa, published an interesting and provocative monograph on *Two Rediscovered Works of Ancient Christian Literature: Gregory of Nyssa and Macarius*. It is a tightly packed and erudite demonstration that both Marcarius and Ephraem Syrus[2]

2[See Outler's extended note on "Macarius" and Ephraem Syrus in came to have their names associated with a treatise, *De Instituto Christiano*, which was actually the work of Gregory of Nyssa. I am persuaded by Jaeger's arguments and evidence. Hermann Dorries and others have not been. Thus, the issue is still arguable but cannot be brought to any definitive conclusion until we have the respective critical editions of Gregory, Macarius, and Ephraem available to us. At the present rate, my only hope is that they will have a perpetual patristics seminar in heaven and that they will admit me to it! This much, however, is clear, Wesley knew and, indeed, extracted the "40th Homily" of Macarius. Now, there is enough consonance between that particular homily and the others, of course, and Gregory's *De Instituto Christiano* that we do not have to wait for a wholly rigorous proof of direct literary dependence to be able to see the basic identity of the views of Christian existence involved. The *genre* of spiritual and ascetical theology in Macarius and in Ephraem and in Gregory is so nearly the same that it seems to me quite safe to conclude that Wesley, in his conscious exposure to Macarius and Ephraem ("the most awakening writer, I think, of all the ancients"—*Journal*, October 12, 1736), had placed himself within the spiritual world of Christian Platonism, in which Gregory of Nyssa stands as the greatest master, among a galaxy of them. I, myself, believe that Wesley was more largely a beneficiary of the *De Instituto Christiano* than he knew; it would be sufficient, however, if we could agree that a general connection and general influence are present.

In 1749, the Cambridge deist, Conyers Middleton, published a four-hundred-page, *Free Inquiry into the Miraculous Powers which are supposed to have subsisted in the Christian Church from the Earliest Ages through Successive Centuries. By which it is shown that we have no sufficient reason to believe, upon the Authority of the Primitive Fathers, that any such powers were continued to the Church after the days of the Apostles.* It was a learned but skeptical review of the accounts in the Fathers of miracles and wonders in their times and oral traditions. Wesley saw, as self-evident, that the logic of Middleton's argument also undercut the idea of miracle in the New Testament itself. Embroiled as he was in his new career as leader of a popular religious movement that absorbed most of his time and energies, he still felt himself obliged to respond and compe-

n26. Cf. Kelly Steve McCormick, "John Wesley's Use of John Chrysostom on the Christian Life: Faith Filled With The Energy of Love" (Ph.D. diss., Drew University, 1984).]

tent to deal with Middleton's argument. Thus, he took off "almost twenty days" in which he produced *A* [102-page] *Letter to the Reverend Doctor Conyers Middleton: Occasioned by his late "Free Inquiry."* It is a hasty piece and no one has ever cited it as a major contribution to patristic literature. But when one recalls that it was nearly fifteen years since Wesley had set foot in an Oxford library for any length of time, that he was more concerned with the threat of Middleton's skepticism than with the details of his arguments, his detailed refutation is at least an interesting demonstration of Wesley's sense of involvement in an area not often cultivated by the generality of folk theologians. Moreover, he wrote with only the baggage of erudition that he still carried with him in his mind, cluttered with the distraction of the Revival. In his conclusion, he defends the "plain men" on whom the weight of traditioning the Gospel had been laid in the early centuries and lists them: ". . . the primitive Fathers: I mean particularly, Clemens Romanus, Ignatius, Polycarp, Justin Martyr, Irenaeus, Origen, Clemens Alexandrius, Cyprian—to whom I would add Marcarius and Ephraem Syrus."

Wesley's assessments of some of the figures in Christian Antiquity were neither conventional nor discriminating. He had a warm spot in his heart for Montanus and produced a spirited short encomium of him in a tract of 1785 in which he opined that Montanus' "real crime was severely reproving those who professed themselves Christians . . . " and were not. In "The Wisdom of God's Counsels" [par. 9], he speaks of Montanus as "one of the holiest men in the second century." He was not even abashed to speak up for Pelagius and to absolve him from Pelagianism, which he regarded as an invention of St. Augustine, for whom he saved some surprisingly harsh words:

> A wonderful saint! As full of pride, passion, bitterness, censoriousness and as foul-mouthed to all that contradicted him as George Fox himself. . . . When St. Augustine's passions were heated, his word is not worth a rush. . . . St. Augustine was angry at Pelagius; hence he slandered and abused him. . . . And St. Augustine was then in the Christian world what Aristotle was afterwards. There needed no other proof of any assertion than *ipse dixit*—"St. Augustine said it."

All of Wesley's heroes from the age of Christian Antiquity are Eastern, and this helps to explain the emphases in his soteriology and spirituality that never were so prominent in Latin

Christianity, and did not always stand in the Anglican tradition in quite the same nuances as in Wesley; few of them were as eager to hold the two traditions of *sola fide* and "holy living" in paradoxical balance as Wesley was. It was from the Eastern Fathers that Wesley learned to conceive of salvation as a process, and of the *ordo salutis* as an articulated continuum of stages, both of "moments" and also of process. He found their concepts of spiritual discipline more appealing and more relevant to the needs of his societies than any of the monastic or pietistic models in Western spirituality. And so he took them as authority for his own designs for a Christian communal life that repudiated state control and forewent hierarchical approval. He felt justified in this rejection of the conventions of church and state control since he had decided that the whole tradition of Caesaropapism was wrong and that theocracy was no better.

But most of all he learned from these early fathers his distinctive pneumatocentric view of grace and of its relevance for understanding the mystery of divine action and human reaction. This provided his doctrines of divine grace and human free will, which had promptly been mislabeled "Arminian." For in the Eastern traditions that influenced Wesley, the grace of repentance and of justification were always understood as the gift of the Holy Spirit—focused, of course, in Christ and the Cross—and "resistible," by God's allowance and design. In Augustine and in Latin Christianity generally thereafter, grace has been understood as the gift of the Father, focused also in Christ and the Cross but, consequently, irresistible almost by definition. Clearly, there is truth in both traditions but they look in two directions. Grace in creation is sovereign *in sese* [in its very self]; grace in repentance and faith is persuasive and, hence, involved in the mystery of our God-given freedom, since "persuasion," in the nature of the case, partakes of choice.

But in the West these necessary distinctions, though they had been formally approved by the Second Council of Orange in 529, were observed only in an occasional maverick like William of St. Thierry. The result was that, in the West, the problem of free will has regularly been bedeviled by notions such as predestination and irresistible grace, final perseverance, "sufficient" and "efficacious" grace or by the obverse notions of man's partially successful defiance of sovereign grace itself. Wesley's awareness of this problem and his suggestions about it were summed up retrospectively in a short tract entitled *Thoughts Upon God's*

Sovereignty (1777), where he distinguishes God's irresistible power as Creator and resistible power as Governor.

This distinctive pneumatology influenced Wesley's ideas of voluntary religious association and reinforced his conviction that the church does not require state support. This is the other side of his conviction that the Constantinian state-church and its successors added up to a sustained disaster. The root notion is the Spirit-filled community and the Spirit-consecrated sacraments in the case of both baptism and the Eucharist. The Spirit-filled believer is not possessed by any mechanical or irresistible force, as in Western concepts of *enthusiasmos*, and this enabled Wesley to repudiate the charges, from Lavington and others, of "enthusiasm" and to denounce false ideas of "enthusiasm" as he did in his sermon "On the Nature of Enthusiasm."

Most importantly, it is this Eastern pneumatology that enabled Wesley to read the Western mystics in such a fashion as to redefine perfection (sanctification, "holiness of heart and life") in terms of the fullness of faith that sustains the fullness of hope that looks toward the fullness of love, in which the believer loves God with so sole a conscious affection that he does not commit deliberate sin or, if he does, he repents and forthwith seeks forgiveness and reconciliation. This is, therefore, not a state of grace so fully achieved as to admit of no further growth, but rather dynamism of grace always opening out toward the unfolding stages of love of God and neighbor. "Use all the grace you have," Wesley would say in *On Working Out Our Own Salvation*, "and God will give you more and more grace."

I call you to witness that I have not tried to portray John Wesley as an expert patrologist. It was his life-long habit to read more hastily than thoroughly. In none of the five fields in which he lived was he a full-fledged scholar in the academic sense of the term. Even in Scripture, where he had a special gift of being able to use an incredible acquaintance with the whole of the biblical texts and ideas to create a homiletical rhetoric with biblical language and his own interlaced in a tightwoven fabric, when he turned to exegesis, he readily borrowed the resources of the commentators in his *Explanatory Notes Upon the New Testament*, and also the *Old*.

What I have tried to stress is that John Wesley was a man of tradition, as well as Scripture, and that, for him, the most influential single segment of tradition was the *corpus* of the early church Fathers. From them he gained a crucial advantage in interpreting Scripture, concordant with his pneumatocentric doctrine of the grace of God in Christ. Last month I was in Australia, and one of the most unexpected developments for me in that visit was the discovery of a Roman Catholic theologian, Father David Coffey of St. Patrick's College, Manly, whose doctorate is from Munich under Karl Rahner and whose published dissertation bears the title *Grace: The Gift of the Holy Spirit*. It was easy enough to guess what general perspective such a study might have had; what was really exciting, however, was Father Coffey's references to the special influence on his study of Professor Heribert Mühlen, whose work in patristic pneumatology in *Una Mystica Persona* and in *Der Heilige Geist als Person* is well known. Here, then, was a pneumatology of grace, shaped by modern existentialism and by patristic personalism. *Mutatis mutandis*, it seemed to me to resemble the special mix in Wesley between "heart religion" and patristic pneumatology. In both, the crux of the soteriology problem is grace, and for both grace is the gift of the Holy Spirit. Father Coffey had just barely heard of John Wesley and had not read one word of his before our mutual discovery. When we parted, he promised at least to have a look at what would be for him a whole new frontier.

And that is all that any program of studies, especially in a field like Wesley studies, would ever presume to hope for. There is no claim here that Wesley was a theologian of the highest order, but only that he deserves a rather different sort of examination and evaluation than he has thus far received by both Methodists and non-Methodists. His rootage in Christian Antiquity suggests a sort of ecumenical relevance that has been confirmed wherever he has been studied by non-Methodists in any depth, in terms of the sources and his use of them. And, given the major shifts in modern theology away from the stark disjunctions of predestination versus free will, Wesley's relevance for the newer formulations of divine-human interaction may be very much more important than anyone has yet noticed. What is most gratifying and hopeful to me in the project of Wesley studies is the representation of Wesley as the special sort of Anglican folk theologian that he was. A proper recognition of this would be a service that he could render to the Methodists who have misunderstood him and also to other Christians who would be edified beyond their present expectations if ever they came to understand him on his own terms.

John Wesley: Folk Theologian

———|———

[1977] With ever deepening forays into the sources, Outler presents the evidence upon which we may judge John Wesley's competence as a theologian. He examines Wesley's teaching on justification and sanctification as a test case of whether his learning was shallow or deep. Outler classifies Wesley as a "folk theologian," a type he carefully distinguishes from both the superficial popularizer and the "theologian's theologian."

It is a commonplace that the history of Christian thought has been mostly concerned with the influence of theologians' theologians, those whose learning and speculative gifts marked off new stages of doctrinal development. By contrast, most of the folk theologians whom we can identify (those not already sunk into history's limbo) have seen as their special task the simplification of the great issues (typically controversial) on behalf of the common people.

I have come to believe that the label "folk theologian" fits John Wesley far more accurately than most conventional interpretations of this remarkable and many-sided religious progenitor.

It is bootless to ask if Wesley might have been a theologians' theologian had he so chosen. It is more useful to survey the largely unexplored range of his sources, tools, and theological culture so that his stature as a folk theologian may be assayed somewhat more carefully than has, so far, been possible.[1]

CONCEALED LEARNING

The crucial fact is that after a shaky start in quest of his true vocation, Wesley became a folk theologian on purpose. In his father's library at Epworth, there was a copy of Bishop Robert Sanderson's *Thirty-Six Sermons* (1689), of which sixteen were addressed *ad aulam* (to his peers), six *ad clerum* (to the clergy), six *ad magistratum* (to a court or civil official), and eight *ad populum* (to the people).[2] Wesley adopted Sanderson's schema but altered its proportions. In his own written sermons (150 of them), there were ten to his peers, one to civil officials, one to the clergy; all the rest

---

[1]The task has already been begun, e.g., Martin Schmidt, *John Wesley: A Theological Biography* (1963, 1972, 1973); *JWO*; Gerald Cragg (ed.), *Doctrinal Writings: The Appeals* (*WJWB* Vol. 11, 1975); Wesley's *Sermons* will be Vols. 1–4, edited by Albert C. Outler; see also Kenneth E. Rowe, ed., *The Place of Wesley in the Christian Tradition* (1976).

[2]The names of Samuel Wesley, Sr., and Samuel Wesley, Jr., appear in the list of "The Subscribers."

were designedly *ad populum* (to the common people). As Wesley put it:

> I write as I generally speak, *ad populum*—to the bulk of mankind—to those who neither relish nor understand the art of speaking . . . I design plain words for plain people; therefore, of set purpose, I abstain from all nice and philosophical speculations, from perplexed and intricate reasonings; and, as far as possible, from even the show of learning . . . My design is, in some sense, to forget all that ever I have read . . . In the following sermons . . . I have endeavoured to describe the true, the scriptural, experimental religion, so as to omit nothing which is a real part thereof and to add nothing thereto which is not.[3]

What is more, he stuck to this program throughout his five-decade career. Most of the quotations in Wesley's writings are uncited (and rarely verbatim). Most of his allusions are unidentified. It is as if he never expected to have a critical edition of his works. What is unmistakable, however, is the erstwhile don turned popularizer, a truly learned man who had voluntarily identified himself with Christ's poor in Britain's slums and mines and fields. "I love the poor," he wrote in 1757; "in many of them I find pure, genuine grace, unmixed with paint, folly, and affectation."[4]

His first religious society in London had been inside "the City" (in Fetter Lane). And yet, for decades after 1739, not a single Methodist society was located in any affluent quarter in any English city or town. Wesley kept a few friends and acquaintances among the middle and upper classes; he often preached in their churches (after the Revival had become "respectable"). But his self-chosen constituency was the poor and the laboring classes; his self-chosen role was as *their* pastor, spiritual director, and theologian.

It was, therefore, inevitable that, in such an enterprise, the

[3]"The Preface" to *Sermons on Several Occasions* (1746), ¶2–6.
[4]Cf., his letters to Dorothy Furley, September 25, 1757. On September 20, 1764, he told a friend, "I *bear* the rich, and *love* the poor; therefore I spend almost all my time with them" (*JWL* VIII:267). See also, his comment in a letter to one of his more sophisticated friends, Brian Bury Collins, June 14, 1780: "You have seen very little of the choicest part of London society: I mean the poor. Go with me into their cellars and garrets and then you will taste their [gracious] spirits."

breadth and depth of his theological competence was concealed both from his followers and his critics alike. His theological education had begun at Epworth and went on apace over the course of eight busy decades. His mother was his first tutor and her eclectic views are reflected in her son's at many levels thereafter. Here is a typical passage (from a letter to John in Oxford, 1732):

> *The Life of God in the Soul of Man*[5] is a good book, and was an acquaintance of mine many years ago . . . There are many good things in Castañiza; more in Baxter. Yet are neither without faults, which I overlook for the sake of their virtues. Nor can I say of all the books of divinity I have read, *which* is the best. One is best at one time, one at another according to the temper and disposition of the mind.

Wesley lived with the classics, quoting them carelessly from memory (who was there to check his texts?) and yet rarely off target. His immersion in Scripture was so thorough that his language is overlaid with quotations; it is not unusual to find whole paragraphs that are scarcely more than graceful interweavings of Scripture texts.[6] His readings in the history of Christian thought range over the centuries, East and West—with many figures and volumes so obscure that one wonders where he found them all. His own recorded bibliography runs to more than 1400 different authors, with nearly 3000 separate items from them (ranging from pamphlets to twelve-volume sets). In the *Sermons* alone, we have listed more than 2500 quotations and allusions worth checking (not to mention the innumerable quotations from Scripture which crowd his pages).[7]

A FOLK THEOLOGY

Out of these incessant readings and reflections and out of the controversies, which he professed to abhor but in which he was

---

[5]The title of a famous devotional classic by Henry Scougal (1677). In the eighteenth century, Lorenzo Scupoli's *Spiritual Combat* (1599) was widely attributed to Juan de Castaniza; see John Newton, *Susanna Wesley and the Puritan Tradition in Methodism* (1968), 136–38.

[6]Cf. ¶4 in "Original Sin": eleven different texts from six different books in twenty-one lines.

[7]Cf. "Plundering the Egyptians," in Albert C. Outler, *Theology in the Wesleyan Spirit* (1975), chap. 1.

constantly engaged, Wesley wrought out a folk theology that goes a long way in accounting for his immense influence. Its heart and center was "the gospel": a call to repentance, faith, justification, regeneration, and "holy living." He was, after all, an evangelist; soteriology is the intense focus of more than half his sermons. There are dozens of characteristic summaries of this "gospel" scattered through his writings, like this one to John Fletcher (March 22, 1771):

> I always did—for between these thirty and forty years—clearly assert the total fall of man and his utter inability to do any good of himself; the absolute necessity of the grace and Spirit of God to raise even a good thought or desire in our hearts; the Lord's rewarding no work and accepting of none but so far as they proceed from his *preventing, convincing,* and *converting* grace through the Beloved; the blood and righteousness of Christ being *the sole meritorious cause of our salvation*. Who is there in England that has asserted these things more strongly and steadily than I have done?

Upon this foundation, Wesley developed a full-orbed theology (with special emphases on Christian morality and culture) that may be fitly described as both "evangelical" and "catholic"—viz., a Protestant soteriology fully integrated with a catholic doctrine of grace ("holiness of heart and life"). There are Puritan elements in the synthesis (the primacy and perspicuity of Scripture, substitutionary atonement, *sola fide* as the *articulus stantis vel cadentis ecclesiae*,[8] the work ethic of thrift, industry and sobriety), but there was also a catholic preference for "prevenience" instead of "election" as a code-word for the divine initiative, specifically as the activity of the Holy Spirit. There is also a consistent denial of irresistible grace and "final perseverance." Wesley's doctrine of "assurance" ("the inner witness of the Spirit") was mystical, but it was also closely linked with "good works"—"faith working by love."[9] From 1738 onward, his doctrine of justification (so he

---

[8]"[The doctrine] by which the church stands or falls." Cf. Friedrich Loofs' analysis of the curious history of this aphorism (often but mistakenly attributed to Luther) in *Theologische Studien und Kritiken* (1917), 90:323–420. In English theology, it appears in Michael Harrison, *Christ's Righteousness Imputed* (c. 1690), 1, and in John Flavel's *Planelogia* (1691), 318 (where it is mistakenly attributed to Chemnitz).

[9]Gal. 5:6. A favorite text, quoted twenty-one times in the sermons alone.

claimed) "differed not a hair's breadth from Calvin's"[10]—and yet even here he seems closer to John Goodwin[11] and Richard Baxter[12] than to any of the English Calvinists (whether "hardliners" like Whitaker, or "moderates" like Davenant). As a hermeneutical rule, he held to the literal sense of Scripture, except where literalism leads to an "absurdity,"[13] and he had picked up Thomas Drayton's idea that every "command" in Scripture should also be construed as "a covered promise."[14]

Wesley had a vast repertoire of obscure lore on which he drew almost casually. For example, in "On Attending the Church Service" (par. 1), he mentions "St. John's *removal* from the earth." This was unknown to Polycarp, Irenaeus, or Jerome; only in a few interior Greek manuscripts is there an "appendix" to the effect that St. John had been translated, like Enoch.[15] Or, again, in "The Good Steward," he refers to "an ingenious man who has lately made a discovery that [the dead] are in a deep sleep from death to the resurrection." This was the iceberg tip of an extended controversy[16] and not a minor point with Wesley. His lively discussions of "the intermediate state" are integral to his eschatology as a whole.[17] Our point here is his *habit* of offhand allusion, without citation.

Wesley was fascinated by the scientific developments that

[10]Cf. "Minutes of the Second Annual Conference, Bristol, Thursday, August 1, 1756," Question 22 ff. in *JWO* 151–52. See also Wesley's letter to John Newton, May 14, 1765.

[11]*Imputatio Fidei* (1642).

[12]He abridged and published Baxter's *Aphorisms on Justification* (1640) in 1765, after Baxter had retracted them, in form if not in substance. Cf. Baxter's *Confession of my Faith* (1655).

[13]Cf. "A Call to Backsliders," I.2.(4).

[14]Cf. Drayton's *The Proviso or Condition of the Promises* (1657), 1–2. Cf. also Wesley's "Sermon on the Mount, V," II.2; "Sermon on the Mount, VII," II.12; and "On Perfection," II.1,2,12.

[15]Cf. "The Acts of John," ¶115, in *The Apocryphal New Testament*, tr. by M. R. James (1953), 270.

[16]Who among his readers would have identified this "ingenious man" as Edmund Law, Archdeacon of Carlisle, who (in a D.D. exercise at Cambridge in 1754, published as an "Appendix" to the third edition of *The Theory of Religion* [1755]) had revived the Anabaptist theory of "Soul Sleep"? How many more would have known Calvin's very early denunciation of "soul sleep" in his *Psychopannychia* (1545)?

[17]Cf., e.g., his sermon "Of Hell," I.4; "The Trouble and Rest of Good Men," Proem., II.6; "The Rich Man and Lazarus," I.3; "On Worldly Folly," II.6; "On Faith" (Heb. 11:1), ¶4.

were making his century famous in the history of science. As early as 1747, he "went with two or three friends to see what are called electrical experiments,"[18] and as he became more knowledgeable, he also became a pioneer in electric shock therapy, which he provided for his people (and used himself).[19] His *Primitive Physick* is a hodgepodge of folk medicine and quackery, but its twenty-three editions in his lifetime prove its popularity and, indeed, its usefulness. Adam Smith's *Wealth of Nations* was published in 1776; Wesley's counterattack against Smith's defense of surplus accumulation was prompt and vigorous—even strident.[20]

WESLEY'S DOCTRINE OF JUSTIFICATION

One is entitled to suspect that Wesley's wide-ranging eclecticism would amount to the same sort of superficial or specious learning with which we are all too familiar in our own standard-brand popularizers. Such suspicions may be tested by a brief analysis of two of Wesley's special interests (justification and "perfection") and their sources.

In an important (if also tendentious) survey, *The Rise of Moralism* (1966), C. F. Allison has traced the polarization in English theology between "faith alone" and "holy living," "from Hooker to Baxter." His own *Tendenz* is for the Calvinist syndrome of "single justification" and for Christ's atoning death taken as "the *formal* cause" of justification—as in Davenant, Downame, Bunyan, *et al.* He sets this over against the tradition of "holy living" as evident in Jeremy Taylor, Henry Hammond, George Bull—and Richard Baxter! It was a tangled controversy—even more complicated than Professor Allison makes out—and Wesley knew it, twist by turn.

At least three interdependent issues were entwined: (1) "single" versus "double" justification, which involves (2) the role of human participation in God's gift of pardon (the essence of

---

[18]Cf. the *Journal* for October 16, 1747.

[19]*Ibid.*, February 17, 1753; November 9, 1756; and December 26, 1765.

[20]Cf. the following sermons written between 1776–1790: "The Wisdom of God's Counsels," 16; "On Friendship With the World," ¶3; "The Danger of Riches," I.19; II.1 ff.; "The More Excellent Way," VI.4; "An Israelite Indeed," I.1; "On Family Religion," ¶16, 17; "On Riches," ¶4; "Causes of the Inefficacy of Christianity," ¶2; "On Worldly Folly," I.4, II.8; and "The Danger of Increasing Riches," *passim.*

justification)[21] and this, in turn, decides (3) whether the imputation of Christ's righteousness is to be regarded as the "formal" or the "meritorious" *cause* of a sinner's justification.[22] Wesley also understood what Allison ignored, namely, that all doctrines of "formal cause" logically entail a corresponding doctrine of election or predestination.[23] Moreover, he had mastered what Allison left unexplored: that rich tradition in Anglican theology that upheld the *sola fide* in terms of *both* a double justification (implying the *fides formata caritate* of Gal. 5:6) *and* the doctrine of "meritorious cause." This tradition stemmed from Erasmus and Johann Gropper, but Wesley knew it best in Cranmer,[24] John Goodwin, William Allen,[25] Richard Baxter, Benjamin Kidder, John Reynolds, John Kettlewell (even Thomas Sherlock).

After Wesley's realization that his own post-Aldersgate doctrine of justification was Anglican after all,[26] he proceeded to develop this special perspective—trying to avoid a break with the Calvinists on his pluralistic principle that, with respect to nonessential points, Christians should "think and let think."[27] After a couple of decades of tension (with Wesley providing his own fair share of provocation), he finally came out in print on the side of "meritorious cause"[28] (his actual view all along).[29] This was the

---

[21]Cf. the sermon, "Justification by Faith," II.5: "The plain scriptural notion of justification is pardon."

[22]Cf. Trent's references to the five "causes" of Justification in COC II:94–95. This was John Davenant's target in his *Treatise of Justification* (1631).

[23]The debate on this point runs back at least to Frith and Gardiner, Cartwright and Hooker, Whitaker and Baro, Davenant and Thomas Jackson, *et al.*

[24]See his abridgment of Homilies I–IV in *The Doctrine of Salvation, Faith and Good Works* (JWO, 123–33).

[25]A "General Baptist" who wrote *A Glass of Justification; or the Work of Faith with Power* in 1658. He later "conformed" and became vicar of Bridgewater.

[26]Cf. JWJ for November 12, 1738.

[27]An oft-repeated slogan for theological pluralism; cf., e.g., "The Lord Our Righteousness," II.20; "The Nature of Enthusiasm," ¶36. See also his "Character of a Methodist," ¶1 (JWW VIII:340), and "Some Observations on Liberty," ¶1 (JWW XI:91)—and at least fifteen other instances.

[28]In "The Lord Our Righteousness" (1766).

[29]This is confirmed in a Latin fragment, rediscovered by Professor Richard Heitzenrater. It has a series of notes for *responsiones* in what must have been an Oxford disputation—on justification!

opening skirmish in what turned into a full scale war in 1770,[30] which continued to rage throughout Wesley's remaining years. From 1778 till his death much of his energies and talent were invested in *The Arminian Magazine*,[31] and this became another curious showcase of his theological erudition and range—without ever being advertised as such.[32]

A crucial issue in any discussion of justification is the meaning and function of repentance. Given a doctrine of "formal cause" and election, repentance can have no antecedent, conditional role in God's "drawing and pardoning" grace. It is the part of the elect to confess their sins and rely on Christ's atoning work as "formal cause." Wesley agreed that repentance cannot be a *necessary* condition of justification (only faith is that)[33]; repentance is not a "good work." But by nuancing the meaning of repentance, he found a crucial place for it in faith's preparation for pardon. *Metanoia* (change of mind) for Wesley is much less a "sorrow for sin" than it is an altered consciousness of one's actual human condition (that is, the lusts and the pride[34] that motivate

---

[30]Cf. *Minutes of Several Conversations Between Mr. Wesley and Others From the Year 1744, to the Year 1789*, Question 77, Ans. #3 (5–6), in JWW VIII:337–38: "We have received it as a maxim that 'a man is to do nothing in order to justification.' Nothing can be more false. Whoever desires to find favour with God, should 'cease from evil, and learn to do well.' So God himself teaches by the Prophet Isaiah. Whoever repents should 'do works meet for repentance.' And if this is not in order to find favour, what does he do them for? . . . (5.) What have we then been disputing about for these thirty years? I am afraid about words . . . (6.) As to merit itself, of which we have been so dreadfully afraid: We are rewarded according to our works, yea, because of our works. How does this differ from, 'for the sake of our works'? And how differs this from *secundum merita operum*? which is no more than 'as our works deserve.' Can you split this hair? I doubt I cannot."

[31]He had accepted the label "Arminian" as reluctantly as he had taken on the nickname "Methodist." But in all his extensive abridgments of theological writings supporting "universal redemption," nothing from Arminius himself appeared in this magazine.

[32]For example, he produced the *only* English translation of Sebastian Castellio's "Dialogues on Predestination, Election, and Free Will" (1st ed., 1578), in Vols. IV and V (1781, 1782). This was a rare book even in Wesley's time; cf. Ferdinand Buisson, *Sébastien Castellion: sa Vie et son Oeuvre (1515–1563)*, 1964, *Appendice, Pièces Inédites*, cxviii, II:498–99.

[33]Cf. "Justification by Faith," IV.1f. and "The Scripture Way of Salvation," III.2, 5.

[34]1 John 2:16 is another Wesley favorite.

our other sins). True repentance, therefore, is the surrender of one's self-sufficiency and the acknowledgment of one's radical need of grace. This is a different notion of the "conditions" of justification than in conventional Calvinism or in the Anglican gospel of moral rectitude. It is an interesting idea in its own right.

Wesley also sought a third alternative to the Calvinist and Anglican polarities by insisting that justification involves both a "real" as well as a "relative" change.[35] From this it followed that sanctification *begins* with justification (more precisely, with regeneration), and that it involves a life *process*—which is always to say, for Wesley, "holy living" springing from the love of God and neighbor. It was this processive idea of salvation—rooted always in faith—that helped Wesley avoid antinomianism (his most vivid aversion) and achieve a dynamic equilibrium between the priority of faith (justification) and the harvests of love (sanctification).[36]

WESLEY'S DOCTRINE OF SANCTIFICATION

It is common knowledge that the most readily misunderstood of all the Wesleyan doctrines was "Christian perfection," the claim that Christians may—and ought to expect—"to be made perfect in love in this life." Our concern here is less important to expound the doctrine than to show how source-criticism can illustrate its development.[37] No Christian has ever denied that "perfection," in some sense or other, is the goal and crown of the Christian life. But there have been unholy quarrels over the proper terms of its "expectation."

The nominalists (Gabriel Biel) with their notions of indomitable concupiscence, Luther (and the Lutherans) with their *simul justus et peccator*, Calvinists (with their idea of the *massa damnationis* [whole company of the damned]) all tended to construe the gospel imperative to perfection" (Matt. 5:48) as eschatological. The

[35]Cf. "The Scripture Way of Salvation," I.4: "In that instant [of justification], we are born again . . . born of the Spirit: there is a *real* as well as a *relative* change. We are inwardly renewed by the power of God."

[36]Cf. "On God's Vineyard," I.5, for a triumphalist claim that the Methodists' doctrine of justification surpasses Luther's one-sided stress, just as their doctrine of sanctification was more amply balanced than that of the Catholics.

[37]Cf. Harald Lindström's admirable analysis, *Wesley and Sanctification* (1946), and R. Newton Flew's historical survey, *The Idea of Perfection in Christian Theology* (1934), chap. XIX.

Westminster Confession of Faith looks forward to it, for the elect, "in the state of glory."[38] On the other side, the Catholic tradition has tended to correlate sanctification with the inherent righteousness imparted in justification.[39] All of these, however, discouraged anything like an expectation of such "perfection" *in this life*.[40] This is why the canonization of "saints" is always retrospective.

The logic here turns upon the common meaning of *perfectus* (and its vernacular cognates) in Latin Christianity. Typically, this has meant some sort of *ne plus ultra* [uttermost point attainable]. In any such sense, perfection is impossible as long as the roots of sin (*fomes peccati*) remain. Such a doctrine of perfection would therefore imply sinless perfection, and most Christians reject this out of hand as presumptuous. The Calvinists avoided such presumptions with their doctrines of election and final perseverance, which Wesley, in turn, regarded as inlets to antinomianism.

What matters is that Wesley was much more fully aware of such complications than has been realized.[41] He comes close, more than once, to expressions that tilt toward sinless perfection.[42] But whenever he was confronted with an explicit argument for sinless—and guiltless—perfection (as in William Cudworth or James Relly), he recoiled and proposed a set of careful qualifications.[43]

The crucial term for Wesley was not *perfectus* but *teleiōs*—a dynamic understanding of "perfecting" that had come to him from early and Eastern spirituality, such as Clement, Gregory of Nyssa, Macarius, Ephraem Syrus, *et al.* In this view, "perfection" may be "realized" in a given moment (always as a gift from God,

---

[38]Chap. IX, ¶v.

[39]Cf. *The Canons and Decrees of the Council of Trent*, Session Six, Canon XXXII.

[40]Cf. St. Thomas, *Summa Theologiae*, II.II, Q.184, Art. 2: "Perfection . . . is not possible so long as we are *in via*, but we shall have it in heaven (*sed erit in patria*)." Wesley had found this, in its mystical dress, in William Law, *A Treatise on Christian Perfection* (1729), read first in 1730.

[41]For example, in Flew, *op. cit.*, and in R. A. Knox, *Enthusiasm* (1950), Chap. XVIII, 422–58.

[42]Cf. "The Trouble and Rest of Good Men," II.4. See also, the Prefaces to the earliest editions of *Hymns and Sacred Poems*, which contain some of the strongest, least nuanced statements on "sinless" perfection in the Wesley corpus (*JWW* XIV:319–30). Cf. also his letters to the Rev. Mr. Plenderlieth, May 23, 1768, and to Thomas Olivers, March 24, 1757.

[43]As in "On Sin in Believers," "The Repentance of Believers," "Wandering Thoughts," etc.

received by trusting faith), yet never as a finished state. "Perfection" connotes two conjoining "powers": (1) the power to love God wholeheartedly, and (2) the power not to commit sin voluntarily ("sin properly so-called," which Wesley consistently defined as "a violation of a known law of God").[44] "Perfection" thus gained might also be lost if ever one's love of God cooled, or if, falling into a "sin of surprise,"[45] one failed to repent forthwith and claim God's mercy.

Everything turns here on the validity of the distinction between voluntary and involuntary sins. If "perfection" is *purity of intention* (as it is in this doctrine), then what of the remains of sin and their corrupting influences upon our best intentions? Thus, even when more carefully qualified (as in Wesley's second sermon "On Perfection" and elsewhere), such a vision of love as a gracious intention triumphant over human passion (even by God's grace) has seemed somewhat reckless to orthodox Protestants.[46] Moreover, their fears have often been justified in the further oversimplifications that turned up in later Methodist "holiness movements"—with their doctrines of "entire sanctification as a second and separate work of grace."[47]

Again, for our purpose here, it is less important to argue for or against this doctrine of sanctification than to understand its background. We have spoken of its Eastern sources—and also of Taylor and Law (add also à Kempis). Another root reaches back into a rich subsoil of English mysticism, as in Richard Rolle of Hampole. More specifically, one can point to Robert Gell's *Essay Toward the Amendment of the Last English Translation of the Bible* (1659), which Wesley had read as early as 1741.[48] This is a sprawling monument of erudition and piety; I have yet to see it in a modern bibliography. Its importance for us appears in its "Appendix" (pp. 785ff.), where Gell adds a sermon on the

---

[44]Cf. "Sermon on the Mount, XI," I.5; "On Perfection," III.9; letter to John Hosmer, June 7, 1761, and to Mrs. Bennis, June 16, 1772.

[45] Cf. "The First-Fruits of the Spirit," II.11–13, III.6. Cf. also William Law, *A Serious Call to a Devout and Holy Life* (1729), 21, and Benjamin Kidder, *A Discourse Concerning Sins of Infirmity and Wilful Sins* (1704), 10.

[46]See *Cautions and Directions Given to the Greatest Professors in the Methodist Societies* (1762).

[47]Cf. J. L. Peters, *Christian Perfection and American Methodism* (1956).

[48]"Surely [Gell] was a man mighty in the Scriptures and well acquainted with the work of God in the soul"; cf. *JWJ* for February 3 and July 19, 1741; see also, April 17, 1777.

possibility of Christian perfection in terms of *pure intention.*[49] Equally interesting are Gell's references to a then familiar controversy in which Thomas Drayton and William Palmer had been condemned for their teachings of perfection in this life.[50]

Such an obscure slice of history is matched by other snippets of evidence of a tradition in English divinity that had correlated the terms "Methodist" and "Methodism" with perfection long before Wesley.[51] Besides these, there is a curious little pamphlet entitled "A War Among the Angels of the Churches" (1693), by "A Country Professor of Jesus Christ."[52] In it, a "sect" labeled "the New Methodists" is denounced for its heterodoxies, such as holy living and perfection. John Goodwin turns out to be one of the author's main targets, the same John Goodwin whose doctrine of justification had so strongly influenced Wesley. It is not recorded that Wesley had ever read this pamphlet. But others had—nor is it a merely fanciful conjecture that the Oxford comics who provided the Holy Club with its unwelcome nickname, "Methodists," had something of this folklore in mind.

THE RELEVANCE OF RECOVERED SOURCES

Obviously, Wesley can be read, and usually has been read, without the broad and intricate tapestry of his sources unfolded as a background for interpretation. This was part of the price he paid for self-divestiture of his theological apparatus. Even so, it is just as this background is recovered and reevaluated that Wesley emerges as a more interesting and impressive theologian than his stereotypes have presented—precisely because he was a folk theologian.

Nor are these gropings for Wesley's sources merely a

[49]"Some Saints Not Without Sin for a Season."

[50]Cf. p. 797, where he cites "Dr. Thomas Drayton . . . and Mr. William Palmer who have published a treatise [on perfection] entitled, *A Revindication of the Possibility of a Total Mortification of Sin in This Life; And of the Saints' Perfect Obedience to the Law of God, to be the Orthodox Protestant Doctrine, etc.*"

[51]Cf. OED, *loc cit.*: Robert Traill (1692): "The new Methodists about the grace of God [i.e., the Amyraldeans of Saumur] had too great an increase in the French churches." William Wake (1686): "Our new Methodists . . . " (i.e., catholic apologists for "holy living").

[52]In the McAlpin Collection (Supplemental Catalogue), Union Theological Seminary Library, N.Y.

pedantic exercise. For now that the old quarrels between Protestants and Catholics (and between Protestants and Protestants) are in process of transvaluation, urgent "new" questions about thorny old problems (like justification and sanctification) are being raised in new contexts of ecumenical dialogue. Such questions have an urgent, equally contemporary correlate: what ought Christians to be urged realistically to expect, and therefore to seek, *in this life?*

Such questions are no longer denominational in their contexts. Theological pluralism is now the actual state of affairs, probably irreversible. We have come to take ecumenical theologizing for granted and thus are closer to Wesley's "catholic spirit" than we have realized.

The problems of our times have no easy answers. But they may be illumined by insights generated by thoughtful transvaluations of our several heritages. In such transvaluations, the contributions of the folk theologians had best be included along with the rest. And, in any such new perspective, John Wesley may yet turn out to be surprisingly relevant, precisely as folk theologian. His mind was prone to oversimplifications, to be sure, but it was richly furnished from all parts of the Christian tradition and he had a special gift for finding constructive third alternatives to barren polarities. All this entitles him to the sort of consideration he has never yet received—alongside other fruitful "doctors of the church," greater and less.

A New Future for Wesley Studies: An Agenda for "Phase III"

———†———

[1985] At the Seventh Oxford Institute of Methodist Theological Studies in 1982 five major addresses were given on the theme "The Future of the Methodist Theological Traditions." Outler's contribution is his most thorough discussion of the historiographical and hermeneutical issues that confront Wesley studies. This is an indispensable introduction for those who would take up the task of "making Wesley credible once again."

In his presentation, President Norwyn Denny warned us against pedantry and dalliance in our undertakings for this fortnight. It crossed my mind, as he was speaking, that *Wesley redivivus* might also have given us a similar admonition—even if, as I think, with a rather different nuance. Once he had alienated himself from this university, Wesley rarely commended that special sort of "leisure" that we have planned for ourselves in this Institute (*scholē*, in its original sense). Besides, his scorn for pedantry, dalliance—*and trendiness!*—was about equal. We remember how both Dr. Johnson and the Countess of Huntingdon used to complain of his busy-ness. Even so, he clung to his academic title as "Fellow of Lincoln College" long after it was appropriate, and he was subject to occasional twinges of nostalgia for "the groves of Academe." For example, in 1772, he could share with his brother a wistful backward glance (*Redde me vitae priori;* Give me back my former life) and pose a curious question: "What have I been doing these thirty years past?"[1] Moreover he had invented a quasi-collegial device of his own (calling it a "conference"); it was designed to function as a sort of institute of theological studies. We would not wish to imitate its format; we would do well to adopt its basic concerns.

On the one side, Wesley was a very public person, accustomed to nearly constant exposure—both to admiring followers who often failed to understand him and to disdainful critics who rarely tried. By stages, he eased into a complex leadership role—founder, patriarch, cult hero of "the people called Methodists"—with effortless aplomb. Meanwhile, he continued to shrug off his critics with at least a slight whiff of self-righteousness. In his old age, he was the best known "private person" in England; he recounts his last visit to Falmouth (at age eighty-six), where "the people, high and low, lined the street from one end of town to the other, out of stark love and kindness, gaping and staring as if the King were going by."[2] Popular reverence had also generated an

[1][Letter to Charles Wesley, Dec. 15, 1772. See *JWL* VI:6.]
[2]*JWJ* , Aug. 18, 1789; cf. other triumphal processions cited in Richard Watson, *Life of John Wesley*, 1831, 168.

astonishing iconography along with a mass of relics and portraitures (unaccountably diverse!). I think, though, that even he might have winced, as I did, at the poster (preserved in The Morley Collection, Wesley College, Bristol) that depicts his bodily assumption into heaven, with a full complement of adoring cherubs and angels!

On the other side, he was an indefatigable author, editor, publisher—and he meant for his writings to be read. For his "plain people," he cultivated a "plain style" (with Glanvil and Tillotson as models) and had become rather smug on this point (cf. his preface to *Sermons on Several Occasions*, 1787).[3] His quotations were copious and careless; his citations were negligent. He oversimplified complex issues with never a qualm. At the same time, he had out a weather eye for more sophisticated readers as well ("men of reason and religion" who shared his own taste for *The Spectator* and *The Gentlemen's Magazine*). Even for his plain people he would drop casual classical tags and allusions, as if to remind them of his academic credentials! But note that he rarely left them untranslated.

It seems to me unlikely, therefore, that he ever expected to be pored over by succeeding generations of scholars or ever to have his sources checked out by nitpicking editors. Why should he have? His own self-understood vocation was that of heralding an updated, simplified version of "the faith once for all delivered to the saints"—in and for his own time and place. His self-chosen role as mentor to the Methodists was geared to their immediate needs and focused on the near future as it unfolded. He was aware of the radical challenges to Christian orthodoxy by the deists and freethinkers, but he died with no more than dim inkling of the drastic transvaluations that were even then reshaping the European mind. He was more deeply influenced by Enlightenment views than has generally been recognized; he was catholic-spirited long before his time. But he was no more the

[3][The first of John Tillotson's fourteen volumes of sermons was entitled *Sermons Preached Upon Several Occasions*. Concerning his style Samuel Wesley had written "Immortal TILLOTSON with judgment scan/. . . ./He always soars, but never's out of sight,/He taught us how to Speak, and Think, and Write." Quoted in L. G. Locke, *Tillotson*, A Study in Seventeenth-Century Literature (Anglistica, IV; Copenhagen: 1954), 149.]

prototype of modernism (as in Umphrey Lee's retrojection) than he was the Calvinist whom George Croft Cell "rediscovered."

Thus it was that the vast bulk of his writings were produced for his own people, with other readers only incidentally in view. This clearly is the case with his *Explanatory Notes* and *A Collection of Hymns for the Use of the People Called Methodists* (1780). It seems also true of *The Arminian Magazine* (1778 et seq.), that marvelous montage of jewels and junk. *The Works* (1771–74) and the *Sermons* (1787–88) may have had a wider audience in mind, as did the *Journal* (from 1735). *A Christian Library* (1749–55) was aimed at a theologically sophisticated public (which throws some light on the fact that it had no more than a single edition in Wesley's lifetime; it was obviously an editorial miscalculation).

PHASE I: THE METHODIST COCOON

The point here is that, in nearly two centuries since his death, the study and interpretation of his writings has been largely a business of the Methodists alone: by them and for them. This self-enclosed pattern helps us identify what we might label "Wesley Studies, Phase I." In it, the chief stress was on the intimate links between Wesley and Methodism. Wesley Studies, Phase I began with a disgraceful contention over Wesley's literary remains between John Whitehead, Thomas Coke, and Henry Moore; it was followed by John Pawson's feckless handling of the surviving manuscripts. We can only guess as to what we may have lost from the original legacy. Much was salvaged by Thomas Jackson, whose editions of *The Sermons* in 1825 (two volumes) and *The Works* (1829–32) are still our chief reliance for more than half the Wesley corpus. The Zondervan reprint's claim (in 1958–59) of being based on "the authorized edition . . . of 1872" is off by a full forty years. Wesley Studies, Phase I, therefore, has been largely dependent on bare texts (some incomplete, some extracted from other authors, some even spurious). It has been staunchly denominationalistic in temper, ardently triumphalist in tone.

The first notable exception here was a biography of Wesley by Robert Southey in 1820. This is still a very interesting essay and certainly the best written of all the Wesley biographies. Its appendix, with its collection of Alexander Knox's comments on Wesley's character and theology is still valuable (and of more than passing interest to a Methodist Institute meeting at Keble College, since Knox was a spiritual mentor to Keble and Pusey and, as such, something of a link between the Evangelical and the Anglo-Catholic Revivals). Southey's unexpected venture (which criticized Wesley's personality but admired his complex contributions to British Christianity) was promptly denounced by John Gibson Lockhart (in *The Quarterly Review*) on the ground that its subject was unworthy of the labors of England's Poet Laureate. Most cultivated Britons were inclined to agree. But the controversy outraged the Methodists and called forth a counterattack in Richard Watson's *Life;* this helped stabilize the Wesley hero cult already flourishing, and which still survives. This cultic aspect has been yet another characteristic feature of Wesley Studies, Phase I—from the great days of Jabez Bunting on down to our time.

Left with Wesley to themselves, the Methodists proceeded to evolve a cluster of stereotypes that we know so well and that have shaped our own images of him: the hide-bound father, the peerless mother, young Jacky marked off as a special "brand plucked out of the burning," the Holy Club, "Aldersgate," the great evangelist taking the whole world for his parish, the invincible debater—and of course, above all, the founder of Methodism. Given Methodist triumphalism and their own biases, *non*-Methodists were content to acknowledge Wesley's remarkable zeal and practical gifts but otherwise to ignore or denigrate him as a theologian. I grew up with encyclopedias and textbooks that were satisfied to link Wesley with Methodism and let it go at that. In the old *Religion in Geschichte und Gegenwart*, there was a short pithy identification of Wesley that still sticks in my mind: *"energisch, herb, und fanatisch"* (vigorous, sharp-tongued, and fanatical).

Methodists, by and large, were content with their patriarch on his pedestal. A pragmatic warrant for this was that, meanwhile, they were enjoying one of the really great success stories in the whole history of the expansion of Christianity. Their triumphalism had much to sustain it. Luke Tyerman said what most Methodists took for granted: "Methodism is the greatest fact in the history of the church."[4] The anonymous reviewer of Curnock's first volume in the new edition of Wesley's *Journal*[5] held the same view: "Methodism is, perhaps, the most extensive religious

[4]*Life and Times* [1870], I:1.
[5]*Times Literary Supplement*, Nov. 18, 1909.

system, outside of Islam, among those who owe their origin to, and still derive an impetus from, the life of one man."

Wesley Studies, Phase I, was, therefore, the scholarly aspect of a denominationalism preoccupied with itself and its founder. Such narcissism still continues; it accounts for an important fraction of Britain's tourist business every year. One is forever hearing Methodists recount their gratification at having walked where Wesley walked, at having stood in pulpits where he preached, at having been in the room where he died—at having had a special showing of those "digs" of his at Lincoln (misidentified as they are). Wesley relics are scattered over the world in museums and homes. Indeed, it would be interesting to know how many in this company have no Wesley relics of their own. For myself, I do not reckon eighteenth-century literary Wesleyana as "relics," but, if you think I should, then even I am something of an iconodule.

In living memory, however, triumphalism has fallen out of fashion (partly because there have been fewer and fewer recent triumphs!). A new ecumenical spirit has spread through the Christian community at large. At the same time, the rise and fall of "Enlightenment Christianity" has brought us to a new post-modern era in which nineteenth-century liberalism seems less and less robust. Thus, with the faltering fortunes of Methodism generally (with welcome exceptions here and there) and with the waxing of ecumenical historiography, Wesley Studies, Phase I, have come to be more and more outmoded. Denominational church history has been demoted; triumphalism has been muted by sophisticated historians as bad form and bad history. The great issues that wracked the sixteenth and seventeenth centuries have been refocused. The Second Vatican Council marked an ending of the Roman Catholic Counter-Reformation. The presuppositions of nineteenth-century liberalism have called for thoroughgoing re-evaluation—despite the persistence of old memories and old labels.

PHASE II: SELECTIVE INTERPRETATIONS

One of the effects of this basic shift in historical perspective has been a representation of the eighteenth century in a new light. This in its turn has prompted a second phase in Wesley studies with less emphasis on the Wesley-Methodist symbiosis and more emphasis on one or more angles of interest in Wesley as a theologian in his own right. Motivations in Phase II have been varied: "ecumenical," as in the studies of R. Newton Flew (*The Idea of Perfection*) and Father Maximin Piette (*John Wesley in the Evolution of Protestantism*, 1937); and "anti-ecumenical," in the sparkling contempt in Ronald Knox's chapters on Wesley (*Enthusiasm*, 1950). In G. C. Cell and Franz Hildebrandt the concern was to link Wesley more closely with Calvin and Luther; in E. P. Thompson, there was a passion to indict Wesley for his social views; in Bernard Semmel, there has been a more credible effort to describe *The Methodist Revolution* as a different sort of social transformation. The shared twin features of Phase II—however diverse otherwise—have been: (1) the concern to rescue Wesley from his Methodist cocoon, and (2) to probe more deeply into one or another basic aspect of his thought and praxis. Here one thinks of John Deschner, Harald Lindström, Ole Borgen, John Walsh, and especially of Martin Schmidt.

One of the negative effects of the weakening of the Wesley-Methodist symbiosis has been the emergence of a full generation (or more) of Methodist theologians whose thought has been touched quite lightly by Wesley himself (save for the purposes of occasional incantation). The list here is long; the easier way to make the same point is to count off the number of contemporary Methodist theologians and ethicists of real stature, who reflect an identifiable debt to Wesley as decisive mentor. How many fingers would such a counting call for? Moreover, there are more and more trendy Methodists who, having helped topple Wesley from his pedestal, now propose to pack him off to history's limbo. Non-Methodists find this a mite baffling. They remember the Wesley hero cult, and they wonder what will happen to a movement that lacks the wit and will to transvaluate its chief legacy.

There is a third subgroup in Wesley Studies, Phase II. These are the Methodist theological partisans of one or another of the current coterie-theologies; their interest in Wesley is confined to his possible use of them as "authority" for their own convictions, rooted in other traditions. This is not to argue for or against this coterie-theology or that, nor even to question the legitimacy of selective appeals to a selected authority. There is a crucial prior question involved and it is a methodological one. How far are these various appellants really interested in Wesley's theology itself? How competently are their appeals grounded in the primary texts taken as a whole? Eisegesis, even in a good cause, is still bad hermeneutics!

One of the distinctive achievements of Wesley Studies, Phase II, has been to lift Wesley out of his Methodist matrix. And yet the question of the reassignment of his place in church history (and in contemporary Christianity) has been largely left open. This suggests two inherent weaknesses in the model (with some notable exceptions, of course). The first is its general indifference to the history of Christian thought as a whole. The other is a partial or biased reading of Wesley so that their separated parts do not quite match his whole. There is a special problem about Wesley's relevance for postcolonial Christianity in Latin America, Asia, and Africa. In these contexts today, he is bound to appear as overlaid by the thick crust of his British provincialism and thus in urgent need of artful and responsible indigenization. But if such a thing can be done with John Bunyan, why not with John Wesley? Besides, there are Charles' hymns to help!

In any case, the question of Wesley's proper place in church history, on the one hand, and in current ecumenical theology, on the other, remains open and a problem. The proposal that Wesley belongs among the really great doctors of the church is preposterous on its face. We know of other figures in Christian history who, in their times and places, were great and shining lights—and yet who now languish in oblivion—save in the most sophisticated summations of Christian memory. One thinks of men like Johann Gerhard, Martin Chemmitz, Johann Heidegger, Francis Turretin, Richard Baxter, and Horace Bushnell—great ones all and now forgotten, to our loss. Will Wesley join them presently—and should he? But if he is not a theological supernova nor yet ready for limbo, what then? How much has he still to contribute to the issues with which we are struggling and those we are passing on to generations yet to come? Questions like these have not yet been fully formulated nor rightly answered to the satisfaction of critical historians or devoted ecumenists. But they have opened up a new horizon of inquiry that might properly be labeled Wesley Studies, Phase III.

PHASE III: HISTORICAL CONTEXT AND
ECUMENICAL RELEVANCE

Such a third phase would not propose to repudiate the positive residues of Phases I and II—although such a phase would be less interested in the Wesley-Methodist symbiosis and more concerned with ecumenical theology and praxis. Its first goal is that of basic reorientation—the repositioning of Wesley in his own time and place, against his larger background, and in as wide a historical context as possible. But all of this is still in order to enable an application of Wesley's relevance to issues in *our* times and *our* futures. Phase III is the effort to get beyond Wesley as Methodist patriarch toward a more fruitful place for him in the larger scene, historical and ecumenical.

For me, such a notion of yet a third phase of Wesley studies was changed from a vision to a program on a summer's day in 1957—in Frank Baker's parsonage in Hull. Two decades before, I had taken a doctorate in patristics and had been engaged in the fruitful absurdity of trying to master the history of Christian thought as a whole (in support of a still more grandiose project: viz., the modern dialogue between Christianity and current secular wisdom, as focused in the human sciences). The point, however, was that nowhere in my education or career had Wesley ever been regarded as other than a great evangelist and denominational founder. For example, my cherished friend and colleague, H. Richard Niebuhr had come by his image of Wesley as a defective Calvinist, largely on the basis of Professor Cell's book, without a firsthand examination of the Wesley corpus itself, so far as I ever knew: "Wesley's essential Calvinism has recently been described by Professor Cell, though it may be that the great Methodist's limitation lay at the point of his frequent unawareness of this [Calvinistic] presupposition of his gospel."[6]

Over the years, I had read Wesley on my own, partly out of loyalty (he was a hero to my father), but more out of a historian's curiosity as to where he rightly fitted into the development of Protestant thought between the Puritans and Schleiermacher. My general impression was of a creative mind in fustian; an antidote to both moralism *and* solifidianism—but not one comparable in theological stature, say, to Jonathan Edwards. When, therefore, in the editorial board of *A Library of Protestant Thought*, we were threshing out a format for that collection of readings, it crossed my mind that Wesley might very well have a volume of his own—just as we had planned for Richard Baxter, Horace Bushnell, *et al.* Jonathan Edwards was already being published by the Yale Press—a project that has now stretched out for more than thirty years.

[6]*The Kingdom of God in America*, 1937, 101.

My proposal drew scoffs from my non-Methodist colleagues, who reminded me that it was I who had proposed the original title for the library, viz., "Protestant *Thought*." Later, when an outside group of specialists in Reformation and post-Reformation history was polled about inclusions and allowable omissions, the project least supported by them was a solo volume for John Wesley. How Wesley got his volume is another story,[7] but it turned out that I got the assignment to edit it. It was then that the real shocks began—especially to a generalist like me, long since accustomed to working on critical editions already prepared by specialists, together with the usual pile of sophisticated secondary literature in which the essential spadework has already been done by my elders and betters. My naïve questions about holographs and sources met with unedifying answers and led to the discovery of how tightly Wesley had been cocooned by the Methodists and how easily ignored by others. The Curnock *Journal* is almost wholly preoccupied with Methodist affairs and not very critical of Wesley's self-serving reportage. Besides, who then could check out the deficiencies in his claims of having decoded the *Diaries*? Sugden's *Standard Sermons* had a few critical comments on Wesley's theology but within a Methodist ambiance that is nearly total. Besides, what Sugden was really interested in was the question of "doctrinal standards" *for Methodists;* this allowed him to ignore the last two-thirds of the sermon corpus.

The secondary literature was dominated by the familiar stereotypes. Critical questions went unasked—or were answered stereotypically. I discovered in England that such primary texts as had survived were in safe enough hands but not then in safe quarters. The contrast between the Wesley archives and the Baxter archives in the Doctor Williams Library was embarrassing. There was no reliable inventory of what Wesley had read nor any convenient collection of his sources. In short, what I had supposed would be a fairly straightforward task turned into a bafflement—and the conviction came readily that Phase III would never unfold if other Wesley scholars had to replicate my experience. Meanwhile, my colleagues nodded smugly at my complaints and hinted broadly that this was a fitting comeup-

---

[7]See "Towards a Re-Appraisal of John Wesley as a Theologian" above, 39–54.

pance for so ill-starred a venture. One of them (a Pascal specialist) mumbled something about silk purses and sow's ears.

In Frank Baker, however, I had finally found a Wesley specialist such as I could never be but who was ready and able to help with my project. He, too, had discovered the limited usefulness of Wesley Studies, Phase I—although he has always been more preoccupied with the man himself and less inclined than I to speak of a "Methodist cocoon." But he had conceived of a new, critical edition a decade earlier and had begun work on a proper bibliography to supersede Greene. Baker's expertise got me over many a hurdle that had balked me up to that point. Thus, with his aid and that of many others (historians, classicists, specialists in English literature) Wesley got his volume in the *Library*—and, for all its flaws (plainer now after twenty years more study), it has continued to outsell the other volumes by a ratio of ten to one and remains the only volume of the eighteen still in print. Many people (including those at the Oxford University Press) have found this unaccountable.

Actually, though, it was I who profited most from this project because in the process, muddled as it was, I had discovered a more interesting theological resource than even I had expected. Here was valuable light shed on many of my other queries: about eighteenth-century linkages between "orthodoxy," "Pietism" and "Enlightenment." The project has gone on enriching my own theological understanding of contemporary issues. Wesley's rhetoric takes a bit of getting used to, but there *is* "plain truth for plain people" in it. There is also a sort of catalytic theology there, designed to interact with other theologies (earlier and later) without losing its own integrity, and without forcing Christian doctrines into a rigid mold. It is a theology less interested in the order of Christian *truth* (as in school theologies generally) than in the Christian *life*. Its specific focus is the order of salvation as an eventful process that stretches across the whole horizon of Christian existence. Its axial theme is *grace*, which makes it Christocentric and yet also preeminently pneumatological. For Wesley the Holy Spirit is the Lord and Giver of *Grace* as well as the Lord and Giver of Life. Thus, "prevenience" is not a stage of grace but the crucial aspect of grace in all its manifestations. It signifies the divine initiative in *all* spirituality, in all Christian experience. Wesley's theology is intensely evangelical but it looks also toward the ethical transformation of society. It is concerned with "third alternatives" to all the barren polarities generated by centuries of polemics. It is a linkage theology between historic orthodoxy and the Enlightenment, between radical Protestantism and ecumenical Christianity. In short, what I had found in Wesley was a theologian who looked better without his halo—who was, on principle, in dialogue with Christians in many different traditions in his own day precisely because he had been in such fruitful dialogue with so much of the Christian tradition before him. He has, therefore, become an important theological teacher for me, and I am convinced that this could happen in other cases. This is why I have kept looking beyond Phases I and II. It has been the warrant for investing two extra decades of drudgery and excitement in the task of making his sermons available in fuller context.

I hope I am not misconstrued as claiming that Dr. Baker, or even Dr. Baker and I, *invented* Phase III. Historiographical perspectives have natural histories of their own. What has happened over the past three decades is the rise of a new sort of interest in the field and folk theology. Other scholars of diverse backgrounds have also discovered Wesley in new dimensions— one thinks of Timothy Smith, Robert Cushman, W. R. Cannon, Richard Heitzenrater, Bernard Semmel, *et al.* One can go on from them to rejoice over the promising crop of younger scholars on whom any new future for Wesley studies really depends.

But it must also be said, however, that Phase III is, up to now, more a vision than an achievement, more of a beginning than a full-fledged movement. This would illuminate Ronald Gibbins' instinctive reflex, in his review of the paperback reprint of the Wesley volume in *A Library of Protestant Thought:* "So much has been written about the life and work of John Wesley that one is always suspicious of *any* new treatment." He could have added, "just as we have grown suspicious of all the old ones."

And yet all of this should help explain my excitement and earnest hopes for this particular session of this Institute and the inclusion in it of a separate working group on Wesley studies. Despite the gains of the past two decades, I am not yet wholly confident that Phase III is here to stay. There are still low moments when I have this sinking feeling of having been playing Sisyphus—the right rock up the wrong hill! On the other hand, the signs multiply that a more favorable reappraisal of Wesley as an ecumenical theologian is taking place. I know of two Methodist universities that have designed special programs in Wesley and Methodist studies—and most of our seminaries are taking this more seriously. Professors Kretschmar and Fries have allotted him a chapter in their new series on classical theologians.[8] There is a respectful footnote in Hendrikus Berkhof's *Christian Faith* (pp. 426–27). Topical seminars have begun to appear on the programs of the American Academy of Religion; one is planned for the next session of the American Historical Association. Conferences on Wesley as a theological resource have been held in Australia; others are planned for in Latin America and elsewhere. A private foundation in the United States is helping to underwrite the graduate education of a score or more of so-called "Wesley Fellows." Last year, a quite discerning question about Wesley *as theologian* appeared in the Oxford Honors Exam in Theology—the first one of its kind that I have noticed since I began to take those examinations as a private hobby in 1939.

Even so, a consensus as to the requisite scholarly definitions of the state of the question in Phase III has yet to be formulated—its agenda is not yet firmly in place. Wesley's impact in contemporary theology is still in the process of being tested. Our work in this Institute could, therefore, make a real difference in opening up a real future in Wesley studies, if indeed, there is to be one.

As I see it, there are at least three crucial issues in any such future:

The *first* is methodological; all theologies claiming to be Wesleyan must be based on the whole Wesley as he was (and not on this aspect or accent in his thought and praxis). Like every other enterprise in historical interpretation, he must be investigated on his own grounds and in accordance with his own theological intentions—which were not, in the first instance, denominational nor sectarian. This would enable us to begin to transcend the tragic polarizations in the Wesleyan traditions in the nineteenth century that still haunt us and hobble our mission in the world. We need to clarify the grounds on which Wesley still stands as an authority for us, insofar as he does. This cannot refer to Wesley's authority in himself; it can only point us to that authoritative complex to which he gave his own allegiance and to

---

[8][Unfortunately, the "allotted" chapter on Wesley was not included in *Klassiker der Theologie*, herausgegeben von Heinrich Fries und Georg Kretschmar (München: C. H. Beck, 1981–1983).]

which we may give ours: Scripture, "Christian Antiquity," reason, and experience.

An inference from this will make a *second* point: Wesley must be read in light of his sources—and therefore within the larger ecumenical perspectives of historic Christianity. He worked in and from Scripture—and so must we—but also the classics, the Fathers, the Reformation and Counter-Reformation, and the contemporary worlds he lived in. He was no antiquarian; more than once I have thought I could hear a few ghostly snorts while I was struggling with an intricate footnote. But he was a man of tradition—and as his way of gathering up and weaving together so much of the Christian tradition is better understood, his theological oversimplifications will be less readily misconstrued. Reading Wesley calls for trifocals: one part of the lens focused on his own background, another on the seventeenth century, and a third on possible projections into the nineteenth and twentieth centuries—in that order. To move from our concerns to his and back again and to call this "Wesley studies" is to miss the richness of the heritage he left us, and to diminish the contributions that we might share with other Christians—and other humans—in our times and in those to come.

Third, however, the justification for the drudgeries entailed in serious Wesley studies must be sought in their prospective relevance for contemporary Christians (and not Methodists alone) in our current commitments to evangelism, renewal, and social transformation. Here, two fruitful ideas emerge as obvious: contemporary theology must be ecumenical and Wesley's is just that. Again, the idea of *development* is central in contemporary historical study (as one can see in Professor Pelikan's magisterial survey, *The Christian Tradition*). We must not claim too much for Wesley's historical consciousness, but we may claim he was more of a pioneer in grasping the idea of development than most of his contemporaries—and felt freer than most to develop his own ideas as the Revival unfolded.

In any future for Phase III, Wesley's role as a folk theologian (or people's theologian) will have to be plumbed more carefully and the secrets of his success in communicating complex notions to simple folk must be sought out. Here was a man who dedicated a competent theological training to the tasks of pastoral leadership of plain people, and who drew much of his own developing understandings from their responses. In such a perspective, his distinctiveness would be more apparent: the Anglican evangelist as devoted to the sacramental means of grace as if he were rector; the eighteenth-century reformer with conscious ties to both the church Fathers and the radical Protestants, and who may be laid alongside other pastoral theologians like Henry Scougal. The result would be a richer sense of theology as *scientia practica* (faith in order to action). This would make it possible, as Wesley comes to be better known, that the traditional Methodist emphasis upon sanctification and perfection could be seen as integrated in a more comprehensive view of grace in the order of salvation. This would then recognize how comprehensive Wesley's view of salvation really was— a continuum of God's gracious acts that reaches from the first stirrings of conscience to the fullness of faith and to the full restoration of the divine image.

The problem of a credible hermeneutics for Wesley is, as I know, a vexed one. Its nub, or so it seems to me, is whether the fact that Wesley never produced a systematic exposition of his theology (and never intended to) is to be reckoned as a weakness to be remedied or as a strength to be exploited. Here, much depends on whether one sets the notion of "systematics" over against its simple antithesis, "unsystematic" and whether one uses the term "eclectic" as pejorative (a synonym for "haphazard"). There is, however, another possibility: viz., to think of theology as coherent reflection upon Christian living, with all its natural divagations. Wesley knew the history of systematic theology, from Peter Lombard's *Sentences* to Philip Melancthon's *Loci* and in the heroic labors of the Protestant dogmaticians. He himself relied heavily on John Pearson's *Exposition of the Creed* (which comes as near to a "systematics" as seventeenth-century Anglicanism can show). But Wesley also knew that the bulk of significant Christian literature, from the Scriptures, to the Fathers, to the classics of devotion, to the liturgies, had focused on Christian *life* and the intimations of Christian truth that could be drawn therefrom.

For better or for worse, then, Wesley *chose* to formulate his teaching in unsystematic forms: sermons, tracts, letters, hymns. He could claim that "every serious man who peruses these sermons will therefore see *in the clearest manner* what those doctrines are which I embrace and teach, as the essentials of true religion" ("Preface" to *Sermons on Several Occasions*, 1746). He could speak of his collection of hymns (1780) as "a little body of *practical divinity*." His axial theme, which organizes all else in his thought, is grace, and the focus of all his thinking about grace is on the order of *salvation*. The real measure of Wesley's mind is the consistency and clarity with which he managed the connections between this axial theme and all the other facets of his thought.

It goes without saying that Methodists and other Christians are, and must be, free to do their theologizing in any genre that they find edifying. This allows for responsible efforts to produce a Wesleyan "systematics" (in the tradition of Watson and Pope), just as it also allows for other organizing principles (for example, in Professor Geoffrey Wainwright's thoroughly Wesleyan *Doxology*). What matters in any case is that all such theologies should bear the marks of careful basic homework in the Wesley texts. This is an equal prerequisite in any other efforts to update Wesley and make him relevant. Thus, I propose a slogan for Methodist theologies (comparable to current trends in other traditions we know): Back to Wesley and his sources, and then forward—with his sense of heritage and openness to the future as one of our models.

In whatever patterns Methodist theologies may continue to develop, it will be crucial for them to strike for new balances between faith and life. It *is* our task "to spread Scriptural holiness over these lands." But *scriptural* holiness has always had the whole trajectory of grace in view—and Methodism has been ill-served by those who have minimized this wholeness for whatever reason. For surely what is most interesting and truly creative in Wesley was his comprehensive vision of the Christian life: life in and from the Spirit (from repentance to justifying faith, to reconciliation, assurance, and regeneration, to sanctification); and life in and under grace as an eventful process punctuated by conversions, disciplined by the moral imperatives of holiness (personal and social).

The future of Wesley studies so conceived depends, more than we may have realized, on a new edition that will enable such studies to go forward more expeditiously than is possible at present. We know how studies in other traditions have been spurred and sustained by critical editions; it is even more crucial in our case. But you should also know that the Wesley Works Project has just now suffered a severely damaging blow. Three volumes have been published by the Oxford University Press and a fourth, now in page proof (i.e., the 1780 "Collection of Hymns"), will be published. But the Oxford Press has now abandoned the project, leaving us with no assured alternatives.[9] It may well be that this Institute could offer counsel and guidance in this crisis—if there is, in fact, an honest consensus among us as to its importance.

New edition or not, however, the future of Wesley studies, Phase III, really depends upon an agreed agenda that could serve all interested scholars in all traditions as a baseline for their own investigations and commitments. Each of us must already have some such agenda in mind, and it is the specific business of Group One to hammer out some such program as part of its *report*.[10] The point to be stressed here is that such an agenda is not the business of antiquarians only but of all men and women who are interested in testing the possible significance of Wesley less as *patriarch* than as *mentor* (along with many others) so that those who seek such a future can bring to it an added richness from the Christian tradition to which Wesley stands as a crucial witness.

Methodists and other Christians have still much to learn about the possible role and function in Christian theologizing of what we have called "the Wesleyan Quadrilateral"—his fourfold guidelines: of Scripture as primal font of Christian revelation, of tradition (Christian Antiquity) as the sum of the collective Christian wisdom in response to the truth revealed in Scripture; of reason as the God-given discipline of ordering our conceptions as cogently as ever we can; of experience as the assurance of God's reconciling love in Christ, received as a special assurance of God's unmerited favor. We have much to gain from a reconsideration of Wesley's correlation of soteriology and pneumatology, the person and work of the Holy Spirit in the Mystery of Salvation.

The way beyond the schisms that still disrupt our oneness in Christ is not a backward step to some older (nineteenth-century) notion of holiness or the social gospel (especially if these were antithetical!). The way forward will come clearer as we recover the Wesleyan vision of Christian existence and all that it entails for faithful Christians in a world where justice must be served or the gospel will not get a hearing. Such a conspectus would provide a fruitful context for all our other concerns in this Institute: for the correlation of salvation and justice conceived in an evangelical mode, for effectual evangelism aimed at social transformation as

[9][Abingdon Press has since continued the Wesley Works Project.]
[10][The report agreed to by Group One appears on page 53 of *The Future of the Methodist Theological Traditions*, ed. M. Douglas Meeks. (Nashville: Abingdon, 1985).]

urgently as personal conversions (and yet not more so!), faith development without a rigid scheme of entelechies, a substantive sacramentalism without sacerdotalism.

No one has yet refuted the validity of Robert Chiles' evaluation of *The Theological Transition in American Methodism* (1965) from its original (i.e., Wesleyan) orientations—in the late nineteenth century and thereafter: (1) from revelation to a rationalistic hermeneutic; (2) from original sin to moral man; (3) from free grace to free will—and I would add (4) from Montanism to Pelagianism. It would also seem that what has happened in mainline American Methodism has its counterparts in other branches of the Methodist movement. It may be that, for some of us, there is no strong will to reverse these deformations, no earnest urgency to recover the form and power of historic Christianity for our times and for our futures. But to desist in these endeavors would be to cut the taproot of our Wesleyan heritage and to foreclose our future as evangelical Christians. On the other hand, if and when such an urgency returns, anywhere in the Christian community, Wesley ought to be accessible as a fruitful resource for Christian self-understanding and hope. If, however, he is to be appropriated as such a resource, he must become better known by more adequate methods of analysis and interpretation. For him to be better known, he must be studied more carefully, in his context and in the light of his sources. Wesley studies, Phase III, is, therefore, aimed at making Wesley credible once again to *our* own plain people and yet also to the whole of the Christian community. This, of course, is no end in itself. The virtue of our heritage must be sought in its power to open a new future where catalytic theologies will do more than polemical ones to enliven the chemistries of Christian thought and action—a new future under the rule of grace.

If any such prospect as this is viable, I cannot think of a likelier place for it to be affirmed than by *this* company, in *this* place, in *this* fortnight. For what, pray tell, are our real alternatives? It is because I see our times as in deep crisis and because I believe that Wesley studies have a positive contribution to make in such times, that I regard this conference as a possible landmark occasion that will call us and others to an even firmer commitment to the recovery of the heritage—as a hopeful prologue to a really new future. Who amongst us would wish for less?

Spirit and Church in the Wesleyan Tradition

—+—

"Biblical Primitivism" in Early American Methodism

---+---

[1988] What happened to Methodism when it crossed the Atlantic? Outler answers this question by showing how the Wesleyan vision of apostolic Christianity worked itself out in the New World. Because American Methodists lacked Wesley's sense of tradition they significantly altered his view of the fourfold character of authority. In Great Britain Methodism had been an alternative to Anglican formalism and Calvinist Dissent; in the United States it became a unique combination of "primitivism and churchliness." Contrasting these origins with the several transformations of twentieth-century Methodism, Outler reflects on the continuing power of the "restoration" and "holiness" ideals in church history.

There are several stereotypical ways to misunderstand early Methodism in America that have continued to seem credible to Methodists and non-Methodists alike, even until now. One is to connect its first century in America too closely with its Wesleyan antecedents in eighteenth-century Britain. Despite the Anglican affiliations of John Wesley, Thomas Coke, Joseph Pilmore, and others, Francis Asbury and the bulk of American Methodists in the early decades understood themselves in terms of modified non-conformity that set them quite apart from the Episcopalians on the one side and other American Protestants on the other. Their Arminian theology set them off from the Reformed traditions generally, and their societal polity (with its connectionalism, itinerancy, and monarchical episcopacy) distinguished them from all the congregationalist and presbyterian traditions. Moreover, they themselves were well content with these "Methodist distinctives," as they called them.

Another misleading stereotype is the supposition that American Methodism in its recent *second* century (1884–1984) amounted to a simple extension of the first. Sweeping social changes and drastic doctrinal reorientations altered the ethos and outlook of mainline Methodism in ways that require a reformulation of almost all generalizations about the early decades, or at least different nuances.[1] Nor will generalizations that are sound enough for United Methodism (since 1968) hold without important revision for the other Methodist bodies in America (e.g., the African Methodist Episcopal Church, the African Methodist Episcopal Zion Church, the Christian Methodist Episcopal Church, Wesleyan Methodists, Free Methodists, Nazarenes, and even less for the pentecostalists-in-variety who also acknowledge a Wesleyan provenance).

Indeed, the Methodist heritage itself has a more shadowy lineage than one would guess from the myths about John Wesley

[1]Robert Chiles, *Theological Transition in American Methodism, 1790–1935* (Nashville: Abingdon, 1964; Lanham, Md.: University Press of America, 1983).

as its founder, *de nihilo*. It goes back at least to the seventeenth-century negations of High Calvinism (as distilled in the canons of the famous Synod of Dort, 1619), gathered under the misleading umbrella term *Arminian*. Its alternative doctrines stressed grace and free will, along with a variety of notions about "double justification" (as with Martin Bucer and the so-called School of Saumur—e.g., Amyraldus, LeBlanc, Cameron, Peter Baro, *et. al.*). We know about this still obscure tradition largely through its critics—the French Protestant Jean Daillé in his *La foi fondée sur Les Saintes Scriptures, Contre les Nouveau Methodistes* (1634), the English Nonconformist Theophilus Gale in *The Court of The Gentiles* (1672), and the Lutheran Johannes Vlach's *Dissertationes novi Methodistae*. An English Puritan critique of this "new *method* in divinity," aimed actually at John Goodwin and Richard Baxter, appeared in an anonymous pamphlet in 1696, *A War Among the Angels of the Churches: Wherein is Showed the Principles of the New Methodists in the Great Point of Justification*. Its author, "A Country Professor of Jesus Christ," was especially incensed by what seemed to him as their "neonomianism," their false doctrines of imparted righteousness in justification and their preference for the doctrine of Christ's atoning death as the "meritorious cause" of salvation, by contrast with the Reformed doctrine of the atonement as justification's "formal cause."

Thus when the brothers Wesley and their friends formed a semi-monastic society in Oxford in 1729 and labeled it the Holy Club, this was bound to remind some of their Anglican critics of those old "new Methodists" and this came to be the nickname (appearing first in 1732) that stuck. Nor is it unimportant that Wesley treated the appellation as a nickname (and preferred to speak of his disciples as "the people *called* Methodists").

It was natural enough, therefore, that when the Methodist movement began to spread as a religious society within the Church of England (in 1739 and thereafter), it would appear as an ecclesiastical anomaly, neither Anglican nor Nonconformist. As friendly a critic as Josiah Tucker (afterward dean of Gloucester) could admonish the Methodists against doctrinal confusion and warn them against the dangers of separation and schism.[2]

[2]Josiah Tucker, *Brief History of the Principles of Methodism: Wherein the Rise and Progress, together with the Causes of the Several Variations, Divisions and Present Inconsistencies of this Sect are attempted to be traced out and accounted for* (Oxford, 1742).

John Wesley, however, was all the more convinced that the times called for an evangelical alternative to the sacerdotalism of "the Church as *by law* established" and to the Calvinism of Nonconformity. He saw his Revival as a providential corrective to the formalism and moralism of the national church; he sincerely believed that the Methodist gospel of grace ("repentance, faith and holiness") was a recovery of apostolic doctrine—still another reform of the Reformation. The Methodists recoiled in horror from the "wars of religion" that had followed the sixteenth-century disruptions, and their memories of religious anarchy in Cromwell's Commonwealth left them suspicious of what they saw as theocratic visions both in Calvinism and in "radical Protestantism."

In America, the Methodists were latecomers (our earliest firm date is 1766), who had blithely lightened their inherited baggage from the Old World. To begin with, many of the first Methodists in the colonies were Irish (some of them Palatine Germans who had first migrated to Ireland and become Methodists there before their further transplantation to the New World). Their primitivism consisted largely in their zeal for Scripture as "the *sole* rule of faith and practice" and their sense of the apostolic church as a perpetual charter rather than as an imitable model.

Once their colonial ties with Britain and the Church of England had been severed, the American Methodists were torn between their tenuous loyalties to John Wesley and their need of a ministry of their own. Inevitably, there were initiatives on behalf of a self-constituted "restoration" (as in the Fluvanna Schism of 1782–83). Francis Asbury, the only English Methodist appointed by Wesley who had remained in America throughout the Revolution, held out for some link in legitimation from Wesley and the British Conference. Wesley, in turn, was prepared to reverse his erstwhile negative views of American independence and moved quickly, on several fronts, to provide the Americans with the makings of a church independent, but still linked with its British heritage. It was Wesley the churchman who dared to act as "a Scriptural *episkopos*" (with what he thought was patristic precedent) and to ordain two elders (Thomas Vasey and Richard Whatcoat), and to ordain his assistant, Dr. Thomas Coke (LL.D.) as general superintendent for America. This trio was to proceed forthwith to the new country and provide a ministry of "Word, Sacrament, and Order" for the Methodist people. With them, he sent along a curious abridgment of the Book of Common Prayer that he had prepared for the new church along with an anti-Calvinist abridgment of the Thirty-Nine Articles; its title was *The Sunday Service of the Methodists in North America* (1784). As a personal blessing and also as an official warrant for all these protocols of continuity, he drafted an open letter "To Our Brethren in America," reflecting his sense of tradition as taprooted in Scripture and developed in his church history: "As our American brethren are now totally disentangled both from the state [the new U.S.A.] and from the English hierarchy, we dare not entangle them again either with the one or the other [note this affirmation of the separation of church and state six years before the First Amendment]. They are now at full liberty simply to follow the Scriptures and the Primitive Church. And we judge it best that they should stand fast in the liberty wherewith God has so strangely made them free."[3] This is the same man who had, a decade earlier, "submitted" his *Collected Works* (1771–74) "to the judgment of Holy Scripture, right reason, and Christian Antiquity."[4]

There can be no doubt that for Wesley, apostolic Christianity was normative or that its restoration continued as an ideal for him and his people. But he was also immersed in church history; he took some sort of continuity of ministries for granted. Was Wesley, then, a restorationist? The answer here hinges on one's understanding of tradition, continuity, and development in church history since the end of the apostolic age. Even the American Methodists, with a far less vivid or rich sense of tradition, understood themselves as reforming a debilitated church rather than reconstituting one, *de novo*. With remarkable self-reliance, therefore, they constituted themselves into the first independent denomination in the new American nation with a title connoting their polity, The Methodist Episcopal Church (1784). Coke and Asbury were elected as their general superintendents (and promptly took on the title "bishop"). They arranged for an itinerant network, tightly connected, from Maine to Georgia, which then was dominated entirely by Francis Asbury, who reigned without a peer for a full quarter century before his death in 1816.

[3]"To our Brethren in America," in *JWL* 7:239.
[4]"To the Reader," in *Works of John Wesley* (Bristol: W. Pine, 1771), 1:vii.

Wesley had supposed that his brethren in America would wish to continue under *his* spiritual direction and theological tutelage, as British Methodism had done so willingly for the preceeding two generations. He also assumed that Dr. Coke, as his delegated *locum tenens*, would be cordially received as the head of the new church, or at the least as Asbury's senior partner. All these assumptions were miscalculations—both of the American temper and of Asbury's temperament.

The Americans were prepared to acknowledge Wesley as their eponymous patriarch, but they were equally resolved upon maintaining their new independence. Asbury assumed the mantle of leadership, quietly eased Coke out of the picture, allowed *The Sunday Service* to fall into disuse—and proceeded to set as distinctive a personal mark on American Methodism as Wesley had done in Britain. His primitivism had no speculative basis. He had next to no sense of tradition, but also no strong convictions about a church in apostasy since the end of the apostolic age. It was, rather, that the Bible served him sufficiently in his personal spiritual hungers and in his passion for awakening and converting souls. In typical Methodist fashion, he added the *Book of Discipline* and the *Hymnal* to "the iron ration" of his preachers. What he had learned from John Wesley (from slight acquaintance and only a brief career in the English Conference) was twofold: that the church is best defined by its commitment to mission and that a religious society is best directed by a single head. In America he came to see how the talents of the preachers could be multiplied by frequent rotation ("itinerancy").

The Methodists were quick to adopt the patterns of Revivals and camp meetings and to put them to good use. On their own, they invented the circuit rider—a Christian militiaman, traveling light, meshed into a grid of Conferences (from local "charge," to district, annual, and general), subject to appointment and frequent reassignment. Until recent times, Methodist preachers were never "called;" they were sent—never "elected" by a congregation; they were received. It was a strange combination—a focus on Scripture and experience as the fonts of authority, together with a monarchical polity within an egalitarian society. What is more, since this unique polity seemed to work so well—not merely on the frontier but in the towns and cities—the Methodists came readily to believe that they had rediscovered the most adequate contemporary analog to polity in the apostolic church.

The Methodists resisted all ideas of the "invisible church"

(this they associated with Reformed notions of *numerus electorum*, the secret number of the elect). They did, however, insist on probationary church membership, plus a strict discipline within the church membership. Their "article of religion" (XIII) on the church, adopted from Article XIX of the Thirty-Nine Articles (itself derived from Article VIII of the Augsburg Confession) was suitably ecumenical: "XIII. The visible Church of Christ is a congregation of faithful men in which the pure Word of God is preached, and the Sacraments administered according to Christ's ordinance, in all those things that of necessity are requisite to the same." In his sermon, "Of the Church" (1785), Wesley expanded the same definition.

> The catholic or universal church is all the persons in the universe whom God hath so called out of the world as to entitle them to the character of Christians—as to be one body united by one Spirit, having one faith, one hope, one baptism . . . [then follows a comment on national and local churches]. A particular church may, therefore, consist of any number of members, whether two or three millions. But still whether it be larger or smaller, the same idea is to be preserved. They are one body and have one Spirit: one Lord, one faith, one baptism, one God and Father of all.[5]

Among American Methodists, this view was focused on "the church of the converted," with constant stress on regeneration and assurance (with frequent allusions to Acts 2:41–47). In Wesley, Scripture and tradition had been integrated, as the mutual interdependence of *revelation* and *interpretation*. No one among the American Methodists, however, knew enough about tradition to appropriate such an integration. Thus Wesley's concept of fourfold authority—of Scripture (as base and font), of tradition and critical reason as hermeneutical pillars, and of experience as confirmation—was drastically altered. Scripture was kept as base and font, but tradition was ignored and reason turned into rationalization (*fides quaerens—argumentum!*). Experience was enlarged beyond its original denotation of "assurance" into emotive concerns of all sorts with an authority of their own (*because* they were emotive). After all, what is there polite to say to a patently sincere assertion: "Deep in my heart, I *know* that . . . "?

[5]"Of the Church," *WJWB*, 3, sermon no. 74, par. 14–15.

Classical restorationism, especially in America, felt bound by "the silences of the New Testament." Methodist primitivism tended to take those silences as concessions to true believers to follow the leadings of their conscience and common sense—within the canons of faith, hope, and love. Methodist ministers were largely self-educated, with biblical perspectives of salvation that discouraged critical study of church history on the one hand and speculative theology on the other. They were bound into a close knit fellowship in which "membership in full connection" in an Annual Conference was distinguished from ordination—and meant a good deal more, in practical terms. And this distinction persists in the Methodist ethos still.

Besides the Articles of Religion supplied by Wesley, the Americans produced one of their own: XXIII, "Of the Rulers of the United States of America"; they declined to attempt any other statements of official orthodoxy. They stoutly rejected the formalism that they saw among the Episcopalians and Roman Catholics. Their eucharistic theology varied from memorialism to the sort of spiritual realism reflected in Charles Wesley's "Hymns for the Lord's Supper." They retained the Apostles' Creed as an optional usage, but quietly dropped the phrase "descended into hell" from their version of it. Some congregations used "the Creed commonly called Nicene" for Holy Communion.

In 1808 the General Conference adopted a Restrictive Rule that forbade the revocation, alteration, or change in the Articles of Religion as well as the establishment of any "new standards or rules of doctrine contrary to our present and established standards of doctrine"—and then resisted all motions designed to specify what those "present and established standards" were. Indeed, this ambiguity still persists. The doctrinal Rule has never been challenged, constitutionally; but this has not prevented Methodist theologians from continuing their theological developments in bewildering variety, with little or no regard to their official Rule. In 1968, when the Evangelical and United Brethren brought their Confession of Faith into the United Methodist Church, it was declared "consonant with the Methodist Articles of Religion" by vote of the General Conference—and a second Restrictive Rule was added that the text of that Confession was unalterable. One might think that this would have made for a stable theological tradition (even a static one!). Everyone knows, of course, that the opposite has actually been the case. In 1972 the United Methodist General Conference approved Wesley's fourfold guidelines as authoritative; in 1984 the Conference mandated a "doctrinal commission" to produce "a *new* statement of United Methodist standards of doctrine."

One can, therefore, see in American Methodism a distinctive mingling of primitivism and churchliness. This has generated an ethos all its own: Methodism has been a sect that became a church without ceasing to be a sect, professing a biblical base. Throughout the nineteenth century, Methodists in general accepted Richard Watson's dictum that Holy Scripture is unique "in its power to communicate divine truths on all subjects connected with our moral state."[6] This impulse to improvisation supported the conviction dearest to Methodist hearts: the church defined as mission. Their enthusiasm and zeal for converts attracted enough adherents so that the Methodist growth rate outpaced the population curve for the first half century; thereafter it led the other Protestant denominations, until an unrecorded day in 1924 when the Baptists edged ahead and have continued on the rise ever since. Earlier on Methodists took their cheerful statistics as proof of their recovery of the original power of apostolic Christianity. Since the reversal of these growth curves, they have had to seek other grounds for self-congratulations.

Given their Anglican origins, Methodists have been especially sensitive to the outright rejection of their ministerial orders by the Protestant Episcopalians, their open scorn of the pretensions of the Methodist episcopate and, therefore, of the validity of Methodist sacraments. This generated a large literature, best represented by Nathan Bangs in his major treatise *An Original Church of Christ: Or, a Scriptural Vindication of the Orders and Powers of the Ministry of the Methodist Episcopal Church* (1837). It was chiefly an argument with the Episcopalians, but its triumphalism was generalized. Bangs was a primitivist of sorts; his claim was that the Scriptures provide the church more with a charter than with a blueprint: "In the course of this investigation, we hope to derive some assistance from the early history of the church, reminding ourselves, in the meantime, of the fallibility of ecclesiastical writers. . . . When we take our leave of the inspired writers, we no longer have an infallible guide."[7]

[6]Richard Watson, *Sermons* (New York: Waugh and Mason, 1835), 2:474; cf. 107, 179, 369.

[7]Nathan Bangs, *An Original Church of Christ; or, A Scriptural*

He distinguished between Scripture itself as revelation and "the primitive church as a privileged witness" as chief aid in the business of valid interpretation. Given this distinction he could stake out the Methodist claim to a biblical authority for their doctrine and polity: "Without presuming to condemn others, we [Methodists] think that we have sufficient authority from the *Scriptures* as to the truth of our doctrine—and from the primitive church as to the efficacy of our polity—so as to do what we have done and as we will continue to do."[8]

What was unmistakably clear in the New Testament to Bangs was the Gospel: the revelation of God's grace in Jesus Christ and of the church's mission to provide witnesses to that Gospel in all places and times. "To the Scriptures, therefore, we must make our ultimate appeal. . . . So far as they lend us their infallible light, and we suffer ourselves to be ordered by it, we shall not be led astray."[9] But note the different nuance here from the similar sentiments of the Puritan Thomas Brooks (1608–80): "I dare not rise above what is written. Where the Scripture is silent, there I love to be silent and where the Scripture hath no tongue, there I desire no ears."[10]

Bangs was, therefore, convinced that Asbury and Coke had been justified "in organizing a church according to the apostolic model." It was a church with a classic trinitarian theology, Christology, soteriology. Yet it was also a church in continuity with the church through the ages. It had itinerant ministers, local elders, and class meetings led by layfolk. Ministers served under annual appointment without appeal and the bishops shared the same bursary with the other circuit riders. Bangs saw Methodism as a leaven among the denominations, "to revive *pure and primitive Christianity*" (a favorite phrase).

Bangs took pluralism and a sort of "spiritual ecumenism" for granted: "It is possible to cleave to our own institutions and yet exercise a catholic spirit toward all who love our Lord Jesus Christ in sincerity. There are superficial differences between Christian communities, but these cannot be felt at the heights which are

Vindication of the Orders and Powers of the Ministry of the Methodist Episcopal Church, 2d, 3d., rev. (New York: T. Mason and G. Lane, 1837), 10–11.

[8]*Ibid.*, 9.

[9]*Ibid.*, 11.

[10]Thomas Brooks, *Works*, 6 vols. (Carlisle, Pa.: Banner of Truth Trust, 1980), 4:374.

above the accidental forms which are created and destroyed, by time."[11]

A generation later, this same tradition was reformulated by a disciple of Bangs, Richard Abbey, in *An Inquiry into the Ecclesiastical Constitution, the Origin, and the Character of the Church of Christ and the Gospel Ministry* (1860):

> The Methodist Church, for instance, is not apostolic because of her confederate character [nor, by implication, would she be if she were congregational in polity]. It is apostolic because, and only because, of her conformity, in faith and practice, to the *religious* doctrines which the Apostles held and taught. This is the test, and the only test, of a CHURCH OF CHRIST.

Or again,

> A church is a *society* of Christians, preaching the Gospel, administering the sacraments and otherwise following Christ.

He concluded then

> that the character of *the primitive church* is to be sought for in the principles of true religion and not in the mode of ecclesiastical association [i.e., polity] into which Christians form themselves.[12]

Both the strengths and weaknesses of American Methodist theology in the nineteenth century may be measured in Richard Watson's *Theological Institutes*, for this single book taught more Methodists what little school-theology they knew than any other (including Wesley's *Sermons* and *Notes*). Its first edition stretched from 1823 to 1829; it then went through five revisions and thirty printings before the century was out. Arminian in substance and Calvinist in form, Watson sought to provide Methodists with what Wesley had chosen not to provide, a systematic theology. His ecclesiology was heavily influenced by William Cave, *Apostolici* (1677)—one of Wesley's favorites. Watson's premise—that "the primitive Christians owed much to what they had learned in the Jewish synagogues"—allowed him to argue that "in all those particulars in which they were left free by the Scriptures, primitive Christians adopted those arrangements for the government which

[11]Bangs, *Original Church of Christ*, 381–82.
[12]Richard Abbey, *An Inquiry into the Ecclesiastical Constitution, the Origin, and the Character of the Church of Christ and the Gospel Ministry* (Nashville, 1860), 33, 80, 112–13.

promised to render it most efficient in the maintenance of truth and piety."[13]

These samplings (in the absence of any influential counter-statements) may be taken as representative of American Methodist ecclesiology down through the century—until the "liberal transitions" toward its end. They reflect a special brand of primitivism that was neither magisterial nor restorationist in its typical form. Its distinctive emphasis was on development: the adaptation of "efficient means" to serve the perennial end of the apostolic mission. It served the Methodists in justification of their ministerial order (against the Episcopalians), of their connectional polity (against all congregationalists), and of their "gospel of universal redemption" (against the Calvinists). Not at all incidentally, this sense of a biblical taprootage remained with the Methodists (sometimes in strangely altered forms) throughout the three transmutations that altered mainline Methodism in the twentieth century out of all comparison with its origins: (1) its eager, if also belated, embrace of the Enlightenment and its theological spinoffs in liberal Protestantism; (2) Methodist enthusiasm for the Social Gospel—the *Social Creed of the Churches* (adopted by the new Federal Council of Churches in 1908) was an adaptation of a Methodist document; and (3) the tragic immoderations of the late nineteenth-century controversies between the "liberals" and partisans of "holiness." There is sad irony in the fact that all Methodists in their bitter differences (always to God's greater glory!) have appealed to the same biblical vision of the peaceable kingdom of God on earth for their authority and vindication, even as they have differed hopelessly in their appeals to the Bible as authority for their rival programs.

After a brief interim of cooperation in the early stages of the Second Great Awakening, the Methodist primitivists and the Reformed restorations (both well portrayed in Arthur Piepkorn's *Profiles in Belief*, vol. 2) tended to go their separate ways. Rice Haggard began as a comrade of James O'Kelly (the first American Methodist to rebel openly against Asbury's pious tyrannies) and ended up as a loyal ally of Barton W. Stone. For all their differences, these two quite disparate traditions have shared the conviction that the essence of the true *koinonia tou Christou* is its

---

[13]Richard Watson, *Theological Institutes: or, A View of the Evidence, Doctrines, Morals, and Institutions of Christianity* (Nashville, 1860).

visible manifestation of faith in Christ and its imperative to be witness to God's self-disclosure in him. This shared tradition is reflected in Thomas Campbell's *Declaration and Address* of 1809— which can have no direct connection with Wesley's earlier "Article." Here is Campbell's definition: "The Church of Christ upon earth is essentially, intentionally and constitutionally one— consisting of all those in every place who profess their faith in Christ and offer their obedience to him in all things, according to the Scriptures, and who manifest the same by their tempers and conduct."[14]

What is to be learned from all this beyond commonplaces about the ironic discrepancies that have always existed between the professions and performances of religious movements? Is it instructive to be reminded that the restorationists began by eschewing denominationalism and then fell victim to its virus? What is the moral to the fact that mainline Methodism began by professing as its distinctive aim the "spreading of scriptural holiness over these lands" and then fell into a preoccupation with organization that has put a premium upon maintenance, and then confounded *that* with mission?

This much at least is clear from almost any reading of this history: that both restoration and holiness are ideals so fructifying that even when tarnished by the kinds of entropy with which we are so familiar as church historians, they still retain their regenerative power as ideals—so that, like the Holy Spirit who inspires them, they defy domestication and continue in their power to spark off new insights and new vitalities in later generations. For always there is a remnant who look beyond old formulae to their still-living powers of refreshment. It is this vision of apostolic Christianity repristinated in later ages (less by replication than reappropriation) that can always find new relevance in new times and circumstances. And if such an ideal—of a vital community of "new creatures in Christ"—still defines God's will for the unity of Christians in time and space, then it might also continue as an urgent, however baffling, task for God's obedient children in whatever history that may still unfold.

---

[14]Thomas Campbell, *Declaration and Address* (Washington, Pa., 1809), cited in A. Piepkorn, *Profiles in Belief* (New York: Harper, 1978), 2:629–30.

A Focus on the Holy Spirit: Spirit and Spirituality in John Wesley

———†———

[1988] "Focus on the Holy Spirit" is the theme of an issue of the *Quarterly Review* that features Outler as the introductory essayist. Beginning with a sketch of the history of Christian reflection on the Spirit, Outler moves to an examination of this theme in Wesley. In contrast to an emotive-psychological interpretation of Aldersgate, Outler shows how Wesley develops through a series of conversion and assurance experiences, all of which affect his understanding of the work of the Spirit. He then sets forth the equilibrium in Wesley's work between spirituality and ethics, and suggests its contemporary relevance for a recovery of the "biblical vision of the *humanum*."

And I believe in the Holy Ghost, the Lord and Giver of Life, Who proceedeth from the Father and the Son; who with the Father and the Son is worshipped and glorified, Who spake by the Prophets.[1]

Any attempted focus on the Holy Spirit is bound to be blurred. The terms for "spirit", in many languages (*ruach, pneuma, spiritus, Geist, esprit,* etc.) point beyond precise denotations. But they also point "behind" self-consciousness, and they point "toward" the radical ineffability of such terms as "soul," "selfhood," "psyche"—whether in reference to the human mystery or to the Encompassing Holy in which [or in whom] we live and move and have our being. Something of this sort seems presupposed in St. Paul's address to the Athenians in Acts 17:23–31. Pneumatological reflection on this aura of human awareness of Holy Spirit has therefore to be an exercise in discernment, and a tricky one, because it can be no more than groping along a pathway between the quicksands of credulity on one side, and the thickets of superstition and magic on the other.

Neither "transcendence" nor "immanence" is a biblical term, but the paradox of their dialectical integration is a biblical commonplace. Phrases like "the Spirit of God" are derivative metaphors from familiar things connoting spontaneity, like breath or wind; they go on to include such elusive realities as life itself (e.g., "the breath of life"). They were then extended to such matters as *human dispositions* (e.g., the "poor in spirit"). On their other side, they point to God's prevenient initiatives in human affairs and history, and here their emphasis is on the *spontaneity* of divine action, whether from beyond or within. Within perspectives such as these, the biblical people felt comfortable with a wide range of anthropo*morphisms*, with a myriad of anthropomorphic

---

[1]"The Creed commonly called Nicene," Article III, as in the Book of Common Prayer of the Church of England (1662), in The Order for Holy Communion.

images, similitudes and analogs. At the same time, they were horrified by various anthropo*centrisms*, for there they could see the sort of overreaching self-centeredness that distorts the primal human vision of transcendence. The original temptation was an attractive promise that our finite limits can be surpassed (as in our contemporary slogans: "you can have it *all*"; "your world should have no bounds"). Thus it is that *idolatry* was and still continues as the archetypal sin of pride-in-action—forbidden by the *First* Commandment.

The ontic pair of human happiness and tragedy have always lived together in the mysterious paradoxes of divine-human interaction. This is reflected in later explorations (as in Origen's theses about an "original righteousness and happiness," or in St. Augustine's opening "confession" ("Thou hast made us *for thyself*"),[2] with its implication that the natural inclination of the human heart is harmony and peace, not in ourselves but in God. And these are echoes of a New Testament idea that humanity is designed for "life in the Spirit" (Gal. 5:25 and 2 Peter 1:4) *because* it is, first and last, God's special project and, above all, a *divine gift*.

It is remarkable how carefully the biblical references to "Spirit" and "Holy Spirit," "God," and "Spirit of Christ" manage to avoid what came later to be called modalism on the one side, and sheer mystification on the other—yet with never an attempted conceptualization that ever pretended to be definitive. One thing is clear, however: in all true spirituality there is a deep moral taproot; the *gifts* of the Spirit (1 Cor. 12:1–13) are correlated with the *fruits* of the Spirit (as in Gal. 5:22–25).

It is a commonplace that in Christianity's emergence (or expulsion) from its Jewish matrix in the later decades of the first Christian century, and with its hazardous ventures into the Hellenistic world, a language about the Holy Spirit's continuing presence and agency in human life and in the newborn church passed into the formulae of Christian worship. It helped to differentiate the new Christian sect from the other *thiasoi* (mystery religions) in the Greco-Roman world with which Christianity was unavoidably associated (and at times confused). All of this happened without a fully realized pneumatological doctrine. The earliest approach to such a formulation appears in St. Irenaeus (in his *Demonstration of the Apostolic Preaching*, I, 1:6). But notice how

[2]*Confessions* I.i.

much pneumatological pre-understanding is taken for granted, as if already lodged in devout Christian consciousness by the seventh decade of the second Christian century:

> And the third article is the Holy Spirit, through whom the prophets prophesied and the patriarchs were taught . . . and the just were led in the paths of righteousness—and whose power in these last times has been poured forth upon humanity over all the earth, renewing men and women to God. Therefore from the baptism of our rebirth comes these three articles, granting us rebirth unto God the Father, through his Son, by the Holy Spirit . . . So, without the Spirit, there is no hearing the Word of God, and without the Son there is no approaching the Father—for the Son is the knowledge of the Father, and knowledge of the Son is through the Holy Spirit.

The early creeds affirmed "Holy Spirit" by title (another instance of how much could be taken for granted). But it was not until the Spirit's full deity was *denied* by the Pneumatomacheans in the mid-fourth century that a major theologian thought it worthwhile to explain it at some length (unless Athanasius' *Epistles to Serapion* may be counted as explanations). This reasoned refutation of tritheism comes from St. Gregory of Nyssa—along with a summary trinitarian formulary:

> It is not possible to confess that Jesus is Lord except by the inspiration of the Holy Spirit. Therefore, Father, Son and Holy Spirit are to be known only in a perfect Trinity, in closest interaction and unity, before all creation . . . [3]

It was in this climate (ca. A.D. 375) that the drafters of the Constantinopolitan revision of 381 were able to flesh out the cryptic ending of the original Nicene Ecthesis of 325 ("And in the Holy Spirit") with the fuller phrasings that have stood ever since, in "The Creed Commonly Called Nicene."

> . . . the Lord and Giver of Life who proceeds from the Father, who with the Father and the Son is worshipped and glorified, who spoke through the prophets . . .

---

[3]Gregory of Nyssa, "On the Holy Spirit; Against the Followers of Macedonius," NPNF 2d Series 5:319ff.); see also his essay, "On Not Three Gods, to Abladius." *Ibid.*, 331–36.

St. Augustine was looking both backward and forward with his lament (ca. A.D. 393) over the neglect of pneumatology (as a doctrine) by the theologians:

> Wise and spiritual men have written many books about the Father and the Son . . .
> With respect to the Holy Spirit, however, there has not been as yet, on the part of learned men and competent interpreters of the Scriptures, a discussion that is full enough or careful enough, to make it possible for us to obtain an intelligent conception of what constitutes the Spirit's special individuality (*proprium*) in virtue of which it is the case that we cannot speak of him either as Son or Father but only Holy Spirit—excepting that they predicate the Spirit as the Gift of God and that we cannot believe that God's gift is inferior to himself.[4]

Some of the obvious reasons for this underemphasis upon pneumatology are instructive. On the one side, there has been the tilt toward various sorts of "domestication" of the Holy Spirit in Holy Church. This goes back as far as Simon Magus, and always it has tended to link Spirit too closely with the institutional church. Eastern Orthodoxy resisted this domestication more successfully than the Latin West—which is one of the reasons for the Protestant preference for the correlation of Spirit and Church in an opposite domestication: Holy Spirit in Holy Scripture. This produced new patterns of authority, with a new guild of certified interpreters of Scripture, with an acknowledged authority "rightly to divide the word of Truth." On the fringes of both traditions, of course, were the champions of "the free Spirit"—from Montanus to Joachim and the Fraticelli, to the Anabaptist "spirituals," to the English Quakers and German pietists and French quietists, down to our current charismatics. But this godly motley have an appalling track record of disruption and fanaticism. St. Paul had forewarned against this (as 1 Cor. 14), but St. Paul has not always been heeded by those with disparate causes that rested on other grounds.

The intent of so impressionistic a prelude as this, thus far, has been to call attention to the fact that, in the history of Christian doctrine, theologians with a special interest in the person and work of the Holy Spirit are something of a rarity.

[4]*On Faith and the Creed*, Chap. IX, 18, 19, 20.

Moreover, even at the level of genius (e.g., St. Bonaventura and Cardinal Nicholas of Cusa) such men and women have drawn down suspicion upon themselves of obscurantism at best or fanaticism at worst. And there has been a tendency toward "enthusiasm," always aimed at lifting the level of spirituality in the church, but, almost as often, spreading abroad the image of a spiritual *elite* whose versions of spiritual superiority have offended other Christians, who themselves find much comfort in deploring "spiritual pride."[5] There is, therefore, no question of even a thumbnail sketch of the hopelessly heterogeneous tradition of "Christian Spirituality." The literature is unmanageable and the story interminable.[6]

It may, however, be allowable for us to pick out an arbitrarily chosen sample of "a focus on the Holy Spirit" that has had an importance of its own and, maybe, a continuing relevance. Moreover, in this particular collection of essays in pneumatology, it may not be inappropriate to select John Wesley for a closer look at an exemplary correlation of "Spirit and Spirituality."

Wesley was neither foremost nor hindmost in the tradition he represented, but he is interesting all the same. The warrant for a brief summary of Wesley's focus on the Holy Spirit is his persistent concern for a *trinitarian* doctrine of the Holy Spirit—a concern that appealed to Scripture, tradition, and to rational argument for his vivid experience of the radical difference between nominal orthodoxy and fruitful Christian spirituality.[7]

[5]As in Ronald A. Knox, *Enthusiasm: A Chapter in the History of Religion* (Oxford: Clarendon Press, 1950), who *defines* his subject as "a chronic tendency in church history reflected in the "clique," where an excess of charity threatens unity—. . ., an *elite*, of Christian men and (more importantly, women) who are trying to live a less worldly life than their neighbors, to be more attentive to the guidance (directly felt, they would tell you) of the Holy Spirit," 1.

[6]Samples of what could be done in special cases, however, can be seen in Henri Bremond's brilliant *Literary History of Religious Thought in France* or in the ponderous beginnings of the current multi-volumed project of *World Spirituality*, edited by Ewert Cousins.

[7]A remarkable current inquiry into this ancient problematic may be seen in Fr. Kilian McDonnell, OSB, "A Trinitarian Doctrine of the Holy Spirit," in *Theological Studies*, 46 (1985):191–227. Here is a challenging and substantive program for what has become an urgent desideratum: an updated pneumatology that includes historical perspective along with the opening horizons of a postmodern and global age. One would not wish to claim that Wesley achieved what Fr. McDonnell is calling for—only that

This is to suggest that Wesley's pneumatology begins with an awareness of the religious and ethical import of a valid integration of Christology, soteriology, and pneumatology; the vital linkage between theo-logy, Christo-logy, and pneumato-logy held together by a consistent emphasis on prevenience of all grace, an habituated awareness of the Holy Spirit as the Giver of all Grace.[8]

John Wesley's pneumatology attempted a balance between spirituality and ethics. It sought the excitements of the free Spirit without abandoning the stabilities of a life ordered by a numinous sense of existence (*coram Deo*). It allowed for the paradox of instant exaltations and the processes of Christian maturation (toward what Wesley called "the plerophory [fullness] of faith").

John Wesley's Britain was working its way through a bad case of burnout (political, cultural, religious) even in a time of exciting colonial adventures and of opening horizons in science and new technology.[9] The intellectual excitements of the age were being generated by the impulses of the Enlightenment. But the state church was suffering from exhaustion after two centuries of nearly fruitless turmoil from the harrowings of the Tudor "Reformations," the holy war between the Puritans and royalists, the bloodbaths of the Civil War, the hysterics of the Commonwealth, the debilitations of Restoration, Old Dissent, and the new deism.

Wesley's first three decades reflect the sort of fruitless devotion that left him deeply discontent. His first "conversion" in 1725—to the lifelong dedication to God, which was never repudiated or outgrown—was not "life-giving." The second (an illuminist experience, in 1727) reinforced his mystical impulses and his Puritan habits of self-examination.[10] There are obvious parallels between the "singularities" of the Oxford Methodists and other patterns of an asceticism-within-the-world with which

he understood some of the same issues and worked at them in something of the same spirit.

[8]See the quite remarkable, even if somewhat difficult, essay of Fr. David Coffey, *Grace: The Gift of the Holy Spirit* (Manly: Catholic Institute of Sydney, 1979).

[9]It still puzzles cultural historians that the Industrial Revolution began in *Britain;* cf. Fernand Braudel, *Civilization and Capitalism, 15th–18th Century,* 2:330–48; 3:555–88.

[10]See, for example, the minute daily and hourly records of his attention to the vicissitudes of his spiritual states in R. H. Heitzenrater's newly edited diaries in *WJWB* Vol. 5, 1988.

Protestant rigorism had sought to replace the monastic flight from the world.[11]

Wesley's most famous experience on May 24, 1738 ("Aldersgate"), has long since achieved an iconic status in Wesleyan hagiography. But it is still worth noticing that Aldersgate was not the transformation of an irreligious man into a man of faith ("an almost Christian" into an "altogether Christian"). Nor was it a triumph of Moravian pietism (the Moravians themselves were quick to deny this). It was not the last of his conversions.[12] It was not even the beginning of the Methodist Revival. And yet one is blind not to see it as a decisive turning point in Wesley's entire life and work, as a reorientation of his sense of mission and a more fruitful harvest in it. Aldersgate was less the reconstruction of Wesley's basic doctrines of God-in-Christ than an unexpected discovery of their power and effects. And its focus was the "internal witness of the Holy Spirit," (as in Rom. 8 and Eph. 2:5, 8–10). Whatever psychological account one may prefer, the theological import of Aldersgate was largely *pneumatological*.

Its story has already been better told by Wesley (in that long *Journal* entry for May 24, *et seq.*) than by any of his biographers thus far. Most of them have ignored the remarkable sequence of lections in the round of his daily prayers for the day—from 2 Peter 1:3–4 at matins (with its stress on divine-human "participation"), followed by a congruent emphasis in the anthem for vespers at St. Paul's (Ps. 130, *Book of Common Prayer*). The actual "Aldersgate experience" came at a reluctant compline and was far less subjective than tradition has it.

Typically, the emphasis has been on Wesley's "warmed heart." But Wesley understood enough of his tightly reined temperament to add a crucial adverb: a *"strangely* warmed" heart. The active verbs in his narration (e.g., *"I felt"*) are misread unless the verbs in the passive voice (e.g., warm*ed*) are stressed even more. Otherwise, the sense of the divine initiative in the whole affair is distorted into something more like a "peak experience" than a providential climax. "I felt my heart strangely warm*ed*"; "An assurance *was given* me. . . ."

Methodist sentimentalists have overstressed Wesley's *feelings*

[11]Cf. Heitzenrater, *op. cit.*; JWJ I:79–105; and *Letters* I in JWLB 25:141–551.
[12]Cf. JWJ, January 4, 1739.

(as so often he did himself, but not here). But Aldersgate and its subsequent developments make more sense if the stress falls on the sheer *givenness* of the assurance of *pardon* (a synonym for "justification"). Thus, the Aldersgate experience was Wesley's personal appropriation of the familiar promises of Romans 8:10–17, 26–28. Nor did it bring an instant comprehension. It took five subsequent decades for his Christian self-understanding to grow and mature. May 24, 1738, was the dramatic turning point in an extraordinary career, from a dedicated perfectionist who seldom succeeded to a wayfarer of the Spirit who seldom failed (at least not in his reliance upon God's upholding Providence).

He had been brought up in a particular tradition of will-mysticism by a mother who was a closet theologian in her own right (and a highly competent one into the bargain!).[13] This heritage continued with him (with altered valences) throughout his life.[14] Before Aldersgate and the early flush of the Revival, his mystical quest had combined with other obsessions to bring him to despair, to bitter complaints against "the mystic writers."[15]

It is remarkable that Aldersgate recedes from sight so quickly in subsequent autobiographical accounts; the reasons for this are not altogether clear. What remains—and has not yet been studied in requisite depth—are the pneumatological overtones, which develop into a sort of theme and variations throughout the corpus and provide a ground-tone in Wesley's version of the *ordo salutis*. In a series of sermons published in 1746–48 he began to sort out the dynamics of his doctrine of grace (prevenient in all its modes—repentance, justifying faith, assurance, regeneration, sanctification) in a perspective that is explicitly pneumatological and implicitly trinitarian. In "The Witness of the Spirit," Discourse I (1746), the emphasis is on

> the testimony of the Spirit as an inward impression on the soul, whereby the Spirit of God directly "witnesses to my spirit that I

---

[13]See for example her letters to him at Oxford, in *Letters I, WJWB* 25:167–68, 178–80, 183–85, 382–83.

[14]Jean Orcibal, "The Theological Originality of John Wesley and Continental Spirituality," in *A History of the Methodist Church in Great Britain* (London: Epworth, 1965), edited by Rupert Davies and Gordon Rupp, I:81–113.

[15]Cf. his poignant memoir of the Georgia fiasco (in Henry Moore's *Life*, I:342) and his attack on William Law, in Baker's edition of the *Letters*, II:25, 540–42, 546–48.

am a child of God" [assurance and reconciliation]. This "Spirit" not only worketh in us every manner of thing that is good but also shines upon his own work and clearly shows us what he hath wrought[16] (I, 8, 10).

Twenty years later, in a revised version under the same text and title, Wesley defends this notion of "perceptible inspiration" against all critics, adding a heightened emphasis on the correlation of the Spirit's witness and its genuine fruit: "inward and outward holiness. . . ." "Holiness" is for Wesley, of course, another term for "true religion . . . the love of God, and of neighbour." Pneumatology, therefore is never merely spiritual without an ethical imperative, or *vice versa*. Personal holiness and social holiness are never disjoined—and their order never reversed.

> Let us never rest in any supposed testimony of the Spirit which is separate from the fruit of it . . . Let us never rest in any supposed "fruit of the Spirit" without the [objective] witness [to filiation] ("The Witness of the Spirit", Discourse II, V. 3–4).

Wesley's refutation of the charges of enthusiasm (as in his sermon No. 37 "On the Nature of Enthusiasm") is to join his critics in rejecting fanaticism, spiritual pride, and all their congeners. Thus, he can stress the *"fruits* of the Spirit" that depend upon persuasion, insight, conviction (Gal. 5:24).

> How many impute things to the Holy Spirit, or expect things from him, without any rational or scriptural ground! Such are they who imagine that they do or shall receive "particular directions" from God, not only in points of importance, but in things of no moment, the most trifling circumstances of life. Whereas, in these cases, God has given us our own reason for a guide, though never excluding the "secret assistance" of his Spirit.[17]

Authentic spirituality is *"A daily growth* in pure and holy religion."[18]

---

[16]The human reaction of faith to grace is conscious (joy): "the soul as intimately and evidently perceives when it loves, delights and rejoices in God, as when it loves and delights in anything on earth," (I:11).
[17]"On the Nature of Enthusiasm," ¶20.
[18]*Ibid.*, ¶39.

In Wesley's religious epistemology, God-*in-se* [i.e., the Divine-in-itself] is unknowable and ineffable. God-language, even when logical in form, is apophatic in function. What we "know" of God is what God reveals in us: in and through God's "works" (in creation and nature); in and through the law and the prophets; in and through Jesus Christ, as the divine *eikon* (Col. 1:15) and *character* (Heb. 1:3). Moreover, it is God as Holy Spirit who is the revealer of all these revelations. As Holy Spirit, God is "Lord and Life-Giver." The operation of the Holy Spirit in regeneration is so radical as to move Wesley to vivid hyperbole:

> When [the new-born Christian] is born of God, born of the Holy Spirit, how is the manner of his existence changed. His whole soul is now *sensible* of God . . . The Spirit or breath of God is immediately inspired, breathed into the new-born soul, and the same breath which comes from, returns to God. As it is continually received by *faith*, so it is continually rendered back by *love* in prayer and praise and thanksgiving. . . . And by this new kind of *spiritual respiration*, spiritual life is not only sustained but increased day by day . . . The eyes of the understanding are opened. . . .[19]

The eyes of faith now *see*, "third ears" are now *opened*. "All the spiritual senses being now *opened*, faith has a clear intercourse with the invisible world. . . . He who is born of the Spirit, dwelling in love, dwelleth in God and God in him."

From the images of birth and perception, he moves on to metaphors of growth and maturation:

> The [enlivened person] feels in his heart the mighty working of the Spirit of God; . . . he is inwardly sensible of the graces which the Spirit of God works in his heart . . . By the use of these, he is daily increasing in the knowledge of God, of Jesus Christ whom he hath sent, and of all the things pertaining to his inward kingdom. And now he may properly be said *to live* . . . God is continually breathing, as it were, upon his soul and his soul is breathing unto God. Grace is descending into his heart, and prayer and praise ascending to heaven. And by this intercourse between God and man, this fellowship with the Father and the Son, as by a kind of *spiritual respiration*, the life of

[19]Sermon 19, "The Great Privilege of Those That are Born of God," I:7–10.

God in the soul is sustained and the child of God *grows up*, till he comes "to the full measure of the stature of Christ."[20]

Rhetoric of this sort is readily distorted when it is psychologized or sentimentalized. The workings of God as Spirit are more deeply inward than self-consciousness can reach; it is prevenient and objective, beyond manipulation. A precondition of valid worship is "the realization that God—the Spirit and the Father of the spirits of all flesh—should discover *himself* to your spirit, which is itself a breath of God—*divinae particula aurae* (a particle of the divine aura).[21]

It is important to note this antidote to obscurantism and its context, specifically its equal emphasis upon the rationality and ethical concerns of authentic spirituality:

> How does the Spirit of God "lead" his children to this or that particular action? . . . Do you imagine it is by "blind impulse" only? By "moving" you to do it, you know not why? No, he leads us by our "eye" at least as much as by our "hand" . . . For example, here is a man ready to perish with hunger. How am I led "by the Spirit" to relieve him? First, by "convincing" me that it is his will that I should and, secondly, by his filling my heart with love toward him . . . This is the plain, rational account of the ordinary leading of the Spirit. . . . Now where this is, there is no dead form, neither can there be . . . All that is said and done is full of God, full of spirit and life and power.[22]

Once one begins to look for them, such gyroscopic balances turn up in almost every part of John Wesley's prose—and throughout Charles Wesley's verse as well.

After the Revival's energies came to be relatively self-sustaining, practical and theoretical questions about Christian maturation began to loom larger than before. These brought with them a shift, not *away* from justification and regeneration, but *toward* the wider horizons of growth and development. This included the tricky business of differentiating between what Gordon Rupp called Wesley's "pessimism of nature" and his "optimism of grace." He took as much as he could from the prophets of the new doctrine of

---

[20]Sermon 45, "The New Birth," II:4–5.
[21]*A Farther Appeal to Men of Reason and Religion,* Part II, III.
[22]*Ibid.,* Part II, III:9.

progress; he denied outright their secularistic premises.[23] In rhetoric and action, he looked more and more to a synthesis of spirituality and social reform (as in his "poor relief" and his anti-slavery crusade). Reform became the social analogue to his soteriological image of "restoration of the divine image."

> The Holy Spirit is the giver of all spiritual life: of righteous-ness, peace and joy in the Holy Ghost—of holiness *and* happiness—by the restoration of that image of God wherein we are created . . . [which always include a communal imperative.][24]

In a paired sermon, "On the Omnipresence of God" (Aug. 12, 1788), Wesley sought to turn traditional abstractions about immanence into vivid metaphors of God's active presence, in and through the Holy Spirit:

> The great God, the eternal, almighty Spirit, is as unbounded in his presence as in his duration and power . . . God acts . . . throughout the whole compass of creation, by sustaining all things, without which everything would sink into its primitive nothing, by governing all, every minute superintending every-thing . . . strongly and sweetly influencing all, and yet without destroying the liberty of his rational creatures (I, 2, II, 1).
>
> In order to attain to these glorious ends spare no pains to preserve always a deep, a continual, a lively, and a joyful, sense of his gracious presence (i.e., *coram deo*) [III, 6].

Notice the absence here of modalism, tri-theism, or spiritual*ism*. As the whole context will show, here is a conscious attempt at a trinitarian doctrine of the Holy Spirit. In his next-to-last published sermon, No. 120, "On the Unity of the Divine Being"—notice Wesley's unacknowledged fidelity to *orthodox* Christian teaching (here and elsewhere, in the tradition of "*Christian* Platonism"):

> True religion is right tempers toward God and man. It is, in two words, gratitude and benevolence. . . . It is the loving God with all our hearts and our neighbors as ourselves . . .

[23]For a brilliant summation of these premises, see Carl L. Becker, *The Heavenly City of the Eighteenth Century Philosophers* (New Haven: Yale University Press, 1932), especially 102–3.

[24]Sermon No. 117, "The Discoveries of Faith," June 11, 1788, par. 7.

This begins when we begin to know God by the teaching of his own Spirit. As soon as the Father of spirits reveals the Son in our hearts and the Son reveals the Father, the love of God is shed abroad in our hearts. Then, and not until then, are we truly happy. We are happy first in the consciousness of God's favour, which is better than life itself; then, in all the heavenly tempers which he hath wrought in us by his Spirit. Again, [we are happy] in the testimony of his Spirit that all our [good] works please him, and lastly, in the testimony *of our own spirits* that, "in simplicity and godly sincerity . . . we have had our conversation in the world."[25] Standing fast in this liberty wherewith Christ hath made them free, real Christians "rejoice ever more, pray without ceasing and in everything give thanks." And their happiness still increases as they "grow up into the measure of the stature of the fullness of Christ" [16–17].

Christianity is that religion which stands or falls by its profession of faith in one God: Lord and creator, Lord and Savior, Lord and Giver of Life. This selfsame God is disclosed in Jesus (and has made him to be both Lord and Christ). Moreover, as Holy Spirit, God has "saved" Jesus from being lost or distorted in history's limbo or obscured in the mist of timeless truths. Any separate focus on tri-unity confounds the uniqueness of Christian truth: "unitarianism," "Christ-monism," "spiritual*ism*." Pneumatology is especially vulnerable to the seductions of anthropo*centrism* (usually in one or another form of credulousness, fanaticism, antinomianism, self-righteousness, pantheism, superstition). In both the biblical revelation and in the Christian tradition, there is an unwearied struggle to conserve the balance and wholeness of God's mystery and self-disclosure. John Wesley was one of those who joined in this struggle in his time and circumstance.

The prospect of contemporary Christianity is grimly problematic. None of its past epochs can serve it well any longer as a norm or paradigm, least of all its notorious mésalliances with Western secularisms and their current debilitations ("the ambiguity of the modern scientific consciousness, the loss of Western political and spiritual dominance, the death of the Western deity of progress . . .; this situation is therefore, quite new . . .")[26] The

[25]2 Cor. 1:12, where *anestraphemen* means something like "lifestyle."
[26]Langdon Gilkey, *Society and the Sacred* (New York: Crossroad, 1981), 13.

nineteenth-century sense of Western "dominance" and "cultural superiority" has been numbed; in more recent times, the human prospect around the globe has been diminished. Concurrently, the clamors of the wretched of the earth can no longer be ignored, even though much of the trendy rhetoric in praise of Christian social activism has been scarcely more than that—trendy rhetoric.

The visionaries and passionaries of our time, in their myriad clamant causes, sound more and more like "enthusiasts" in Wesley's pejorative sense (i.e., benevolent souls who will good ends without being prepared to identify and accept the necessary means, or the primal motives, that could convert their goodwill into effective action). More and more the options between "The New Age" of human self-realization[27] and the New Age of God's rule and God's righteousness stand opposed—and the crux of the matter seems, once more, the ancient choice between the Tempter's promise ("you shall be as gods") and the promise of the Paraclete ("When he, the Spirit of Truth is come, he will guide you into *all* truth," John 15:26–27; 16:13). There is a nonnegotiable difference between the idealized human potential as the prescription for a human ethical agenda (as in Feuerbach), and the biblical vision of the *humanum* restored in and for its primal design—by its Designer. For this latter possibility, it is the power and grace of God in Christ that can bring us to that finally realized Rule of God (*apocatastasis*) foreseen in Acts 3:21 and 1 Corinthians 15:24–28. Betimes, come weal or woe, it is our privilege to live in the assurance that "the grace of our Lord Jesus Christ, the love of God and the communion of the Holy Spirit" really *is* with us and the whole People of God, *always*.

[27] As in *The 1988 Guide to New Age Living* and the bi-monthly *New Age Journal*.

Pastoral Care
in the
Wesleyan Spirit

———†———

[1971] As a frequent speaker in Pastors' Schools, Outler sought the full engagement of pastors in the reappropriation of the Wesleyan theological heritage. In this essay he calls for a renewed awareness of the effective healing ministry that appeared in John Wesley's pastoral work, which bore rich fruits in the practice of the early Methodist societies, classes, and bands. Outler shows how the Christological mystery of the "fully human" informs the Wesleyan perspective on Christian growth and nurture. He encourages contemporary pastors and counselors to make use of present-day psychological wisdom, but he urges them to temper this with a theological vision of the human "plight and promise," which transcends "temperament and technique."

Even with my warm advocacy of Wesley as a rich, and neglected, resource for our times, it would never cross my mind to urge him on you as a model of "mental health," as that phrase is commonly understood today. He was a driven man and a driving man. His emotions were checkreined and conventional. He never mastered the arts of love or even close friendship. He was uncommonly self-possessed but not really self-understanding. He was authoritarian to the core.

What interest, therefore, can this man have for a modern pastor or for a contemporary concept of "pastoral care"? "Neurotic, heal thyself!" might seem the easiest way to dispose of such an uptight little martinet. Maybe—except for the demonstrable fact that a whole host of men and women were very greatly aided by him in their search for just exactly what we have come to call "mental health" and "social adequacy." The annals of the Revival are replete with the records of persons who found God and grace—and themselves!—in Wesley's preaching, in his societies and bands, in his queer mix of stern judgment and unfeigned acceptance, of "rebuke" and reassurance. He was incessantly the pastor; his sense of responsibility for his flock knew no respite (as we can see from his *Journal* and *Letters* and also ample testimony from others). The fruit of it all was an impressive increase of mental and emotional stability in a myriad of lives—in testimonies and tangible evidence of joy and human effectiveness—that deserves to be accounted for. There's no use denying the rich harvest of Wesley's healing ministry—and yet it can scarcely be explained by reference simply to his personal "charism" or "clinical techniques."

I pose this generalization in this way because the data involved push us far more deeply into the mysteries of Christian psychotherapy than any of our current theories have penetrated. I hope it goes without saying that I have no adequate theory now to propose and thus explain Wesley's "secret." My utmost hope—audacious enough!—is that some of my comments on this specific example in the larger paradox of authority and freedom may prompt deeper insights on your own, whether in your understanding of Wesley or in your own self-understanding (or both!).

The obvious point to begin with is Wesley's deep intuitive awareness of growth and nurture as utterly crucial in all meaningful human experience. Individuals are born to grow and develop. Growth is life's most decisive "sign." Stunted or deviated growth is a human blight. Hence, Wesley's constant exhortations to his people to grow: to go on growing, from wherever they were on toward their full human potential. This is clearly a part of what he meant by "Christian perfection" and also why he insisted that it might be sought and expected "in *this* life." But it was his equally clear conviction that *human* growth and maturation are not automatic or autonomous. To become fully human—in Wesley's view—requires Christian nurture (education, socialization, a series of "conversions"); nurture is a *social* process. Wesley's own childhood had taught him that man is not a solitary creature. He requires being cared for, and this care must be personal and loving, but open to widening vistas of social experience. This means that small groups are the natural and optimal settings for personal and interpersonal maturation: first the family and then the opening, widening arc of voluntary associations and involvements.

We have already pointed out that Wesley's "societies" fared better than other revival movements in the eighteenth century because of their distinctive provision for the Christian nurture of their members. And it was precisely this pattern of small-group discipline and nurture that became Wesley's principal agency for pastoral care. He was proud of being *chief* pastor to "the people called Methodists" but never their *sole* pastor. It was part of his genius to divine and delegate pastoral responsibility throughout a widening network ("connexion") of local groups and leaders, under his overall and diligent supervision. Thus he was able to multiply and disperse his pastoral influence in quite extraordinary ways.

After 1738, at least, he was convinced that authentic Christian experience begins with "conversion"—and by "conversion" he meant a decisive moral and spiritual event (or series of events) in which faith and the inward assurance of sins forgiven gave the new believer a new frontier of trust and hope. "Conversions" might typically have gradualistic antecedents, but the event itself was discontinuous and climactic. Wesley and Bushnell *might* have understood each other—if Bushnell would have allowed that faith is both taught *and* caught, oriented in either case toward real decision, real change, real consequence in Christian living.

Conversion, then, is the chief aim of Gospel preaching. But Wesley was equally emphatic: "Converts without nurture are like stillborn babes." "Follow the blow," he said, "never encourage the devil by snatching souls from him that you cannot nurture." And so the natural follow-up of conversion was membership in a "class" or "band."

The history of the religious societies in England, in the last quarter of the seventeenth century and the whole of the eighteenth, is a fascinating chapter in the larger history of the Christian cure of souls. These societies had appeared in the wake of the Stuarts' downfall and their prime purpose was stimulus and support for those who sought more from their faith than they had found in the Church of England. They were not "little churches inside the big church" (*ecclesiolae in ecclesia*) as the Lutheran pietists in Germany called them. Their members usually held the established church and her priesthood in moderately high esteem. They were not, therefore, rivals to the church or substitutes for her sacraments. Rather, they offered a complementary experience of intense personal exposure to faith and grace, over and beyond the typical apathy of nominal Christianity.

The chief agenda of these societies was "prayer and devotion"—readings, testimonies, interrogations. But they also encouraged people in opening their hearts in sensitive response to the opened hearts of others.

When young Charles Wesley and George Whitefield formed the Holy Club at Oxford, they had ample precedent—even in Oxford. And then later, when John attempted to organize his Savannah parishioners into spiritual bands, he was combining the format of the religious societies in England with the Moravians. Back in England, he and Peter Böhler founded a society in Fetter Lane three weeks before "Aldersgate"—and in the following November we find Wesley writing to James Hutton about some of the problems in the latter's "band." Incidentally, Wesley's main point, in this letter, is that the secret of group dynamics is for *every* member of the group to feel, and be, responsible for every *other* member. Hutton had been advocating special "monitors" in each band (Moravian-style) to serve as official "reprovers." Wesley argues against this relegation of a duty common to all Christians to any single person in the "band."

Experience in these early societies tended to be rather snug and cozy; they were not eager to expand or hive off. But once Wesley's revival movement finally got going, his new circumstances made the old patterns almost immediately obsolete. New methods for the care of souls in quantity—increasing quantities!—had to be improvised and here Wesley's psychological genius shows up impressively. Taking his cues from the old societies, Wesley adds three new features: (1) weekly collections for expenses and the poor, (2) systematic study and interpretation of Scripture and theological tracts, (3) systematic mutual interrogations. One gets the flavor of these exposures from "The Rules for the Bands" formulated in 1744:

The design of our meeting is to obey that command of God, "Confess your faults one to another, and pray one for another, that ye may be healed" (Jas. 5:16).

To this end, we intend:

1. To meet once a week, at the least.
2. To come punctually at the hour appointed, without some extraordinary reason.
3. To begin (those of us who are present) exactly at the hour, with singing or prayer.
4. To speak each of us in order, freely and plainly, the true state of our souls, with the faults we have committed in thought, word, or deed, and the temptations we have felt since our last meeting.
5. To end every meeting with prayer suited to the state of each person present.
6. To desire some person among us to speak his own state first, and then to ask the rest, in order, as many and as searching questions as may be concerning their state, sins and temptations.

Some of the questions proposed to every one before he is admitted among us may be to this effect:

1. Have you the forgiveness of your sins?
2. Have you peace with God through our Lord Jesus Christ?
3. Have you the witness of God's Spirit with your spirit that you are a child of God?
4. Is the love of God shed abroad in your heart?
5. Has no sin, inward or outward, dominion over you?
6. Do you desire to be told of your faults?
7. Do you desire to be told of all your faults, and that plain and home?

8. Do you desire that every one of us should tell you, from time to time, whatsoever is in his heart concerning you?

9. Consider! Do you desire we should tell you whatsoever we think, whatsoever we fear, whatsoever we hear concerning you?

10. Do you desire that, in doing this, we should come as close as possible; that we should cut to the quick, and search your heart to the bottom?

11. Is it your desire and design to be, on this and all other occasions, entirely open, so as to speak everything that is in your heart without exception, without disguise and without reserve?

Any of the preceding questions may be asked as often as occasion offers; the five following at every meeting:

1. What known sins have you committed since our last meeting?

2. What temptations have you met with?

3. How were you delivered?

4. What have you thought, said, or done, of which you doubt whether it be sin or not?

5. Have you nothing you desire to keep secret?[1]

In his annual rounds, Wesley would meet with the bands in each place—and would often winnow them of uncooperative or inactive members. But the constructive genius of the process was its provision of meaningful things that ordinary people could do for themselves and others—and in so doing, make a significant contribution. Band and class leaders were chosen in and by the group process. It was in the bands and classes that people who were faceless and worthless in the streets outside the chapel found respect, dignity, and a new vision of God and of the human possibility.

Here we come to the heart and soul of the Wesleyan view of the cure of souls: his concept of human nature, of basic human relationships—to God, neighbor, and self. Here, too, we see Wesley's notions of the nature of grace and, consequently, of "growth *in* grace"—of the growth process in which people come to recognize themselves as *truly* human and have their hopes raised of becoming *fully* human. It was less Wesley's special skill

[1]*JWO* 180–81.

at counseling, or managing the group process, that defined this crucial contribution. It was, rather, his special vision of the human possibility that made the decisive difference, that compensated for the hypertensions of Methodist zeal and dogmatism.

To grasp this vision, one must ask what Wesley understood by the Pauline phrase, "the hearing of faith"—the moment of actual conversion. Those who finally hear the good news of the Gospel in their hearts—really hear it!—are those who, up to that "moment," had been desperate, either from guilt or ennui or empty complacency. They were, as Wesley says, "dead" (as also their religious beliefs, however orthodox and observant, were "dead"). At best, they were "almost Christian." The essence of sin, however experienced, was alienation from God—a spurious perception of God's wrath, or mercy, or absence. This is sin's bitterest fruit, the source of its blighting power. Sinful humanity imagines itself as able to save itself (i.e., self-deceiving) or else as already lost and abandoned (i.e., deceived by guilt). The transit from the death of sin to the life of faith is made possible by the miraculous discovery (God's gift on God's terms) of God's personal love and care, pardon and free grace—of God's accepting and expecting love. The new man and woman in Christ now know themselves as children of God—and realize that *this* is what it is to be truly human: an "image of God," a special creature, a divine project—an individual creation: identified, sustained, and consummated by divine grace. The human self is not a thing—a homunculus inside an animal skin. It is a unique mystery, inspired and sustained by God. We are created and held in creation by God, moment by moment, for life's full span—and this whether we live in rebellion or trust. In either case, we are in God's providence. There is no other ground or end of being.

The spectrum of Christian views about human selfhood is wide and diverse—and each view generates its own theory about the dynamics of growth and fulfillment. Wesley was heir to a tradition that ran back through central Anglicanism, through the Oxford nominalists, back to a late-patristic slogan that has served as slogan for a major strain in Christian anthropology: "He who lives up to what is truly his best, God will not deny him a measure of graces" (*facientis quod in se est, Deus non denegat gratiam*). Denounced by Luther and Calvin as being virtually Pelagian, this view differs widely from Pelagius but also differs from the Reformation anthropologies that see the self as invincibly concupiscent (Luther) or inherently idolatrous (Calvin).

This Wesleyan version of Christian synergism begins and ends with God—with God's sovereignty, initiative, and untrammeled freedom. But it understands the creation of humanity as a special and specific enterprise of God—in which humanity's identity, freedom, and transcendental orientation are all constitutive of the *humanum* itself—not canceled, or cancelable, by sin, even when corrupted and perverted, as it regularly is.

The human *in se*—what truly is the human "best"—is, therefore, God's doing and, as such, morally meaningful. And whoever lives and acts according to the highest leadings of his or her created nature (*in se*) is assured of the sustenance and sanctions of divine grace. This is the true meaning of God's prevenience: not only that God loves us no matter what (although God does), but that God's grace anticipates us at every turn—from conception and birth through all our crises to destiny's final climax, creating and holding open possibilities of health and growth and self-fulfillment, never imposing mere arbitrary determinations of character or moral action. We are not just what we will and choose (i.e., the basic error of the existentialists). We become what we will and choose within the atmosphere and options of God's grace (prevenient, cooperating, encompassing). We cannot save ourselves. What we can make of the human possibility is regularly and inevitably tragic and subhuman. Secularism is the final betrayal of humanity's hopes of becoming fully human—and the meaninglessness of life, apart from faith and grace, is a grim confirmation of this.

In this sense, we are justified (and have the way opened to Christian maturation) by faith *alone*, with no antecedent merit or claim. Wesley rules out all possibilities of *self*-understanding and *self*-acceptance prior to and apart from the perceptions of faith— that we are the selves we are because God has made us so, keeps us so, is making our "perfection" possible (by divine creation and recreations) by the multifaceted actions of grace; prevenient, justifying, sanctifying.

When we see ourselves in *this* light, it makes a crucial difference in our *self*-estimate and in our resultant attitudes toward fellow humans. Our self-loathing is reduced (can *we* despise what we know God *loves*?). But then also our loathing or envy or misperceptions of others are corrected, since they, too, are "brethren for whom Christ died." One is prevented from swinging to the opposite pole of secular confidence and hope: the supposition that the human potential is somehow inherent and therefore somehow eternal, *in se.*

Here, then, is a paradox: our radical dependence upon God ("for life and breath and all things" and for personal identity as well!) and yet also, on the other side, our meaningful independence, moral freedom and agency. These two dialectical insights generate the specifically human experiences of the transcendental outreaches of human curiosity (the unrestricted desire to *know*), of freedom (the hunger for an open future) and of love (the need for harmony: within the self, with God and with our human environment). The people of faith realize that they exist from and for God, moment by moment (with no exceptions conceivable) and they are *willing* to exist in this dependent relationship (which is one way of defining "faith"). But they must also realize that they have been created to act responsively and responsibly within the human order: in terms of reason normed by truth, freedom normed by justice, love normed by community. This, then, is the true liberty of Christians, their true joy and blessedness. This is what it means, or would mean, for people to become *fully human* (i.e., "perfect in love in this life").

By teaching people to understand themselves in this light— this special perspective on sin, grace, and human perfection— Wesley helped them to a self-understanding that liberated them, more or less, from the strictures of the dependency patterns fostered by his own authoritarianism and rule-ethic. What strikes one repeatedly about the reactions of his followers to Wesley is their typical absense of servility or sycophancy. Somehow he managed to give them room to swing free, and rejoiced with them in their responsible use of their freedom, intelligence and *self*-control. And this, one might think, gets nearer the essence of "mental health" and "self-authentication" than most of the formulas we hear about nowadays.

Some light is shed on all this by the curious fact that Wesley never set much store by intense and symbiotic "I-thou" relationships (which sets him off sharply from most other pietists, before or afterwards). The fact is that he mistrusted *bi*lateral relationships, save as they were sublated in some wider group setting or, most significantly of all, in a *tri*adic relationship with God as the transcendent reference between every human "I" and "thou." His reason was that typical I-thou bonds make for ascendency-dependency relationships between persons. Despite all ideal aspirations, one of the partners dominates or is dominated, absorbs or is absorbed, leans too much or is leaned upon. And so Wesley took more care than most autocrats in discouraging knee-jerk discipleship. Always his stress is on the vertical reference to God's truth and grace that transcends and judges every human master and all disciples. In this appeal to the lordship of Christ over all, he was able to encourage real parity in co-discipleship.

In psychotherapy generally and in pastoral care especially, the trickiest of all problems (given a relative competence in clinical theory and technique) is the management of what is called "transference" and "counter-transference"—those patterns of inordinate attachment and/or resistance of patients to their therapists, and vice versa. One of the most ambivalent of all questions in the cure of souls (old style and new) is *whose* soul is being "cured"—the pastor's or the pastored—and the answer is often so ambiguous as to raise legitimate doubts about much of the enthusiasm with which some pastors invest disproportionate time with a *few* of their flock, leaving the large majority to fend for themselves.

One interesting place to notice Wesley's theory of promoting human dignity *in God* is in his *Letters, Journal,* etc. He never wheedles, never blathers, is seldom intimate. He commands, directs, reproves, argues, appeals. Always he is pointing beyond himself to a higher authority to which his reader has equal access—to Scripture and its rational interpretation, to prayer and conscience, to God and his revelation in Christ. And always he is nudging his reader toward a more profound experience of his or her own, of freedom and responsibility. It is this consistent respect for the voluntary principle, even when related to his own authority, that confirmed his concern that his disciples be free under God.

But *under* God and God's righteous rule in human hearts and the human community! Wesley's most vivid abhorrence, apart from flagrant sin itself, was antinomianism. This was because of his conviction that when individuals become laws unto themselves—when the *in se est* is interpreted as autonomy or inherent goodness—they have already corrupted the terms of their real existence as *God's* children and have begun to stultify their true humanity (which exists solely in relationship to God).

But Wesley was also very much a man of *this* world. He takes the sweet bye-and-bye for granted; indeed, he counts on it, quite conventionally, for eventual redress of earth's inequities. But he never dwells on it and he is loud and clear that the hereafter must never be proffered as an excuse for the Christian fecklessness here below. Thus, he is moved to correlate the cure of souls with Christian manners—mental health with social aplomb and self-possession. This is the main motive in his otherwise impertinent advices about clothes and cleanliness, about diligence and thrift, about pride of craft and stewardship. He repeatedly makes the point that conspicuous and wasteful expenditure, or slackness, or improvidence, all belie bad faith and unfreedom. He decries fashion, partly because it is wasteful, but also because its slaves are un-free. Clothes are for comfort and decency, not for decoration and display. Food is for nutrition, not for gluttony. This was Wesley's general doctrine of temperance, which never stretched to doctrinaire extremes. He was no advocate of self-punishment, no partisan of the shabby, sloppy, or shaggy (although he wore his hair long—and clean!) His point, consistently, was that Christians' habits should support their commitments—for the sake of their Christian witness and service in the world.

I'm very much aware that there is not much of Wesley as pastor that will translate, word for word, into the language and practice of pastoral care in the modern world. For one thing, patterns of authority and leadership have altered out of all recognition since the eighteenth century. For another, all ancient notions of values and moral judgment have been rendered newly problematic, as if from scratch. The dominant views of psychology and personality have changed. The Rogers and the Maslows and the Glassers of this generation have not read John Wesley much, and even if induced to try they would not find him *simpatico*. The theory and practice of group dynamics has taken new directions since Wesley's time—some of them fruitful, some rather ridiculous.

There would be no point, therefore, in my commending Wesley's way with people for mere imitation. But, for that matter, I'm not prepared to recommend much of what passes currently as pastoral psychology and pastoral care—largely because these fields have lagged behind the revolution in the human sciences (anthropology, biology, personality theory, etc.) that keep on forging ahead with such bewildering complexity.

And yet I am more convinced than ever that the basic substance of the Wesleyan view of the incredible journey from the *barely* human to the *truly* human to the *fully* human is one of the richest of all available options. By comparison to the doctrines of humanity's radical evil and its virtual passivity in relation to its ground of being, here is an anthropology that affirms and promotes full humanity. By comparison with all reductionist estimates (the naked ape, "computaman" or whatever), here is a human agenda that recognizes self-transcendence in utter seriousness and sees Christian faith and trust as the most natural terms for healthy, human living. If ever we are to find the way between the praise of God that denigrates the human and the praise of humanity that would banish God, it will most probably lie along the lines of the sort of synergism that Wesley did not invent but did help to develop in ways that are still significant.

Do you remember, from your own ordination service, or from listening to others, the quaint words of the bishop's charge to us as "elders in the Church of Christ"?

> You are to be "messengers," "watchmen" and "stewards" of the Lord: to teach and to admonish, to feed and provide for the Lord's family; to seek for Christ's sheep that are dispersed abroad, and for his children who are in the midst of this evil world. . . .
>
> And if it shall happen that the church, or any member thereof, do take hurt or hindrance by reason of your negligence, you know the greatness of the fault. Wherefore see that you never cease your labor, your care and your diligence until you have done all that lieth in you, according to your bounden duty, to bring all such as shall be committed to your charge unto perfectness in Christ. . . .

[Incidentally, Wesley heard these very same words from Bishop John Potter when he ordained him priest on 22 September 1728.]

Now, obviously, this Elizabethan rhetoric can, and must be, demythologized and remythologized in terms to suit our own times and our own current theories about the care and cure of souls. But if our reformulated commitments somehow fail to include an equivalent vision of the human in God—a comparably fruitful understanding of Christ as God's clue to the full reality of our humanity, a vivid stress on God's presence not merely in personal or mass experience, but peculiarly in dynamic groups— then our patterns of pastoral care could be "competent" and still be barren. If, in our zeal for freedom, we fail to ground and limit our freedom within our existence as God's creatures, we shall find ourselves aspiring to what we cannot provide. If, in our hunger for dignity for all and peace for the world, we fail to call individuals to a recognition of their true worth (*dignitas*) as rootage in God's gratuity and grace, we shall find ourselves self-righteously asserting our own dignity, with all sorts of flimsy rationalizations as *self*-justification.

In the Christian cure of souls, the aid of all the human wisdom in the arts and skills of graceful human relations is indispensable. The pastoral counselor who is unfurnished with the best the human sciences can contribute is by so much a discredit to the calling. But the one thing needful, in all the changes and chances of psychological theory, has been a true vision of the human plight and promise—as this is revealed in Christ and lived out in the community of the Word, the sacraments and Christian comradeship. Given *this* vision in a context of freedom-loving *self*-respect and freedom-granting respect for others, there are some deficiencies in temperament and technique that may not be fatal—as we have noticed in Wesley's case. Without such a vision, the most equable temperament in the world, and the best techniques, will not suffice to lift personal existence beyond itself to a glimpse of the human mystery encompassed by the divine. And if you cannot do this for others, what are you doing in the office of pastor or counselor to them?

The word of grace is not a psychological gimmick or panacea. Religious cant is often a reinforcing agent in mental illness and emotional disturbance (not so much as it was, because of the fading relevance of traditional religious language). The Gospel is no more a specific for schizophrenia than for cancer. What matters, though, is that all people, well or ill, live by their notions of who they are, how they came to be, what they are up to, and where their real destinies are cast. Here, at least, Christian pastors have something to offer that extends all their other services and transcends them—and in such ministrations, the Wesleyan perspective is as relevant today and tomorrow as it was to men and women two hundred years ago.

Speaking of the ordinal, as we were a moment ago, I often think of its closing collect as one of the more meaningful of my daily petitions. As you may know, Cranmer borrowed it from the Gelasian Sacramentary and stuck it in here rather arbitrarily— which means that it is all too rarely noticed or used. It just might, however, be the proper peroration to this effort of ours to assess our own pastoral office in the Wesleyan spirit.

Prevent [anticipate] us, O Lord, in all our doings, with thy most gracious favor, and further us with thy continual help, that in all our works, begun, continued, and ended in thee, we may glorify thy holy name, and finally, by thy mercy, obtain everlasting life; through Jesus Christ our Lord. Amen.

Methodism's Theological Heritage: A Study in Perspective

———┼———

[1969] In order to locate Methodism's distinctive emphases within the faith it shares with other Christians,
Outler focuses on Wesley's "synergism"—a unique
combination of the evangelical accent on God's sovereignty and the catholic affirmation of human agency. Relating
this synthesis to the whole sweep of Christian thought,
Eastern and Western, ancient and modern, Outler is able
to show its distinctive role in Wesley's doctrinal perspective. Later Methodism, he argues, loses its theological
self-understanding by succumbing to an erroneous history
of its Arminian "label" and by forgetting its Anglican
heritage. This results in an eclectic borrowing of doctrinal
fashions and a theological anthropology at odds with the
original Wesleyan sense of the Divine-human paradox.
Although he recognizes the continued relevance of a
Wesleyan theological paradigm, he does not pull back from
the possibility that Methodism's true destiny is to lose its
life in catholicity.

Even in a revolutionary age, the past is still prelude to the future. What is more, our freedom for that future depends at least partly on our present self-understanding in the light of our traditions and corporate experience, since these control our perspectives. In the case of a historical entity like Methodism, any realistic look ahead demands a careful retrospect: a synoptic view of the theological past that we share with all other Christians and an identification of those distinctive emphases, if any, that we may call our own.

In any such essay in perspective, the Methodist ecumenist had best walk warily. On the right is the gaping pit of denominational triumphalism with its claim that the Methodists constitute a doctrinal species all their own, with some sort of divine right and duty to defend their differences to the death. Such a claim is doubly false, as a matter of fact and as a matter of ecumenical principle. Directly on the left, however, is the miry swamp of doctrinal indifferentism—the blinkered assertion that Methodists have no unique doctrinal contribution to offer the whole church, that *all* our concerns are practical, missional, social. This, too, is false, in fact and on principle—and the principle has a significant bearing on our ecumenical involvement. Speak as ardently as you will of the primacy of mission over doctrine (in my view, a wholly gratuitous disjunction), and it is still true that *the Christian message is the Christian mission* and that the measure of mission is not mission itself but rather *the hearing of faith* (cf. Rom. 10:17). If it is true, as I hope to show, that the Methodists have, or had, a distinctive understanding of what goes into "the hearing of faith," then it would follow that our particular understanding of that message affects our understanding of the Christian mission. And if it is also true, as I have argued for thirty years, that it is Methodism's manifest destiny to lose its denominational life in a more vital, catholic community of Christians ("that the world may believe"), then it will matter immensely if we can make our "death" truly meaningful: an offertory of our best gifts to the wider union—and I keep hoping that this will include our intellects along with our hearts and muscle!

This is why, therefore, I make bold to propose a bare-bones

sketch of the thesis that Wesleyan Methodism has a unique and identifiable doctrinal emphasis of considerable import both for mission *and* ecumenism; that this "doctrinal emphasis" does not add up to a singular *system* of doctrine, whole and entire, but is rather a delicate balance of emphases and accents, which is all too often out of kilter but which remains relevant for our part in the ecumenical dialogue. In short, Methodist doctrine has a distinctive style of integrating the evangelical stress on God's sovereign grace and the catholic accent on human agency in the history of salvation. There may be nothing very original about the several elements in Methodism's doctrinal stance, but the way they were put together and have been held together *is* unique—and so also the way in which they have been allowed to fall apart!

One graphic way of seeing this point about the difference between separate theological *systems* and unique *configurations* of doctrine is to run a simple experiment in ecumenical cartography. Take any of the theological "maps" in common use and try to locate Methodism on it. The most obvious feature on any of these maps is the great divide between the Catholics (Orthodox and Roman) and the Protestants, and it will scarcely occur to anyone to put the Methodists "over there," on the Catholic side, despite the fact that Wesley was an Anglican, was often denounced as a "papist" and openly avowed his indebtedness to Catholic spirituality. Over on the Protestant side, there is first of all the Lutheran domain, with no place for us there, either—despite our joint professions of loyalty to the *sola scriptura* and *sola fide*. Alongside them is the broader expanse of Calvinist territory (embracing important client groups like the Baptists and the Campbellites), but we don't really fit there—despite Wesley's affinities with some elements of the Puritan tradition.[1] Ever since Wesley denounced Whitefield (1739) for preaching "the decrees," the battle between sovereignty and agency has been joined, much mellowed of late, but not at all forgotten.

Then there are the scattered enclaves of the Protestant Radicals who, once penned up, have since scattered abroad and, in America more than elsewhere, have deeply affected their neighbors in matters of ecclesiastical polity. Methodists have deep affinities with Radical Protestantism. We, too, began as a religious

---

[1]Cf. Robert C. Monk, *John Wesley: His Puritan Heritage* (Nashville: Abingdon, 1966).

society. We, too, have our martyrs and self-righteous memories of having been put upon by the high and the mighty. We, too, set great store by "heart-religion," "the community of the Spirit," "we-group fellowship," and the like. But in England we grew up inside a national church, and in America we grew into an "establishment" of our own—with our "connectional system" as a hallmark of our identity. Besides, many of the Radicals tended to construe Christian experience in mystical terms that offended Wesley mightily.[2]

This leaves us, then, with only one remaining segment on our map—inscribed *Ecclesia Anglicana*—and both we and they shrink from our being spotted *there*. We were never welcome in our homeland, and two centuries of schism have complicated our relationships of affiliation and disaffiliation. We began as a religious society within the Church of England, never more than tolerated. Wesley tried to hold his societies inside the church,[3] except for the Americans whom, finally, he had to consign to the vagaries of a strange providence.[4] But the Wesleyan style of evangelism was discordant in the Church of England, and the Methodist understanding of ministry and the sacraments antipathetic. In the resultant love-hate relationship that developed, the Anglicans lost their most forceful "evangelical" party and the Methodists forfeited their original "catholic" context.

If, then, we are not Catholic in any formal sense, or Lutheran, Calvinist, or Radical, what on earth are we, theologically? Here we ourselves have added to the confusion. To begin with, we accepted the Lutheran and Calvinist view that theology is and ought to be speculative and systematic (albeit biblical, of course): the heroic attempt to discover, expound, and defend that one true *system* of Christian truth that *must* be lodged somewhere in Scripture and tradition, and to do this by means of abstract conceptualizations ordered into a comprehensive whole. But then we backed away, as if by instinct, from any such enterprise so described.[5] As a result, we have tended to discourage (and to

[2]Cf. *JWJ* I:420 (January 24, 1738).
[3]Cf. *Reasons Against a Separation from the Church of England* (London, 1758); see also *A Preservative Against Unsettled Notions in Religion*, #13 (Bristol, 1758).
[4]Cf. *JWL* VIII: 238–39 (September 10, 1784).
[5]This is what Wesley meant by "orthodoxy"and why he denied to it any normative authority. "Orthodoxy, or right opinions, is, at best, but a

denigrate) theological speculation and scholarship at any level much beyond that of practical utility. Then, in an obvious compensatory reaction, we proceeded to develop a positive pride in our lack of theological prowess.

Meanwhile, what with the nagging of the Calvinists, we adopted as our own their pejorative label for us: "Arminian." This has been doubly confusing. It suggests that Arminius must have been one of Wesley's major sources—and therefore ours—and it implies that Methodism may accurately be classified as a subspecies of Aberrant Calvinist (which was Dort's verdict on Arminianism). Both of these implications are false.

It has, therefore, been "doing what comes naturally" for Methodism to evolve through two centuries with a minimal *theological* self-consciousness. Her spokespersons usually have been content to emphasize such particular accents as "religious experience," "assurance," "holiness," and the like, and they opposed various contrary views and practices in other traditions (formalism, predestination, believer's baptism, etc.). But they stopped short of claiming that the Methodist position amounted to more than a peculiar *configuration* of common Christian doctrine. Latterly, however, this lack of a distinctive theological self-identity has prompted patterns of borrowing from other doctrinal traditions and fashions, especially from European Protestantism (Lotze, Ritschl, Barth, Bultmann). For the most part, however, these transplants were not wholly successful—partly because of a native streak of anthropological doctrine that is characteristic of Wesley and the Anglicans, which produces an emphasis that is not easily understood or explained in the terms of the classical Protestant syndromes. There is a problem here that deserves our careful pondering. It bears on the fact—or what I take to be the fact—that Methodism's share in the history of theology has yet to match its true potential. If we are to improve our record in the future, we had best try harder to understand our past.

Let me suggest, therefore, that Methodist theology, generally speaking, may best be understood as a peculiar brand of evangelical Christianity, with origins in a catholic environment and with its evolution (especially in America) within the milieu of

very slender part of religion, if it can be allowed to be any part at all" *JWW* VIII:249. "As to all opinions which do not strike at the root of Christianity, we think and let think" *JWW* VIII:340.

modern secularism. Its most distinctive theological characteristic has been its doctrine of God's grace (the active presence of God's love in human existence) in which the prime concern is a vital synthesis of the evangelical stress on God's sovereignty and the catholic emphasis on human agency: a dynamic mix of prevenience, justification, regeneration, and holiness. In other words, when Methodists talk about the ancient paradox of God's ways with humanity, they have their own recognizable way of trying to explain it all.

This way turns on a notion that has its roots in biblical thought and also a long history down through the unfolding of Christian doctrine. It is an unstable idea; and it has generated a teetering effort to keep to the twisting ridge that runs between the lowlands of moralism and what Wesley called "solifidianism."[6] It would take a whole book to spell this out with anything close to adequate argument and documentation—a book not yet written, and one that may never be. But some of the landmarks of that history are reasonably clear, and they do add up to what I hope may be a useful comment on the future of theology in the Methodist tradition in an ecumenical age.

Christianity is a gospel: about God and humanity, and about Jesus as God's special agent in the drama of our salvation. It presupposes a radical defect in the human condition and thereby poses a subtle question about the residual capacities of "fallen man" within the order and purposes of God's grace in God's ongoing creation. In their perennial wrestlings with these questions, Christians have turned up a genuine paradox: God's undisputed sovereignty *and* our undeniable responsibility. In every system of Christian doctrine, God's sovereignty is asserted or assumed; there are no humanists in Holy Writ nor in the company of the church's accredited teachers. And yet also and equally, there is the recognition of human agency as decisive in the mysteries of both sin and redemption. From the J story of Yahweh and Adam in their first unequal confrontation (Gen. 3:9–23) down to the Revelator's vision of "a new heaven and a new earth" (Rev. 22), there runs the insistent theme of God's prevenient and prevailing grace, in the sustenance of God's creation and in "providence" for rebellious creatures. "For it is by grace you have been saved, through faith—and this *not* from yourselves, it

[6]Cf. *JWJ* II:174; see also V:244.

is the *gift* of God—not by works, so that no one can boast" [Eph. 2:8, 9, NIV, italics added]. And yet the human share in this process is utterly crucial. Salvation is an interpersonal affair. The human condition is ruinous, and yet its residual *dignitas* prompted God to give us freely of costing love in Jesus Christ. It is God, of course, who works in aid of all our willings and doings; *all* our powers are created, and God is their Creator and Sustainer. And yet their God-chosen purpose is to involve us deeply in holy history, to *work out our own salvation* with fear and trembling (cf. Phil. 2:12).

Through crisis after crisis this paradox has persisted, and Christians have dealt with it in as many different ways as they could conceive. In the East, the tendency was to stress God's image in us, spoiled by sin but not negated—the human capacity for participation in the divine perfections.[7] All of this was based on the assumption that grace is omnipresent in creation ("a sacramental universe"); hence, the normal mode of faith's appropriation of grace is worship and communion. In Orthodoxy, the chief human work is *leitourgia* (worship in its broadest and deepest sense); the chief human end is *teleōsis* (perfection, the fullness of the human possibility).

In the West, the Pelagian controversy polarized the Christian mind and moved Latin orthodoxy over to a one-sided emphasis on the gratuity of grace. The unhappiest consequence of that tragedy was the strength it gave to the notion that *any* version of divine-human synergism could easily be smeared by calling it "Pelagian." The Second Council of Orange (529) and Boniface II (531) proceeded to confer semi-dogmatic status upon the triumphant Augustinianism that had emerged from the ruins of the Roman Empire. But what of the "natural" capacity for grace, if any? What happens, or can happen, in the human heart in the way of preparing it for "the hearing of faith"? This was a question of great urgency and moment in the church's mission ventures in a barbaric society. It makes a great deal of difference how you preach to the unconverted whether you assume or reject the premise of God's grace as prevenient, preparatory, and morally active in human existence, always and everywhere.

[7]Cf. David L. Balás, *Metousia Theou; Man's Participation in God's Perfections According to St. Gregory of Nyssa* (Rome: Libreria Herder, 1966), and Lars Thunberg *Microcosm and Mediator: The Theological Anthropology of Maximus the Confessor* (Lund: C. W. K. Gleerup, 1965).

It was in such a missional context that there emerged in the sixth and seventh centuries a maxim for Christian missionaries that modified the prevailing Augustinianism: *Facienti quod in se est, Deus non denegat gratiam* (God does not withhold grace from the person who is doing what is truly "him"—*in se*).[8] The expression was a coinage of biblical and patristic sentiments, and in its earliest usage (before Anselm) it referred exclusively to the purely natural human activity (*in se*) that disposed the soul toward justification proper (*gratia infusa* [infused grace]). The power that enabled a person to do anything positively (*in se*) was the grace of creation (*concursus Dei*,)[9] one of the functions of which was the preparation of the human will (*habilitas passive*) that normally precedes the gift and reception of saving grace itself. Is not the man who opens a window to let in the sunshine responsible in some sense for lighting the room, even if he is not responsible for the sunshine?[10] There is no such thing as saving grace (*meritum de condigno*) in human virtue, but there is a sort of "congruent merit" that goes with the *facere in se est*.[11]

This was a way of urging that human nature, even at its worst, is never wholly bereft of grace.[12] Sin has spoiled but not effaced the *imago Dei*. Even in its alienation, the human heart is being stirred and drawn by the immanent action of God's Spirit. We can, and must, do what we can in response to these

---

[8]Cf. A. M. Landgraf, *Dogmengeschichte der Frühscholastik* (Regensburg, 1952–54), I:1, 249–63. See also H. A. Oberman, *HMT*, 132–45. [Cf. Outler's discussion of the *in se est* tradition in "Pastoral Care in the Wesleyan Spirit" above, 177–90.]

[9][*Concursus Dei*, i.e., the "concurrence of God"; a corollary of the doctrine of God as the first, efficient cause. For any contingent creature to act, the divine will, which continues to support all contingent being, must concur in the action. See Richard A. Muller, *Dictionary of Latin and Greek Theological Terms* (Grand Rapids: Baker, 1985), 76.]

[10]Cf. *Landgraf, Dogmengeschichte*, 258–59.

[11][Outler is referring to the scholastic distinction between *meritum de condigno* (merit of worthiness), and *meritum de congruo* (merit of fitness, or congruity). The former refers to conduct that earns genuine merit because it is the product of grace; the latter refers to a proportional merit based on human free will. See below, 200. Cf. Reinhold Seeberg, *Textbook of the History of Doctrines* (Grand Rapids: Baker, 1958), 122f.]

[12]Cf. George Matheson's familiar hymn, "O Love that wilt not let me go," and St. Thomas' famous maxim, *gratia non tollit naturam, sed perfecit* [Grace does not destroy nature but perfects it].

promptings and leadings—and God will "pre-vent" (go before) us in love and promise.

This, of course, takes human agency for granted—and thus falls athwart the Augustinian view of what the human *in se* actually is. In those terms, *in se* means depravity and self-deceiving pride. Any virtuous operation of a sinful person's *in se* can issue only in *vitiae splendidae*, "splendid sins."[13]

As Europe began to come of age (in the twelfth century), there gradually arose a new naturalism—a spin-off from the revolutions in science, technology, and philosophy that accompanied the importation of Arabic-Aristotelian secularism into the collapsing feudal society that had never been more than half-converted. The resulting collision of cultures and worldviews set off the most profound crisis of the Middle Ages, with repercussions that still echo in our own bemused ears. The controversy (miscalled "Averroistic") was fought on the highest level of abstractions: the eternity of the world and matter, the unicity of the intellect, the mortality of the soul, etc. But at urgent issue were the distillates of two rival lifestyles: the transcendentalism of traditional Christianity and the basic naturalism of "the new philosophy." It was the special vocation of Thomas Aquinas to absorb the full force of this secularizing challenge—so powerful that it fascinated both the intelligentsia and the rising bourgeoisie—and to convert the otherworldly traditions of early medieval Christianity into a new "theologically founded worldliness," in Josef Pieper's interesting phrase.[14] A vital element in this Thomistic synthesis of nature and grace was the premise of the *facienti quod in se est*.[15]

But the immobilists were panicked by the threat of this new secularism. Three years to the day from Thomas' death, Averroism was roundly condemned by the Archbishop of Paris in an indictment that also contained several key propositions that had been affirmed by Thomas himself. This suppression was instigated and approved by Pope John XXI and was quickly followed by an even more explicit anti-Thomist condemnation by the Archbishop of Canterbury. Together, they amounted to a powerful

[13]Cf. *JWO* 150, 440.

[14]Josef Pieper, *Guide to Thomas Aquinas* (New York: Mentor-Omega, 1962), 117; cf. 118–19.

[15]Cf. *De Veritate*, Q. 28, arts. v-viii. English translation: *Truth* (Chicago: Henry Regnery, 1954), III:380–96.

attack on the universities of Paris and Oxford where the new naturalism was rampant. They also had the effect of tainting the reputation of the *Doctor Angelicus*. The cause of Christian naturalism went under a cloud. The next move was up to the transcendentalists.

Presently, then, with Duns Scotus and the nominalists, a new theological compound begins to emerge: radical empiricism (in logic) in support of radical transcendence (in theology). For the nominalists, reason is reliable only within the narrowest limits. Faith is able to soar above these limits and to mark out the distinctions between the twin manifestations of God's freedom: *potentia absoluta* and *potentia ordinata*. God's sovereignty was indicated by the *potentia absoluta*; God's *self*-limitations were signified by the *potentia ordinata*. Thus human agency reappears in nominalism in a strange and curious way. As Professor Oberman has explained it in his excellent *Harvest of Medieval Theology*, the nominalists (and especially Gabriel Biel, Luther's mentor in philosophy) held both divine sovereignty and human agency in desperate balance—allowing for the congruent merit of humanity's natural love of God was a significant preparation for the condign merit of God's saving grace (God's unmerited gift)—and the key to this nominalist synthesis was the *facere quod in se est*![16] This was an unstable mixture of a radical supernaturalism and a moderate moralism—yet it also had a very special relevance to the then current issues of social and political conflict between the papacy and the empire.

Now there are two points that make all this obscure history relevant to our present theme. The first is that it was *nominalism* that Luther and Calvin learned and rejected as the only philosophy worth learning and rejecting. Indeed, both the *sola scriptura* and the antinaturalism of the great Reformers derive in important measure from their ambivalent reactions to this particular philosophic outlook. They took over its transcendental theology; they rejected its humanist anthropology outright and vehemently. Luther's violent aversions to "natural" theology and morality were stirred by the dangers he saw specifically in the *facere in se est*. Compare his *Disputation Against Scholastic Theology* (September 4, no. 157), especially Theses Six, Ten, Fifteen, Twenty-six, Twenty-eight, Thirty-three, Sixty-one, Eighty-eight, Ninety-one,

[16]Cf. Oberman, *HMT* 120–45.

Ninety-seven,[17] together with his attack upon Erasmus in *The Bondage of the Will* (1525), and you can recognize Luther's radical aversion to synergism of every sort. Then, in Calvin's contention (*Institutes*, Book I), that apart from *saving* grace the human will is at odds with God by "nature," that the human mind is (*in se*) an inveterate idol factory, one may see the climactic rejection of the *facere in se est* in classical Protestantism. Thereafter, no version of divine-human synergism would have a welcome place among the strict Lutherans or Calvinists.

The second point that touches us is that the nominalist cause, lost in Protestant Europe, survived in England, and combined with the spirit and substance of the Erasmian reform program to supply the Anglican Reformation with its most distinctive theology. Nominalism had deep roots in England and especially in Oxford. Scotus was an Oxford man; his major work is aptly titled *Opus Oxoniense*. Ockham was trained at Oxford, and four of the five identifiable targets of Thomas Bradwardine's *De cause Dei contra Pelagium* were English and Oxonian.[18] As a philosophy, nominalism was the fibrous root of what became "British empiricism" (Bacon *et seq.*); its theological residues fertilized the special brand of "faith *and* good works" that became the hallmark of the central Anglican tradition in which John Wesley's mind was formed. All this suggests, and this is the nerve of my thesis, that there was a native-born tradition of Christian synergism in Europe and England long before Arminius and the Synod of Dort—and that it was *this* tradition that nourished Wesley. Such a thesis had already been put forward by a historian whom Wesley read: Peter Heylyn in his *Historia Quinquarticularis* (1660). Against the Puritans, Heylyn rejected the label "Arminian" as a designation for Anglican theology, on the ground that the Church of England never had been Calvinist. Since "Arminian" denotes an aberrant version of Calvinism, it is a misnomer when

[17]Thesis Twenty-six: "An act of love is not the best way of doing 'what in one lies.' . . . . Nor is it a method of repenting and drawing near to God."

Thesis Thirty-three: "And that is a false dictum, too, which alleges that to do 'all that in one lies' is to remove the obstacles to grace (against certain teachers)." *Luther: Early Theological Works*, James Atkinson, ed., Library of Christian Classics (Philadelphia: Westminster, 1962), XVI:266–73.

[18]Cf. Gordon Leff, *Bradwardine and the Pelagians* (Cambridge: Cambridge University Press, 1957).

applied to *Ecclesia Anglicana*. Heylyn makes a correlative point, too: that, beyond its own native traditions, the Church of England owed its foreign debts mainly to Erasmus, Melanchthon, and Bucer. It was neither Lutheran nor Calvinist.[19]

There is no denying that Heylyn's history overall is partisan and tendentious, but on these two points he had a good case. The two great charters of "central Anglicanism" had already been drafted before Arminius and Dort—in the Edwardian *Homilies* (1547) and in Richard Hooker's *Laws of Ecclesiastical Polity* (1594–97). In both of these the Methodist reader will recognize a familiar version of the Great Paradox, an argument based on scriptural grounds as decisive in all questions theological, that original sin does not obliterate the *imago dei*, that salvation is God's gift "with no merit thereunto antecedent," that good works follow just-ification, and yet that human cooperation is decisive with the whole process: preparation, reception, and harvest. The medieval maxim (*facere in se est*) is not repeated verbatim; its presence as premise is everywhere.

Elsewhere I have tried to indicate the ways in which Wesley, across a lifetime, sought and found a way between the equally unacceptable extremes of moralism and "solifidianism"; how he maintained a rigorist doctrine of original sin along with a generous conception of prevenient grace; how he correlated and distin-guished justification, regeneration, and sanctification; how he stood off antinomianism of every kind; how he championed the cause of universal redemption.[20] On justification, he found "not a hair's breadth" of difference with Calvin and Luther;[21] on sanctification, he approved the pre-Tridentine Romans. Only the Methodists, said he, had got the hang of holding the two to-gether.[22]

That Wesley was a synergist can scarcely be denied unless "synergism" be defined in terms exclusively Pelagian. This, of course, was exactly what the Moravians and others tried to do to him, both before and after Aldersgate. But Wesley went on his

[19]Cf. *The Historical and Miscellaneous Tracts of the Rev. and Learned Peter Heylyn, D.D.* (London, 1681), 505–634.

[20]*JWO* 3–33. See also, Albert C. Outler, "Theologische Akzente," in *Der Methodismus*, "Die Kirchen der Welt," VI, C. Ernest Sommer, ed. (Stuttgart: Evangelisches Verlagswerk, 1968), 84–102.

[21]*JWO* 78. See also 136–40.

[22]*Ibid.*, 107–8.

way unruffled by this, and the Methodists, generally, have followed his emphasis on grace at work among the virtuous pagans and his implicit appeals for preaching to the unconverted in terms of that prevenient, preparatory grace that can be assumed active even in the unheeding heart.[23]

In the blurred days before Aldersgate, it was Peter Böhler, probing the causes of Wesley's infirm faith, who identified and deplored this strand in Wesley's background: *Mi frater, mi frater, excoquenda est ista tua philosophia* (My brother, my brother, that philosophy of yours must be purged away).[24] This was not, in the first instance at least, a blanket repudiation of *all* philosophy as such. Rather, as the context shows, it was a specific hit at what I would like to call the *"transactional* synergism" that Wesley had grown up with. Its main confidence was that if individuals behaved according to their highest lights (*facere quod in se est*), their claim to saving grace had the status of a *right*. It was *this* "philosophia" (itself a misinterpretation of the *Homilies*) that had sterilized Wesley's dedication and zeal since his conversion in 1725. This is what had to go, and this is what did go at Aldersgate. What came in its place—but not all at once—is what we might call *"covenantal* synergism," in which both prevenient *and* saving grace are recognized as coordinate providential activities of the one true God of love who, in divine love, makes and keeps covenant with the faithful. This doctrinal transformation continued to develop from his first encounter with Böhler until his first decisive results as a revival preacher in the spring of 1739.

Aldersgate, therefore, did not signify Wesley's abandonment of the *in se est* motif in his account of the drama of salvation. The proof of this is his vigorous repudiation of what he called "the German stillness,"[25] his prompt counterattack against the Moravians, his withdrawal from the Fetter Lane Society, and his move to the Foundery. One might even say that the Methodist societies began a protest movement in favor of the *facere in se est*.[26]

The climax of this particular quarrel came in the famous debate with Zinzendorf (June 16, 1741) in Gray's Inn Walks in

[23]*Ibid.*, 231–37.

[24]*JWJ* I:440 (February 8, 1738): "I understood him not, and least of all when he said, *Mi Frater*, etc."

[25]Cf. *JWO* 221, 347, 353–54.

[26]Cf. *JWJ* II:328–31; see also *JWO* 357ff.

Holborn.[27] The point at issue, accepted as such by both men, was whether *any* of the works of grace are inherent, or if *all* are imputed. Said the Count, in a fine fury:

> I know of no such thing as inherent perfection [the final implication of *in se*] in this life. This is the error of errors. I pursue it everywhere with fire and sword! I stamp it under foot! I give it over to destruction! Christ is our only perfection. Whoever affirms inherent perfection denies Christ. . . .
>
> W. Isn't every true believer holy?
>
> Z. Indeed. But holy in Christ, not *in himself*. . . .
>
> W. It follows, then, that he is holy *in se*, doesn't it?
>
> Z. No. No! Only in Christ! Not holy *in se*. No one has any holiness *in se*.[28]

We will remember that Wesley's heart was strangely warmed while "one was reading Luther's preface to the *Epistle to the Romans*."[29] And it is well not to forget the deep affinities between Wesley and Luther as touching the heart and marrow of the gospel of faith. But these two great men stood poles apart in the total configurations of their doctrines and their practical conceptions of evangelism, Christian nurture, and holiness—and the polarity was focused in this issue of the human *in se*.[30]

Again, in relation to Calvin and the English Puritans, it is true that Wesley was deeply indebted to the modified Calvinism of Amyraldus and his colleagues at Saumur. And yet the longest and most painful controversy of his life—zealously protracted by the American Methodists throughout the nineteenth century—was with the Calvinists about predestination. Here again, the *casus belli* [cause for controversy] was divine prevenience and human agency. *The Arminian Magazine* (which monopolized Wesley's literary output from 1777 until his death) was the cockpit of the conflict. The bite of the Calvinist critique, which has been all too successful in fixing the theological stereotypes by which Methodists have been subsequently judged and have all too often

---

[27]Cf. *JWO* 367–72.

[28]It seems most unlikely that Zinzendorf had ever read Luther's September, 1517, *Disputation*—but here he is echoing even its language; see above, 200.

[29]*JWJ* I:475 (May 24, 1738).

[30]*JWO* 366.

judged themselves, was that Wesley's profession of justification by faith was nullified by his overgenerous allowance for the human *in se:* that, in effect, he was either a poor theologian or else a Pelagian heretic. Wesley laid ream to ream in reasoned refutation of all this, but occasionally he was provoked to a dangerous candor: "Who was Pelagius?" asked one of his loyal but uncomprehending followers, prodded by Calvinist scorn. "By all I can pick up from ancient authors," Wesley retorts, "I guess he was both a wise and an holy man."[31] In a sermon written at the height of the controversy (April 28, 1784), he let fly with this annoyed outburst:

> I verily believe, the real heresy of Pelagius was neither more nor less than this: The holding that Christians may, by the grace of God, (not without it; that I take to be a mere slander,) "go on to perfection," or, in other words, "fulfil the law of Christ."
>
> "But St. Augustine says:"—When Augustine's passions were heated, his word is not worth a rush. And here is the secret: St. Augustine was angry at Pelagius: Hence he slandered and abused him (as his manner was) without either fear or shame.[32]

This is scarcely a balanced judgment, even for Wesley. But it reveals the intensity of his conviction that his own version of the paradox of sovereign grace and human freedom fell safely inside the orbit of orthodoxy and was not to be discredited by defamatory labels. One of the very best among the sermons of his old age is entitled "On Working Out Our Own Salvation" (1785).[33] Gabriel Biel could not have written it, but he would have understood it. Luther and Calvin would have rejected it out of hand.

In all of this, however, Wesley never faltered in his faithfulness to the Protestant premise of God's sovereignty and the gratuity of grace. On this score, he was as consistent as in his advocacy of the catholic tradition of human agency, and even more insistent. His constant stress on the *sola scriptura*, on justification by faith alone, on private judgment, and on the rights of nonconformity drew harsh criticism from the traditionalists in the Church of England, and this might have fitly ranked him with other Anglican evangelicals (Harris, Whitefield, Lady Hunting-

[31]Letter to Alexander Coates, July 7, 1761. *JWL* IV:158.
[32]"The Wisdom of God's Counsels," *JWW* VI:328–29.
[33]*Ibid.*, VI:506–13.

don's chaplains, *et al.*)—except for their objections to his emphasis on divine-human interaction. In the other direction, Wesley had important affinities with the catholic traditions of the Nonjurors and High Churchmen in the area of prayer and devotion, but his Puritan brand of sacramental theology and church polity was plainly alien to them. He was a defender of reason in theology, and yet he stood at odds with Joseph Butler and even with a moderate like "John Smith," who roundly denounced his doctrine of "perceptible inspiration."[34] He understood himself as missionary and evangelist, an "extraordinary messenger" raised up in, and for the service of, the Church of England. During his lifetime, therefore, he compelled the British Methodists to seek and find their sacraments in the Established Church, although the course he set for them was almost bound to lead to eventual separation.

In America, the Methodists quickly organized themselves after the Revolution into the first "American" church—"Methodist Episcopal"—with a set bias against their Anglican background. The result was that the fact of our Anglican heritage has never been a vivid resource for our self-understanding as a denomination. Despite our repressed memories, however, Methodist preachers and theologians continued their development of the Wesleyan synthesis of divine gratuity and human agency. By now, however, the term "Arminian" had lost its force as an epithet and had been adopted as a proud badge—supported by the revised history that the Methodist commitment to human moral agency actually stemmed from Arminius and the Remonstrants. Our first systematic theologian, Richard Watson (1781–1833), begins his *Theological Institutes* (1823) with a chapter on "Man as Moral Agent" and concludes it thus:

> Those actions which among men have almost universally been judged *good*, have the implied sanction of the will of our wise and good Creator, being found in experience, and by the constitution of our nature and of human society, most conducive to happiness.[35]

[34]Cf. the correspondence between Wesley and "John Smith" in Henry Moore's *Life of John Wesley*, (London, 1824–25), II:277–322.
[35](Nashville: Southern Methodist Publishing House, 1860), Part I, i, 10.

This is later connected with prevenient grace: "His [the human individual's moral] agency, even when rightly directed, is upheld and influenced by the superior power of God, and yet so as to be still his own."[36] This comes at the end of one of the longest sections in the book, which is—what else?—a refutation of Calvinism!

The core of Thomas Ralston's *Elements of Divinity*[37] is found in his three center chapters:

XVIII. *Calvinism and Arminianism Compared*
("The atonement so extends to *all* men as to render salvation possible for them," p. 238.)

XIX. *The Moral Agency of Man*
("The whole history of the fall, in the light of reason, of common sense, and in view of all that we know of the Divine character and government, proclaims, in language clear and forcible, the doctrine of man's free moral agency," p. 249.)

XX. *The Moral Agency of Man—Objections*
("So far from being absurd in itself, it [the doctrine of free agency] presents the only consistent illustration of the Divine attributes, and the only satisfactory comment upon the Divine administration," p. 257.)

William B. Pope, the most eminent of all nineteenth-century Methodist theologians, says nothing about the *quod in se est* maxim and yet teaches its import with triumphalist enthusiasm:

This hearer of the Word has a preliminary grace in the roots of his nature. . . . Redemption is universal and goes back to the root of [human] nature.[38]

[Methodism] has, however, more fully and consistently than the Remonstrant system, connected the universality of grace with the universality of redemption.[39]

There is, doubtless, to be sometimes found in men not yet regenerate, . . . in men not even decided in their choice, something of moral excellence.

[36]*Ibid.*, Part II, xxviii, 610.
[37](Louisville: Morton & Griswald, 1847).
[38]Pope, *Compendium of Christian Theology* (New York: Phillips and Hunt, 1881, III:366.
[39]*Ibid.*, 80.

On the whole, it may be said that the doctrine [of man's fallen nature] thus stated is the only one in harmony with all the facts in the case: it omits nothing, softens nothing, evades nothing.[40]

Miner Raymond, a key figure in Methodism's belated reception of the new European liberal theology, is still more explicit:

> The universal consciousness of sin and of obligation to virtue proves that the race, as a rule, have, in actual, personal possession, all the elements essential to a moral character. . . . Whatever is essential to moral obligation is not left to the contingencies of a man's circumstances. . . . Power, or ability to bring something to pass; intelligence, or ability to apprehend an end and its means; free-will, ability to do or not to do, and an apprehension of obligation, constitute the elements of a moral action, and all men are conscious of possessing these elements.[41]

Raymond marks the bare beginnings of the impact of German Protestant liberalism on American Methodism. Within two decades this influence had become a dominant one, with the result that the traditional Wesleyan synergism was swiftly transformed into a different type of theological anthropology. German liberalism was a metamorphosis of Lutheran and Reformed traditions and, as we have seen, not at all the same thing as the traditional Anglican version of the grace and nature paradox. Consequently, the experience of American Methodists turning "liberal," or whatever, has typically an odd and off-key character.

Let me say once more—because it *is* a ticklish point, easily misunderstood—that it is no part of my argument that synergism is the whole story about Methodist theology; it is not even its heart and spring. Of conscious and set purpose, Methodists have claimed as their own the main core of common Christian belief and then have produced a special mix of its catholic and evangelical elements. Out of this came Wesley's version of the doctrine of "salvation, faith and good works,"[42] the crown of which was his doctrine of perfection ("the fullness of faith," the hope of becoming fully human). And it might be worth remarking

[40]*Ibid.*, 82.

[41]Raymond, *Systematic Theology* (Cincinnati: Hitchcock and Walden, 1877), II:314–15.

[42]*JWO* 123–33.

that, in this view, holiness is related to sanctifying grace much as the *facere in se est* is to prevenient grace.

What I do mean to urge, however, is that Wesley's accent on synergism affected the internal balance of his doctrinal perspective, that it generated its own distinctive hermeneutic for interpreting the Christian message as a whole, that its conscious practical concern is to serve the twin tasks of evangelism and Christian nurture, which have always been our main business in the world, even when we have not done them well.

There is, however, still another side to this problem of Methodist synergism and our role in the ecumenical dialogue. The Methodist theological complex has never been a stable entity by itself–and was never meant to be. In Wesley's own time, it was contained and sustained by the doctrinal and liturgical context of the Church of England, which provided the Methodist societies with a sacramental environment. Outside such an atmosphere Methodism has had perennial problems of theological identity that have encouraged an eclectic drift. This is obvious in the motley crowd of borrowed fashions in doctrine that we have sported from time to time: pietism, revivalism, fundamentalism, liberalism, neo-orthodoxy, existentialism, radical theology, neoclassical theism (you name it; we've got it around here somewhere!). For more than half a century now, it would seem that Methodist theologians have felt some sort of compulsion to marry outside the clan. Concurrently, the fate of the scholarly study of Wesley and of Methodist constitutional history has sagged from bad to worse—so that, for example, the job of a badly needed critical edition of Wesley's *Works* (which the Oxford University Press has promised to publish and which would be of genuine ecumenical significance) is now languishing for want of adequate personnel. Or, again, supposing that such a strange impulse arose, where would one go for training as a Wesley specialist?[43] This is not mere grumbling on my part. The consequences are serious—all the more so in a time when so much useful work is being done in the primary sources of the other Christian traditions, in an ecumenical style and on behalf of an ecumenical theology.

In any case, it is clear that the Methodist doctrinal perspective was not meant to stand on its own, apart from all the others.

---

[43][For Outler's later view on the state of Wesley Studies see "A New Future for Wesley Studies: An Agenda for Phase III" above, 127–44.]

It works best in a wider and more catholic context where the humanist drag of the *in se* tradition is, or can be, redeemed in a sacramental order where grace and the means of grace are integrated in a visible and universal covenant: "unity, witness, and service" (to borrow a phrase from the New Delhi Assembly of the World Council of Churches). But by the same token, the Wesleyan heritage also profits from the constant criticism and correction of the evangelical emphasis on faith as a sheer gift, the evangelical horror of idolatry and ecclesiastical egoism. Thus, our constant need of challenge from the Lutherans, Calvinists, and Radical Protestants!

There may be those who find this description of the Methodist theological configuration unpromising or unimpressive. It does suggest a real deficiency, as if Methodist theology *needed* an ecumenical context in order to do well. And that, precisely, is my point, and I see at least two ways in which it is relevant to our future. In the first place, that future must surely lie with those who conceive theology in ecumenical terms above all else. The day of denominational theologies is over. The least productive of all theological approaches is the one that asks, "Which, among the rival options before us, is the one true system of doctrine?" Yet this has been our general habit in the Christian community for at least the past four polemical centuries. There is no call for Methodists to deprecate or jettison their heritage, nor offer to swap it off for something better. This witness that I have spoken of is still vital and relevant—never more so than today, and tomorrow—for its possible correction and balancing of traditions that lie to its right or left. We have a vital linkage with every major bloc in Christendom, and yet our independent mission in the modern world continues to cast us in a role that needs to be maximized within a catholic whole: as catalysts, critics, and pragmatists.

There is still another count on which our heritage can have prepared us for a hopeful future if we will claim and exploit it rightly. Is there a more obvious and massive problematic in modern theology than the escalating interest one sees everywhere in a credible doctrine of human nature (*in se*)—this vivid preoccupation with the human side of the divine-human relationship, with our place in nature and society, with our responsibility for human culture, with the equivalence of salvation and human fulfillment? Pelagianism and synergism are no longer "dirty words" (secularism is the latest sacred cow!)—which accounts in large part for the swift eclipse of neo-orthodoxy within the last decade. And yet the old nemesis remains, and has already begun to strike back: humanity's preoccupation with itself is the threshold of the declension into humanism; glib talk of human fulfillment (what Wesley called, in a different context, "holiness of heart and life") may readily lead to the disparagement or denial of grace. "The death of God" is a natural event in any situation where the divine-human relationship is construed in terms of disjunctive *rivalry*!

There is, therefore, a vital mission in the modern world for a theology in search of catholicity, a theology that struggles for the balancing of the divine-human paradox, a theology that holds the middle between fideism and moralism, between "evangelical" and "catholic," between the pneumatic and sacramental dimensions of the church. This cannot mean an antiquarian return to Wesley or to anybody else as arbitrary authority. Wesley was the first to repudiate *that* sort of thing. Even so, there is still something about his way of doing theology that is still open to us as paradigm: (1) to ground it all in Scripture; (2) to match it all against the centuries and the Christian consensus; (3) to keep chording the keys of grace and agency together; (4) to remember, always, the aim of it all: effective mission in the world, effective service to the world for which Christ died. For us and for our future, is there a conceivable alternative more promising?

Do Methodists Have a Doctrine of the Church?

———†———

[1964] Originally published as the lead article in a volume that came out of the 1962 Oxford Institute on Methodist Theological Studies, this essay sets forth Outler's provocative view of the temporary character of Methodism's ecclesiastical existence. He portrays Methodism as an "evangelical order" working best in a larger catholic environment. This temporary movement of "mission, witness, and nurture" now finds itself in a "detraditioned" state of questionable ecumenical status. For the present lack of Methodist consensus about ecclesiology he prescribes a renewed understanding of Methodist origins and the revitalization of Methodism's historic mission in a move forward toward catholicity.

In the way it is posed here this question is a trap for the unwary. The answer "yes" says too much; "no" says too little. "In a manner of speaking," which is more nearly accurate than the other two, seems nevertheless, equivocal. Like many another formally indeterminable question, however, this one is important and it becomes more poignant at every new turn of current church history. Far from being an academic affair amongst ourselves, the shape and thrust of Methodists' notions about the church and about themselves as members of it have deep and wide repercussions, not only in the management of our own internal affairs but in our relationships with the rest of the Christian community in our time.

Thus, I was willing to undertake what I recognized as an ambiguous assignment—not because I have an unambiguous answer to offer or the "true doctrine" of the church to propose. The discussion of this question is useful only because it unfailingly bestirs a cluster of cognate questions, the consideration of which might serve to illuminate what I take to be our real problem: Methodism's place and mission in the current situation of Christianity-in-crisis. The following comments, therefore, are intended to provoke reaction—less to themselves than to the problems they point to. I am far less interested in winning your agreement than I am in the possibility that you may be provoked, even if in a contrary fashion, to join with me in the basic reconsideration of Methodist ecclesiology, which our present circumstances clearly require of us.

Nor have I tried to guard each sentence from the embarrassment of specific qualification and possible amendment. Overcautious lectures make for dull discussions. It might be well, however, to make the otherwise impertinent comment that what is here presented is actually less impromptu and impressionistic than its rhetoric may suggest to certain proper academics!

In the beginning the people called Methodists had no distinctive doctrine of the church—for the very simple reason that they did not need one (and it is a clear rule in church history that Christians do not *think*—i.e., construct doctrines—unless they *have* to). The early Methodists were not a church and they had no intention of becoming one. They understood themselves to be one among a number of religious societies and revival movements in the eighteenth century dedicated to the salvation of souls and the cultivation of the Christian life in its utter seriousness. The specific terms of membership in these societies had no *ecclesiological* reference ("to be saved from their sins and to flee from the wrath to come"), and this by design. The overwhelming majority in the United Societies were already nominal members of the church of England or had at least been baptized therein. John Wesley was a staunch churchman—prepared to be irregular and inconsistent but also to defend his irregularities and inconsistencies on what he took to be *Anglican* principles. Charles Wesley was an actual bigot on the point of conformity. Such ecclesiological notions as the rank-and-file Methodist may have had were strange mixtures of attachment to and alienation from the national church.

This meant that if they had no fully formed or peculiar *doctrine* of the church, they did have a peculiar *problem* in and with the church to which they were related—that is, the Church of England. In its simplest terms, it was the problem of how to be an evangelical order (or society) within a "catholic" (or quasi-catholic) church, which steadfastly refused to sponsor or even to sanction their order and their enterprise. Professor Shipley summed up the early Wesleyan conception as *a ministerium extraordinarium* within the *ministerium ordinarium* of the Church of England. It was *this* notion of being divinely commissioned "extraordinary messengers" that provided the frame for the characteristic organization and program of the original societies. Wesley could "look upon all the world as [his] parish" because, as he explained in a letter of James Hervey, "thus far I mean, that in whatever part of [the world] I am I judge it meet, right, and my bounden duty to declare, unto all that are willing to hear, the glad tidings of salvation. This is the work which I know God has called me to. . . ."[1] In similar vein he could say to his lay assistants: "You have but one business: that of saving souls." It was this limited but central objective that justified the Methodist ecclesiological irregularities—field preaching, lay preaching, Wesley's extra-pa-rochial, supra-diocesan pattern of supervision and control, extemporary prayers in worship, et cetera. Moreover, it justified the

[1][On the *ministerium extraordinarium* and the letter to James Hervey, see *JWO* 19–21, 70–73.]

Methodists' continuing existence as a religious society within the Church of England, despite the latter's massive disapproval of them. It was on this principle that Wesley deliberately designed the pattern of Methodist preaching services so that they would be liturgically insufficient, leaving the Methodist people still dependent on the priests of the national church for the sacraments and the full round of Christian corporate life. Wesley never tired of insisting: "We are *not* Dissenters; we are *not* Sectarians; we will not separate!"

But what were they—these people who were in but not of the eighteenth-century Anglican establishment? They puzzled and offended many an Anglican leader—both the good ones, like Butler and "John Smith" and Edmund Gibson—as well as the bigots, like Lavington and Warburton and Church, who raised the cry of "enthusiasm" and let it go at that. Moreover, the Methodists were a sore puzzle to the Dissenters, who could not understand why such vigorous advocates of holiness would not "come out from among [the corrupt national church] and be separate." It was, therefore, inevitable that as time went on an increasing number of Methodists—though always in a minority—began to regard their situation in the Church of England as anomalous and intolerable. But Wesley knew what the Methodist societies were intended to be and he set himself to make and keep them so, an evangelical order defined by their unique *mission:* "to spread scriptural holiness over these lands."

Once he was involved in it, the Revival dominated the rest of Wesley's life—his preaching, theologizing, writing, publishing, his private and social affairs. He was convinced that the Methodist societies were the chief human agencies of the Revival—and that this was their importance and justification. They were also his hope of reforming the Church of England—not by overthrowing the establishment or even capturing it—but by their actual performance of the church's essential mission, where this was going generally by default. Whatever else Methodism ever was or has since become, its first and most decisive identification was as an enterprise of Christian mission, witness, and nurture.

John Wesley's own doctrine of the church, like the rest of his theology, was an interesting amalgam. Its solid, consistent core was hewn from bedrock deposits in the Anglican tradition, laid down by the tradition of anti-Roman English "catholics"—such as John Jewel and Richard Hooker. For example, the decisive motifs of Jewel's ecclesiology, as seen principally in his controversy with

Thomas Harding, may be summarized under five heads: (1) The church's subordination to Scripture; (2) The church's unity in Christ and the essentials of doctrine; (3) The notion that paradigmata for ecclesiology should be drawn from the patristic age; (4) The apostolic doctrine; (5) The idea of a *functional* episcopacy (as belonging to the church's well being rather than its essence). Each of these motifs re-echoes in Wesley whenever and wherever he refers to the *form* of the church and to its *continuity in historical existence*. The grounds on which Hooker justified and approved continental ordinations are precisely those on which Wesley proved to his own satisfaction that an *exclusively* episcopal polity was not original or classical Anglicanism.

Wesley's view of the church as *a community of liturgy and devotion* was framed from such diverse sources as the Catholic Nonjurors (Hickes, Kettlewell, Ken, Nelson) and the Puritan masters of devotion (Scougal and Baxter). His ideas about the form and administration of the church came, not from the Puritans nor the Dissenters, but from the so-called *latitudinarians* (Stillingfleet, Lord King, Tillotson, *et al.*). Wesley's vision of an evangelical society serving the church almost against its will was a creative synthesis of Anthony Horneck's vision of a church reformed by "religious societies," from the Lutheran and Moravian pietists, from the fourth-century seekers after the perfection of the Christian life, and from the Society of Jesus—about which he had curiously mixed feelings. His sacramental theology was borrowed outright from his father's *Pious Communicant*—from which he took his *Treatise on Baptism*—and from Daniel Brevint's *Christian Sacrament and Sacrifice*. The influence of the continental Reformers in this particular area is never more than indirect—and that from the Protestant moderates (Bucer, Peter Martyr, Melanchthon) mediated largely through Cranmer (*Homilies*), Jewel, *et al.* This goes with his generally dim view of Luther, his *implicit* rejection of Calvin's concept of the New Testament model of the church, and his *explicit* rejection of the sectarian ecclesiologies of the Protestant left wing.

The three primary texts for what we might call Wesley's *resultant* ecclesiology are Sermon LXXIV, "Of the Church"; LXXV, "On Schism"; and the *Minutes* of 1745. Important auxiliary texts are his sermon "On Numbers 23:23" and the one on "The Ministerial Office." There are certain accent points in these texts, which I would like to recall in the framing of the basic hypothesis of this essay.

The catholic or universal church is *coetus credentium*—the entire company of men and women whom God hath called out of the world to give them the power of living faith. The Church of England is that part of this whole company who are inhabitants of England. In this connection Wesley affirms the *positive* meaning of Article XIX but then goes on to reject its negative implication— for, strictly construed, the article excludes members of the Church of Rome from the church catholic, and this Wesley was unwilling to do.

In the sermon "On Schism" Wesley distinguishes between *diversity* amongst Christian groups, and *disunity*. The New Testament sense of "schism," he maintains, is neither more nor less than an alienation of Christians from each other in heart and love—even "though they still continued members of the same external society." Such a "division of heart" may, however, lead to or occasion "schism" in its common usage: *"causeless separation from a body of living Christians. . . ."* "It is only when our love grows cold that we can think of separating from our brethren. . . . The pretences for separation may be innumerable, but want of love is always the real cause; otherwise, they would still hold the unity of the Spirit in the bond of peace."

To those who urged that communion with the Church of England was in itself corrupting—and so concluded, "You ought to separate from the Church of England"—Wesley replied:

> I will make the case my own. I am now, and I have been from my youth, a member and a Minister of the Church of England; and I have no desire nor design to separate from it, till my soul separates from my body. Yet if I was not permitted to remain therein without omitting what God requires me to do, it would then become meet and right, and my bounden duty, to separate from it without delay. To be more particular: I know God has committed to me a dispensation of the gospel; yea, and my own salvation depends upon preaching it. . . . If then I could not remain in the Church without omitting this, without desisting from preaching the gospel, I should be under a necessity of separating from it, or losing my own soul. . . . But, setting aside this case, suppose the Church or society to which I am now united does not require me to do anything which the Scripture forbids, or to omit anything which the Scripture enjoins, it is then my indispensable duty to continue therein. (Sermon LXXV, "On Schism.")

In the *Minutes* of 1745, and in connection with the question of his own status as chief pastor and bishop of the Methodist Societies, Wesley thus summed up his concept of church *polity:*

> The plain origin of church-government seems to be this. Christ sends forth a preacher of the gospel. Some who hear him repent and believe the gospel. They then desire him to watch over them, to build them up in the faith, and to guide their souls in the paths of righteousness. Here then is an independent congregation, subject to no pastor but their own, neither liable to be controlled in things spiritual by any other man or body of men whatsoever [so far, bare-bones, bed-rock Congregationalism].

> But soon after some from other parts, who are occasionally present while he speaks in the name of Him that sent him, beseech him to come over and help them also. Knowing it to be the will of God he consents (complies), yet not till he has conferred with the wisest and holiest of his [original] congregation, and with their advice appointed one who has gifts and grace to watch over the flock till his return [in his absence].

> If it please God to raise another flock in the new place, before he leaves them he does the same thing, appointing one whom God has fitted for the work to watch over these souls also. In like manner, in every place where it pleases God to gather a little flock by his word, he appoints one in his absence to take the oversight of the rest, and to assist them of the ability which God giveth. These are Deacons, or servants of the church, and look upon their first pastor as their common father. And all these congregations regard him in the same light, and esteem him still as the shepherd of their souls.

> These congregations are not strictly independent. They depend on one pastor, though not on each other.

> As these congregations increase, and as the Deacons grow in years and grace, they need other subordinate Deacons or helpers; in respect of whom they may be called Presbyters, or Elders, as their [common] father in the Lord may be called the Bishop or Overseer of them all.[2]

This is, of course, a quite fanciful account of the actual history of the first and second centuries of the Christian church. It

[2]John Bennett's copy of the Minutes of the Conference of 1744, 1745, 1747, 1748. Publication of the Wesley Historical Society, No. 1. London, 1896. Published for the W.H.S. by Charles H. Kelly.

is, however, an almost exact account of the rise of Methodist Societies from 1739 to 1745—and of Wesley's understanding of his own role therein.

The story of the long struggle over separation is gnarled and knotted. I do not myself know all of the requisite data for its intelligible rehearsal. As far as I know, these data do not exist in any accessible form. Nobody has ever put together Wesley's testimony with the corresponding testimony of both his opponents and partisans. There are, however, visible salients in the story—the conference of 1755, where John barely averted a determined push toward separation; Edward Perronet's mischievous doggerel in *The Mitre*; Charles Wesley's horror of separation and his subsequent withdrawal from the Revival (on *this* score more than any other); the increasing clamor of the lay preachers to be treated as equals to the ordained clergy. These serve partially to account for the fact that separation was a perennial issue, renewed at *every* annual conference of which we have a record from 1755 to 1790.

Shortly after the conference of 1755, Wesley wrote to a fellow evangelical clergyman, Samuel Walker (September 1755), in defense of his evangelical order within the Church of England, "irregularities" and all. His main point with Walker is that these so-called irregularities are, each one, functions of the evangelical mission of Christian witness and discipline—and are not necessarily symptoms of dissent. What he would very much like to negotiate, he says, is "a method . . . which, conducted with prudence and patience, will reduce the constitution of Methodism to due order, and render the Methodists under God more *instrumental to the ends of practical religion*" (italics mine).

In all these comments—and everywhere else that I know of—we find the essential *notae ecclesiae* [marks of the church] characterized in a distinctive way. This is what I would call the *classical Methodist* (Wesleyan) *ecclesiology*:

1. The *unity* of the church is based upon the Christian *koinonia* in the Holy Spirit.
2. The *holiness* of the church is grounded in the discipline of grace, which guides and matures the Christian life from its threshold in justifying faith to its plerophory in sanctification.
3. The *catholicity* of the church is defined by the universal outreach of redemption, the essential community of all true believers.

4. The *apostolicity* of the church is gauged by the succession of apostolic doctrine in those who have been faithful to the apostolic witness.

Significantly, and at every point, Wesley defined the church as *act*, as mission, as the enterprise of saving and maturing souls in the Christian life. This vision of the church as mission was to be realized and implemented within the Anglican perspective of the church as form and institution. Moreover, Wesley took some pleasure in appealing from Anglicans drunk to Anglicans sober— from Butler to Jewel, from Lavington to Cranmer, from Warburton to Hooker—and from everybody to the *Articles*, the *Homilies*, and the Book of Common Prayer!

The Methodists did become a church, however—after all and on their own—by a complicated process, which it is partisan to defend and fruitless to deplore. For what it is worth, I might remark in passing that I feel acutely embarrassed as a Methodist who is also a historian because of the lack of an adequately critical, adequately comprehensive rehearsal of British or American Christianity in the half century from 1790 to 1840—and of Methodism's role in that history. Such a thing would be a very useful contribution to modern church history and to ecumenical understanding. It might supply yet more evidence for the thesis of C. H. Dodd's now famous letter about the *"non-theological* factors" that have complicated and frustrated the quest for Christian unity.

What we can say, however, is that Methodism's transition from society to church came in the bright morning of the branch theory of the church, when the analogy of competing business companies made good sense to Christians as a parable for the rivalries of their several sovereign and autonomous "denominations." Moreover, the evolution of Methodism as a denomination proceeded under circumstances which have engendered lasting bitterness between Methodists and Anglicans—exacerbated by the atrabilious tempers of the Tractarian controversy. The effect of this was to push the Methodists into the arms of dissent with something like enthusiasm so that they came quickly to be almost indistinguishable from the other free churches in most observable respects.

The historical patterns of this transition from society to denomination are tangled and vary widely from country to country and from time to time. It first began in the United States, then in Great Britain and elsewhere. One of the most interesting instances was in Canada, where the evolution of Methodism took yet another course from that in the States or in Britain. This needs to be understood if the later development of the United Church of Canada is to be understood. In every instance, however, the transitional process involved a series of borrowings and symbiotic adaptations. Typically, when Methodists have felt a lack in matters ecclesiological they have looked about for whatever seemed handy and truly useful—and then proceeded to adapt it to their own uses and purposes (often quite different from the original). Examples of this sort of thing in American Methodism are (1) "episcopal polity," (2) the scheme of representation and delegation in the Conference system, (3) the written Constitution of 1808, and (4) the patterns of frontier expansion and settlement. In England (or so it seems to an American who is scarcely expected to understand such things—really!) Methodists came to be increasingly so far estranged from the Church of England (for reasons that have varied from pique to righteous indignation) that they found themselves readier to adapt to the patterns of dissent and sectarianism. This tendency in Methodism after Wesley to borrow from left and right gave rise to a theory of the church as a *coincidentia oppositorum* [coincidence of opposites]. As William B. Pope put it,

> To [the church] there are certain attributes assigned. . . . These qualities are Unity, Sanctity, Invisibility, Catholicity, Apostolicity, Indefectibility, Glory. But we also find by the side of these . . . qualities in some measure their counterparts or opposites: such as Diversity, Imperfection, Visibility, Localisation, Confessionalism, Mutability, and Militant Weakness. Hence we gather that the true church of Christ is a body in which these opposite attributes unite.[3]

One way and another then, Methodism in the nineteenth century evolved from an evangelical order in a catholic (or quasi-catholic) church into a low-church Protestant denomination or congeries of denominations, but always with subtle differentiations from its congeners—those groups that were more nearly linear descendants of the continental Reformation. As firmly committed as other Protestants to *sola scriptura*, the Methodists were also Arminian and anti-antinomian, and thus never *quite* like the Reformed traditions in their interpretation of *sola fide*. The

---

[3]*A Compendium of Christian Theology*, III:266–67.

theological consequences of this were very considerable—as Dale Dunlap has shown in his Yale dissertation.

In America the Methodists were low church to begin with, differing violently with the Baptists—and later the Campbellites—on such matters as "believer's baptism," immersion, and "the connexional system," but becoming very familiar to them in many other respects, e.g., in social typology and ethos. In the present century—for such are the vagaries of ecclesiological ecology—the well buckets have reversed themselves, and now American Methodists have been drifting toward congregational autonomy at a great rate, while the Baptists and the Christians are on their way to becoming almost as connectional as the Methodists used to be. Moreover, there are both Baptist and Christian congregations that now dedicate infants—and a great many Methodists who baptize them with what looks and sounds as if it were the same basic theory of what is going on, or *not* going on! At the same time, however, both British and American Methodists still preserve selected, mutilated remains of the Book of Common Prayer for various ritual and ceremonial purposes. In the current revival of interest in liturgical reform a good deal of it is patently imitative. My point is that if we are to understand the anomalies of Methodist ecclesiology—or anything else doctrinal in Methodism—we must take this deep-seated symbiotic tendency into account.

Nevertheless, in this history of being a church without having been intended to be one, there are landmarks which remind us that Methodists, when they really face up to the task of self-understanding, usually recover their racial memory of the evangelical order that once upon a time was raised up on an emergency basis to extend and deepen the reach of the gospel witness in uncommissioned service to the church's essential mission. To do the work of the church in default of the church's being the church in its ideal fullness—if we take Richard Watson and William B. Pope as exemplary, as on this point I think we can—we quickly discover that, for each of them, ecclesiology is an auxiliary concern claiming very little of their genius or originality, which is devoted in large measure to what might nowadays be called "the theology of evangelism."

For Watson the first business of theology is to exhibit the derivation of doctrine from revelation—and so to connect the preaching of the gospel with its source. The bulk of the *Institutes* (Part I) is devoted to the authority of the Holy Scriptures and to

"Doctrines of the Holy Scriptures" (Part II)—with "Redemption" (II, xix-xxix) the vital core of the entire system. In "The Institutions of Christianity" (Part IV) he expounds a view of the church as a spiritual fellowship of believers that (should never be "established" but must have powers of government and discipline—all of them *functional*. Baptism is interpreted—as in Samuel Wesley—in covenantal terms, to be administered to infants, and normally by sprinkling. As for the Lord's Supper, he concludes that Article XXVIII, in its 1662 version—and without certain particular expressions in the liturgy—"must be taken to be the opinion of the Church of England upon this point, and it substantially agrees with the New Testament" (Part II, 667).

For Pope the heart and center of Christian truth is soteriology, and this as grounded in the atonement and expressed in the Christian life of faith and holiness. Pope's doctrine of the church is frankly eclectic and mediating—taking the Anglican *Articles* in their pre-Laudian interpretation, but interpreting their consequences in a staunchly Non-conformist temper. His liveliest comments come when he describes the church as the organ of the Holy Spirit and the matrix for the maturation of faith. Here he homes in on the Methodist class meeting (in one of his rather rare positive references in *The Pecularities of Methodist Doctrine* [1873], pp. 18–19):

> Throughout the world, but especially in Great Britain, the Methodist people hold fast the tradition of a Christian communion which confesses the name of Jesus not only before men generally, as in the Eucharist, but in the assemblies of the brethren themselves. Not that we have a monopoly of this kind of fellowship. Meetings for mutual confession, and edification and counsel have always been aimed at in the purest ages and purest forms of the Church: but *we are the only community that has incorporated them in the very fibre of our constitution.* Growing out of our society character, this institution we have aimed to interweave with the organization of the Church also: not yet with perfect success but with results that encourage *the hope of perfect success.* As it is rooted in our ecclesiastical economy, so it is rooted in the affections of our people. No form in which the social element of Christianity has found expression has enlisted more universal enthusiasm in its favour than the old class meeting. Other forms of confederation have been gloried in, lived for, and sometimes died for, in the history of Christendom. But I question if any institution, grafted on scriptural precepts,

has ever commanded such widespread and pervading homage of all orders of the devout, or approved itself by such practical and irresistible evidences of good, as the Methodist class-meeting. . . . Incautious and unskillful hands have been meddling with it of late; but in vain. It may admit of much improvement in detail and in administration, but its foundations are secure and inviolable.

Would to God he had been right on this last point!

In the twentieth century Methodism, in America at least, has undergone a radical metamorphosis, which naturally affects any ecclesiological reflection that goes on within our ranks or about us by others. It is an oversimplification in the direction of the truth to say that this was chiefly the effect of German-Enlightenment theology assimilated into a tradition which had lost its vital traditionary linkage with classical Methodism. One way of describing the outcome of this development would be to say that we have passed beyond the gravitational field of our historical origin and are now in what might be called a condition of weightlessness as far as our peculiar history is concerned—a detraditioned state of mind and polity. In America at least, Methodism is an "established church" (in the sociological sense) in which the maintenance and expansion of the establishment has become an undeclinable prime duty for almost everyone associated with it.

Ecclesiologically speaking, however, we are a church after the order of Melchizedek. Estranged from our Anglican heritage— for reasons that range from cogent to paranoid—having no blood ties with any other mode of catholic Christianity (as the Lutherans and Calvinists have even in their *anti*-Romanism), and having become too "worldly" and middle-class a movement ever to make genuine common cause with the Radical Protestants and the Pentecostalists, we are Christians whose institutional forms are uniquely our own but whose theological apparatus has been assembled from many quarters—whose place in the ecumenical movement is painfully equivocal.

For all this derivative and symbiotic behavior there remains a deep, almost instinctive awareness among us that our foremost and final justification for being the church that we are is still precisely the same as the justification for our having first been an evangelical order within *ecclesia Anglicana*—namely, Christianity in dead earnest, distinguished chiefly in our evangelical concern for the Christian mission, witness, nurture—"holiness of heart

and life." I cannot myself point to any contemporary ecclesiological formulation or formula that I would now acknowledge as *the*
"Methodist doctrine of the Church." But I honestly think I can
recognize a constant and comparatively consistent concern
amongst Methodists that strikes me as characteristic and peculiar.
The church is "a company of faithful men" (i.e., *a movement with a
mission*) "in which the Word rightly preached [evangelism] and
the sacraments duly administered" [worship], together with
everything else that is relevant and requisite to getting the rightly
preached Word truly heard and the duly administered sacraments
rightly received (Christian *discipline*, or nurture). Our *notae ecclesia*
are, therefore, evangelism, worship, discipline. It interests me to
notice that whenever the motif of *the mission of the evangelical order*
is mentioned in an assembly of Methodists, it strikes a responsive
chord, even if in contexts that are sometimes faintly bizarre. In the
crucial and profound debates over the issues currently paramount
in the Faith and Order Commission of the World Council of
Churches, for example, one sometimes gets the impression that
the Methodists are not really listening—at least, not with their
"third ear." But when someone speaks incisively about the church
in essential action, even the most over-institutionalized Methodist
in "the connexion" snaps to attention—and feels at least a fleeting
impulse to report for duty.

The drift of these comments is that Methodism has never lost
the *essence* of a *functional* doctrine of the church but that, by the
same token, it has never developed—on its own and for itself—
the full panoply of bell, book, and candle that goes with being a
"proper" church properly self-understood. This makes us *une
église manqué* [a failed, incomplete church], theoretically and
actually. But this raises the question of our relations to other
denominations, which is to say our ecclesiastical "foreign relations"—those that we maintain within the pan-denominational
pattern of the World Methodist Council or those we share in the
interdenominational patterns of the World Council of Churches
(and, *mutatis mutandis*, national and regional councils of churches).

It is by now a commonplace that the ecumenical movement
is one of the great facts of current Christian history. It is also
common knowledge that Methodists have had interesting
difficulties in finding and taking their place in the full round of the
operations of the World Council of Churches. In the process some
fairly stupid stereotypes have emerged that go on generating or
perpetuating what the psychiatrists call a parataxic relationship

between Methodists and non-Methodists. I, for one, am rather weary of them, but they continue to haunt us at conference after conference.

I have suggested that there is not now, and there has not been for at least two generations, even a modicum of a *consensus fidelium Methodistica* in ecclesiology. In respect of the ministry, more Methodists would agree on the main issues relating to the minister's *role* than on the theological basis of the ministerial *office*. As for questions about apostolicity, catholicity, episcopal polity, the meaning of ordination, and the power of the keys in discipline and excommunication, et cetera—there is no recognizable consensus anywhere and no conceivable prospect of one.

Thus, in America at least, Methodists still practice infant baptism by effusion—but the vast majority would balk at both the premises and consequences of Wesley's *Treatise on Baptism* if they were confronted by it. As for the Eucharist, there is a wide area of confusion in respect of the nature of sacramental grace and on God's presence and action at the Table of the Lord.

As Methodism goes on being—and having to be—a church, it will be increasingly harassed and embarrassed by the consequences entailed in the tension between *ecclesia per se*—institutional maintenance and management—and *ecclesia in actu*—proclamation, nurture, and service. If this continues for the next half century as it has for the last, we shall be in a sorry shape for sure. If we go on borrowing and patching and playing with pious gimmicks, we shall not only become ridiculous in the eyes of yet older *poseurs* in our divided Christian family, but our proud claim to a valid heritage may very well become suspect.

One of our difficulties, I suggest, is that Methodism's unique ecclesiological pattern was really designed to function best *within* an encompassing environment of *catholicity* (by which I mean what the word meant originally: the effectual and universal Christian *community*). We don't do so well by our lonesome as some other denominations appear to do—and for a good reason. Preoccupation with self-maintenance distracts us from what is actually our peculiar *raison d'etre*. This is why a self-conscious and denomination-centered Methodist is such a crashing bore to all but his own particular kith, kin, and kind.

Methodism arose as a divinely instituted project—*ad interim!* There can be no doubt that the Wesleys, and most of the early Methodists, understood their enterprise as the effort to meet an emergency situation with needful, extraordinary measures. As with the eschatological views of the New Testament Christians, the "emergency" has lengthened and the "emergency crew" has acquired the character of an establishment. But we lose perspective whenever we forget that we are still more deeply rooted than we realize in the motifs and spirit of the eighteenth-century origins. We need a catholic church within which to function as a proper evangelical order of witness and worship, discipline and nurture. Yet, it is plain to most of us that none of the existing unilateral options are suitable alternatives to our existing situation. The way to catholicism—i.e., Christian unity—is *forward*—toward the *renewal* of catholicity rather than in *return* to something that has lost its true status as truly catholic. Meanwhile, since we *are* a church, it is more than a practical convenience that requires of us that we try to act responsibly in the exercise of our churchly character. This means, among many other things, the reconsideration of our own traditions and their role in that *traditionary process* by which Christianity lives and maintains its authentic continuity with the Christian past and its openness to the ecumenical future. It also means a major reconsideration of the obligations we have as a church in respect of *catechetical instruction*, in more adequate provision for group discipline and therapy, in the ministries of the general priesthood and of the meaning of our own representative priesthood. Almost above all else, it means the acceptance of the liturgical and sacramental obligations of being a church for so long as God requires it of us, pending a really valid alternative of authentic Christian unity.

Every denomination in a divided and broken Christendom is an *ecclesiola in via* [church in pilgrimage], but Methodists have a peculiar heritage that might make the transitive character of our ecclesiastical existence not only tolerable but positively proleptic. On our pilgrimage toward the actualization of the unity in Christ that God has given us and still wills for us to have, we can take both courage and zest from the fact that what we really have to contribute to any emergent Christian community is not our apparatus but our mission. Meanwhile, however, we must ourselves beware lest, in this business of having to be a church while waiting for the church that is to be, we should deceive ourselves by falling further into the fatuity that this business of "being a church" is really our *chief* business!

The Mingling of
Ministries

———†———

[1968] Outler's life-long personal pilgrimage toward unity
and catholicity is evidenced in this study-paper written for
the Consultation on Church Union. Addressing the ecumenical problem of moving from the recognition of "valid"
ministerial orders to "mingled ministries," he offers a
series of proposals that might allow a path between the
false alternatives of reordination on the one side and
indifferentism on the other. Outler argues for a concept of
"validity" grounded in the Spirit. This means a catholicity
that combines theological integrity with a refusal to
repudiate the separate traditions that have mediated
Christian identity. His loyalty to the Methodist tradition is
clear, yet he suggests a Spirit-guided traditioning process
by which the divided churches might experience "death
and resurrection in the Christian tradition."

It is a commonplace by now that the last ecumenical enemy to be overcome is the disparity of ministerial order in our divided churches. Given the current realization that a disciplined theological diversity goes with the genius of Christian thought, something better than a wan hope arises that an adequate doctrinal consensus is at least conceivable—that doctrine, as such, is not the final barrier to our recovery of Christian unity. The proof of this, is the relative ease with which chapter I of the Consultation on Church Union's "Principles" was put together. By the same token, "worship" and "sacraments"—at least theoretical statements about their essential meaning and functions—are no longer widely felt as insuperable obstacles.

The case for "structure" stands on different grounds. Here, our primary concern is not the vital essence or the mission of the church, but rather its practical management—i.e., the clutch of political, economic, psychological means that might best serve the church's missional ends. Ecclesial means and ends are morally coordinate, of course; but the structures of the church are not themselves ingredient in the knowledge of our salvation. Their forms—and, above all, their spirit—are not ecclesiologically neutral, but the measures for their efficacy come from the philosophical virtues of prudence and justice rather more than they do from the theological virtue of charity, as such. At any rate, there is no sound theological reason known to me that requires a negative prognosis for more unified church structures than our present COCU churches exhibit. One might hope that whatever structures are evolved *by* the managers will not be designed chiefly *for* the managers (as most ecclesiastical arrangements are).

In the matter of ministry and ministerial order, however, we have a fearful tangle: doctrine, human feelings, "spiritual" convictions that cannot be compromised, cherished practices that cannot readily be reconciled. Here the burden of our separate histories weighs heaviest upon us: the promise of a radically new future is offset by the specter of betrayal and repudiation of our past loyalties—the shame of dishonoring those who gave us whatever Christian identity we have. At the heart of it all is the crucial conviction of each of the separated ministerial orders—a conviction vital to their vital exercise—that each of them has been honored and blessed in their actual operation by the Holy Spirit, in some honest measure of validity. This sort of conviction cuts both ways: a minister who had come to regard his or her ordination as invalid would have no problem about the *mingling* of *that* ministry with others; similarly, those who regard their own orders as exclusively valid can scarcely negotiate the mingling of such superior credentials with other orders deemed invalid or fatally defective. Here, then, is the crunch. None of us in COCU is disposed openly to deny the validity of the ministerial orders of the other member churches (or are we?)—but we have no visible or familiar precedent for translating this implicit recognition of *valid* orders into *mingled* and *shared* orders. The ghost in this machine is pathetically obvious: it is the haunting fear of *re*-ordination, which is sustained by the fear of disloyalty to and repudiation of what we have been. If *re*-ordination is the price of union, many of us will simply have to forego it, in calm good conscience. Ordination, in any of its theories, is a non-repetitive sacrament (or sacramental, or ordinance or whatever). *Re*-ordination, in any *strict* sense, is therefore a contradiction in terms—or else it is an agreement that what had passed before for ordination had been a mistake, "absolutely null and utterly void," as the Romans have said of Anglican orders. This means *repudiation*, not only of those who ordained you but also a denial of the blessings of the Spirit upon your ministry, modest and irregular as it may have been, and this is pneumatologically intolerable. One preliminary conclusion, therefore, is quickly and clearly come by: there can be no mingling of ministries in COCU (or otherwise) if any of the ministries involved is to be repudiated or abandoned, on principle or by licit implication. I have no problem with the fact that, in some sense of the term, my Methodist orders are "irregular"—or even "defective," in the specific sense that they do not amount to an authorization by the whole People of God, to act representatively in and for that whole People. They are not, and never have been, *plene et perfecte* [full and perfect]. But these orders were received in good faith; they have been exercised in good faith; they have been honored, far past any personal merit of mine, by the Holy Spirit. I could, quite conceivably, renounce them and so resume my "lay" (i.e., private) status in the general Christian priesthood. But to repudiate them in exchange for another "set" would be an offense against the integrity and *true* catholicity of the church that would require such a thing of me.

My lifelong devotion to the cause of Christian unity has never included *this* as an acceptable means to a passionately cherished end.

This would seem to bring us to an impasse, especially between those who claim to be able to validate my defective orders and those who are eager to have the representative range of their existing orders enlarged (made more truly universal), *not*, however, at the price of abjuration. If, for example, it were allowed that the Protestant Episcopal Church does in fact possess "the historic episcopate in apostolic succession" (a supposition contrary to fact in the eyes of Roman Catholics, officially, and most Orthodox), how then could Methodist ministerial orders be mingled with Anglican—in the light of the muddle of 1784 and thereafter? And how can Anglican orders be mingled with Presbyterian and Campbellite ordinations—standing as they do in traditions that have, at least in times past, conscientiously rejected the typical Anglican concept of succession? The easy—and insupportable!—answer is: *re*-ordination or more bluntly, *ordination*. If this is all that we have to negotiate, then we are wasting our breath—and, more tragically, our hope.

Mutatis mutandis, if it is allowed that congregational, presbyterial and episcopal ministries are all valid and fruitful in some sense and in varying ways—not in accordance with the personal qualities of the clergy involved but in virtue of their representative office and character as "authorized ministers" of Word, Sacrament and Order—how then are such differences and defects as may be alleged against them (e.g., their incomplete representativeness) ever to be reconciled or repaired?

The first point we'd do well to agree to forthwith is that there is no *status quo ante* in our separate histories to which we can all return, so as to allow a fresh start from scratch. Our histories, in this sense, are quite irreversible. Our only way is forward; our only hope is "convergence."

A second point is almost as important: the amiable blurring of basic differences in church polity will lead only to trouble, in either of two alluring courses toward disaster. One of them waves the banner of indifferentism and exhorts against unworthy caution: "What's the difference; go ahead and m-e-e-r-r-ge! Love and the Spirit will conquer all." Then there are those, on the other side, who say, "Let's everybody ordain (or re-ordain) everybody else and then let the *Holy Spirit* unscramble the resulting exchange of ministerial status!" Both proposals are actually smokescreens:

the first conceals a willingness to cancel the historic meaning of ministerial order (which would actually amount to the abandonment of the ecumenical quest itself); the second simply postpones the time when somebody will claim that *they* re-ordained (or ordained!) "the others," or else somebody complains that *they've* been *had*!

A third point is so obvious as to be banal, yet it is all too easily underestimated. We haven't got forever to stand patiently in this increasingly acute frustration. If the hunger for *ecclesial* unity (real unity: *communicatio in sacris* [communication in holy things]) is not satisfied in the reasonably near future, it will mutate and seek out alternative satiations—as our "secular" and "underground" ecumenists are already reminding us.

One way through this impasse that I think I see, if only in a glass darkly, begins with a first premise that the Christian unity we are actually seeking is parity of membership and ministry— nothing less, surely, and not much more, really. Give us an open community—of all who

> are baptized with water and in the Triune Name, who confess Jesus Christ as Lord and Savior, who congregate to hear God's Word rightly preached and to receive Christ's sacraments duly administered, who serve the Great Commission (Matthew 28:19-20) in word and deed, and whose lives manifest God's ministry of reconciliation in Christ (2 Corinthians 5:18-20), are members of Christ's Body, the Church, and truly "members one of another" (1 Corinthians 12:27; Ephesians 4:25).[1]

Give us a church that would hold that *any* person in *any* church with such "marks" is rightly and fully a member in any *other* church that holds the same. Then, would we not have a Christian community that could defend itself against the usual distortions of ecclesiastical monarchy, oligarchy or monopoly?

How far are we *now* from some such parity of membership, in theory and practice? It is a fact (or is it?) that all ecumenically minded Christians—and their churches—recognize and acknowledge the validity of the *baptisms* and the confessions of faith in Jesus Christ as Lord of their separated Christian brothers and

[1]"Marks of Church Membership," Resolution on Ecumenical Commitment, The United Methodist Church. General Conference, 1968. *Daily Christian Advocate* (April 29, 1968), 280.

sisters, at least in some other churches. This recognition of baptism is not (or can it be?) by reference to "clinical" and "lay" baptism, *in extremis* [i.e., baptism performed at the point of death]. If so, who has been conning whom for how long? If baptism is a dominical and universal sacrament and yet does not require a representative (i.e., ordered) ministry for its *usual* administration, then why an ordained ministry at all? But if such baptisms are deemed valid and if baptism is regarded as a sacrament or dominical ordinance, then such acceptance of another's baptism truly is *communicatio in sacris*. But if, again, we are in actual (even if limited) sacramental communion with each other in terms of our mutually recognized baptisms, what then of the validity of those *ministerial orders* of those who administered those baptisms admitted by us to have been valid? Valid baptisms imply valid orders! This, in my view, is the first and crucial step on our way to a mingling of our ministries in yet fuller and more perfect representativeness. For if an Anglican minister acknowledges the validity of the baptisms I have performed—and *vice versa*—then our ministries are already and undeniably mingled on this level and to this extent, before and apart from re-ordination, or ordination, either way.

The *next* step on this same way is trickier. It has to do with confirmation or the completion of the implicit commitments of baptism by the voluntary acceptance by the baptized person of those commitments: his or her appropriation of the life in Christ into which baptism had been the initiation (and this would be the case in "believer's baptism" as well, in a somewhat reversed fashion—i.e., "confirmation" there usually *precedes* baptism). The ancient church (so Dix, *et. al.*) taught that baptism and confirmation were two parts of the *one* sacrament of Christian initiation, or else twin sacraments of initiation, both vitally complementary—neither truly meaningful without the other. If this is the case, can they then be divided so that one church can recognize another's baptisms and still deny their confirmations—which is to say, deny the parity of their church membership? The answer, of course, is "Yes, they can and they do!" Is this not the official position of the Anglicans *vis-à-vis* members of other churches in COCU? But on what ground and by what justification? Can it be that the same minister who is somehow authorized to administer valid baptism is somehow disqualified from confirming or receiving that same baptized person (or another) into the church? If so, why? To acknowledge baptism and deny confirmation makes a mockery of any proposed *parity of membership*. To accept *both*, however, would point the way, however dimly, toward a conceivable formula for a parity of both membership and ministries as well. This is why one can say that the extent to which "irregular" baptism/confirmation has come to be acknowledged as *valid*—i.e., parity of membership—is an almost exact measure of the ecumenical progress we have made in the past half century. Ecumenical dialogue, *par cum pari* [equal among equals], can mean nothing less than dialogue between members of the Body of Christ. Anything else is sort of refined religious toleration—and if this is what ecumenism is all about, it's a sham and a sell.

Now, suppose we could agree, even roughly, that members of the ordained ministry are related to the "general priesthood" (1 Peter 2:5, 9) as their authorized surrogates for the entire community of the baptized, for the specific purposes of representing that entire community in pastoral, sacral, and corporate offices that manifest the community as a whole. Such a ministry is representative in two ways: (1) representative of Christ who through his Spirit dwelling in the church, continues his earthly ministry in, for and through the pilgrim People of God; (2) representative of this *People* in those official and symbolic manifestations of their consensus in Word, Sacrament, and Order and their united action in Christ's name, in witness and service. Ordained men and women are, therefore, the symbols and agents of the *catholicity* of the church—or the *lack* of catholicity of the particular church whose orders they bear. Both the chief problem and the chief hope of the ecumenical endeavor is to extend the catholicity of ministerial orders of the divided churches until they become coextensive with the catholicity of the People of God entire.

There must, of course, be specific and identifying marks of such authentic representation, and the crucial question here is whether such marks must be chiefly *formal* (e.g., the imposition of hands, the *porrectio instrumentorum*, episcopal or presbyterial election, etc.) or chiefly *functional* and pneumatic—or what mixture of both? I would suggest that the *substance* of authentic representative ministry lies in three concurrent manifestations of God's calling and "ordaining" a person to exercise the office of *representative* minister in the church of Christ. The first, of course, is spiritual *vocation*—the clear, compelling sense of interest, aptitude and commitment, not to those general goals of "service" and "human welfare" that are imperatives for all baptized Christians, but to the specific endeavors (in all their variety) appropriate to the sacral representation of the People of God. This sense of "calling" must be matched, however, by comparable spiritual *gifts and graces*, for a truly representative ministry. A man or woman must have the requisite objective talents and qualifications and these must be open to candid assessment by responsible authorities in the church. Good intentions without supporting competences corrupt the church even before they go on to pave the nether regions. But where there is a genuine call, together with the requisite gifts and graces, there must also, thirdly, be spiritual *"fruits"* (Gal. 5:22–23)—accessible evidence of effective performance of the tasks and roles of representative ministry (cf. Matt. 7:16, 20).

Men and women with such spiritual vocations, gifts, graces and fruits are presumably more likely to be valid ministers, *with or without formal ordination*, than those who may possess formally regular ordinations and who lack one or more of the "marks" of the called and ordainable ministry. But if this *is* the case, then the ministries of those whose marks and fruits of the Holy Spirit are manifest and verifiable could somehow be *mingled* without the reimposition of hands by a suitable act of mutual acknowledgment (say a *real* Kiss of Peace!) that would indeed be a service of *reconciliation!* Why not? If it were alleged and believed that such a mingling was agreeable to the will of God, whose spirit has blessed and honored these orders now to be mingled, what doctrinal consideration would suffice to deny that what the Spirit has honored no church ought rashly to dishonor?

It is the painful truth that our separate histories have resulted in divided ministries which few of us have chosen *because* they were divided or *because* they were "irregular" or "defective"—or, indeed, in the presence of really open alternatives in the range of choice amongst holy orders we had before us—as far as any specific *doctrine* of holy orders is concerned. One would think that the number of intentional and principled *schismatics* in the ministries of the COCU member churches must be reckoned as a minority. For example, when I accepted the Methodist orders I now have, I did not consciously *exclude*, or reject, other ministerial orders; a more fully catholic ordination was not a live option under the actual circumstances—and it still isn't. Over the years, I have had an honest and ardent *votum* [prayer] both for membership *and* ministerial *orders* that would be universally representative; indeed, this *votum* is one of my less ambivalent and befuddled ecumenical motivations. But the only hope I have of this lies in the mingling of my ministry with that of others through an ordination of the Holy Spirit—still the first and final arbiter of ministerial order in the church of God.

By the same token, though, the ministerial orders of my separated brethren are also themselves plainly defective in *their* catholicity, in greater or lesser degree. Even if one ignores the Roman and Orthodox rejection of Anglican orders, the Anglicans still represent a smallish fraction of the Christian community (as small even as *that* is in the human community at large). The Presbyterians represent a somewhat larger fraction, the Congregationalist churches a smaller one; Methodists are more numerous but not always self-consciously concerned to be "catholic." But what does *this* signify? Our own respective defects are not simple functions of our minority status. The fact is that none of us can quite confidently report a fully responsible trusteeship of the Christian heritage that we have received (or have had accessible). Our separate histories have been too narrow or divisive for that. In this sense, *none* of us is apostolic, *plene et perfecte.*

It is simply not the case, therefore, that in COCU (or any other ecumenical negotiation) we are dealing with any one instance of one (or more) fully adequate ministerial order(s) capable of and favorably disposed toward conferring the fullness of that perfect order on eight other ministries whose orders are so far defective that they cannot be deemed valid without some such reparation. Any proposal for mingling our ministries must, therefore, begin with the mutual recognition of all of them as valid, at least in point of their *ministerial intention* (i.e., the intent and authority truly to represent the People of God, etc., etc.). The warrant for this would be our recognition in them of the marks of a called ministry and the blessings of the Holy Spirit in their ministries.

It might then proceed to a mutually consented formulation of those canons, criteria, and commitments that belong to the character, office, and exercise of faithful ministry in the church in the name of Christ. Its crucial point would be that it is the Holy Spirit who makes valid ministers—in and by the church but not by any ecclesiastical *opus operato* or even *opus operans.* This prescription for valid ministry would become a cause for conscientious subscription by all those currently in orders in the COCU member churches—and, in this sense, it would serve as "the examination by the church" that is presupposed, in some form or other, in all the ordinals. This would settle the primary question of *validity*—or, perhaps, it would amount to the existential *confirmation* of the mutual recognition of orders that already has been implied by our mutual recognition of *baptism* and by our ecumenical experience of worship and work together. Men and women now "in orders" who declined such a subscription or failed to pass such an examination would be demitted from the ministry, as quietly and gracefully as might be, before the Service of Reconciliation. It would then suffice to devise a liturgical "happening" in which our *vota* [prayers] for catholic orders would be offered to the Spirit—the Lord and giver of order in the church!—for the Spirit's honoring, blessing and renewal!

What makes holy orders *holy*? Answer: their being sanctified by the Spirit—in the call, gifts, and blessings. What else? What makes holy orders *catholic*? Answer: their authorization and acceptance by the whole People of God. Who else? What makes holy and catholic orders *apostolic*? Aye—there's the rub! For apostolicity has to do with the unique history of the Christian church—with the circumstance that the *style* of its aboriginal *koinonia* was shaped by apostolic individuals in the "apostolic age" and that the persistence of the good essence of this "apostolic style" has been a perennial factor in the avowed purpose and claim of the church in history, chiefly because of the very continuity of the church, as the extension throughout history of the apostolic witness to Christ turns on the fact of its apostolic rootage. From the beginning the continuity of this style has been the most obvious measure of orthodoxy, deviation from it the surest sign of schism or heresy. This was the deepest concern of the traditionary process; indeed, tradition and apostolicity have always been correlative notions (the one the process by which the other is preserved). And in the tradition of apostolicity, the notion of strict, unbroken continuity was variously maintained; sometimes by the presbyters, sometimes by the presbyters-cum-bishop, sometimes by the bishops (until the Reformation). In the beginning, "episcopal" and "presbyterial" were closely related (the synonymous usage of "presbyter" and "*priest*" does not occur until the early Middle Ages!). The succession of one's orders from an apostle, or apostolic church, was a powerful presumption in favor of one's *regularity* and *authority* in holy orders. Irenaeus is the classic advocate of the decisive importance of episcopal succession; his views were widely shared, in his own time and thereafter, and form the substance of the theory of strict succession, then and now.

But there is an all-important distinction to be made between the episcopal succession as the *regular, normal, proper* mode of apostolic and presbyterial continuity and this same episcopal succession as the *strictly exclusive mode* of apostolic continuity and validity. For this would presume that the demonstrable fact of such a mode was historically verifiable; it would also presuppose a literal continuity of episcopal succession throughout all ages since the death of the last apostle, with no breaks, lacunae, hiatus—and with no taint of heresy, schism or excommunication! Who will argue that *this* case can be made *on historical grounds*—either for the penumbral zones of the second century or for the long haul of the papal succession, or for the limited case of the presbyterate of Alexandria, or for the presbyterates of the Reformation churches, or in the continuity of ministerial order and function in the history of missions (e.g., Church of South India, etc.)? I find it agreeable on many grounds to accept and cherish the historic episcopate as ingredient in the good order of any truly catholic and apostolically oriented ministry. It is one of the principal modes of continuity and collegiality that has contributed to the *regularity* and concord of ministry in the church. But the notion that episcopal ordination is an absolute prerequisite for ministerial *validity* is a manifest *non sequitur*—on grounds historical, ecclesiological or pneumatological.

If, then, the new church is to have "the historic episcopate"—and this, I take it, is already a prior agreement in the "Principles" (p. 48)—then it must be achieved by means of a *per saltum* [a breaking through] acceptance, *by all*, of the validity of those existing ministries already in COCU, and already recognized by all as *valid*. This, then, could and should be followed by some sort of reinstitution of the process of *regularization* of the ministry of the united church in its consequent polity and practice. Its ordinal should provide for as much apostolic traditioning as possible. Such "breaks" (*salta*) have occurred before—in Alexandria, in the Dark Ages, in the early decades of the Anglican Reformation! The one proposed here for COCU would be a rather more spectacular *saltum* than some others, in terms of the interims and numbers involved, but it would not be really different in ecclesial or pneumatological *principle*. If Rome and Constantinople were able to cancel a five-hundred-year-old excommunication without repudiations, maybe Anglicans and Methodists could manage to do as well.

In this way, the Episcopal Church could indeed supply to the united church and its ministry its distinctive treasure of the historic episcopate—and this would be most welcome and edifying!—but not to the existing ministries of the churches that would form the union. The Episcopal Church would be expected to acknowledge—with any reservations she felt that fell short of veto—the *validity* of such ministerial orders as conformed to the canons of faith, calling, and qualifications that might be devised for the united church. Other churches would be expected to acknowledge that, henceforth, episcopal consecrations in the united church would always be shared in by bishops in "the apostolic succession" (with whatever reservations they may have, short of veto, as to the historic *fact* of *this* succession in the Episcopal Church). Thus, in due course, ministerial order in the united church would become *regular*—but the question of their *validity* and efficacy would remain to be determined on the same grounds as have really been applicable since St. Paul's calling and commission.

One of the practical consequences of this argument is that, in the formation of the united church, a service of mutual ordination or re-ordination would be ruled out—as hopelessly ambiguous both in theory and probably interpretation. There is, however, a conceivable alternative that might be less ambiguous and might be more creative. The church is a covenant community and in the genesis of the "new" church a "new covenant" of mutual understandings and commitments—*including the ministry*—could be drawn up and subscribed to by all. Its burden would be to express our mutual acceptance of each other (as churches, as fellow members and fellow ministers in Christ's body) and to spell out the implications of these acceptances—in doctrine, liturgy and in the tangle of our several histories that we are bringing into the new church to be transformed into a new history (and a new ministry). It would speak, presumably, about the discrepancies between our professions of a valid ministry and our performance in it (not chiefly because of the defects in our orders but because of our disobedience to the Spirit!). It would specify our rightful expectations of the new ministry in the new church; it would celebrate the precious offertory that each church brings to the treasury of the new (including over diverse accents in *ministerial style*)—and whatever else rightly needs sublation and sanctification in this venture of ours in submitting our separate traditions to the Holy Spirit for death and resurrection in *the Christian tradition.* In this way, or something like it, we could dramatize our best intentions, confess our faults, identify our convictions as to the *source* of our new-found unity and project our future as far as our own voluntary dispositions can affect it. It could be a brave beginning in the new life of the new church—catholic, evangelical, and reformed: a good omen that it would be more nearly one, holy, catholic, and apostolic than any of our member churches now is.

The two most urgent *theoretical* questions posed by this alternative on which its *practical* conclusions turn are:

1. The theology of confirmation—or reception into the membership of the church. Are baptism and confirmation (or reception) so far separate that one may be allowed as valid and the other denied—except in extreme or abnormal case? If the answer is "Yes; it has been so taught and practiced," the next question is whether we have here a negotiable issue, or one that has already been settled. How much discussion, and what kind, would be necessary for some sort of consensus here? And if we could conclude that our mutually accepted baptisms constitute significant and valid *communicationes in sacris,* is this an analogy for some sort of mutually acknowledged eucharists? If we could get *that* far, or even in sight of such a goal, we might then be home free.

2. The winnowing of our existing ministries in preparation for their mingling. Ought this to be done—and, if so, how? I realize the danger of self-righteousness (the Gideon-complex, Donatism and all the rest!) in the proposal that the new church would be itself more likely to be reformed and renewed if its ministry was literally re-formed and re-newed in its genesis—not by a canceling of order and continuity but a winnowing of those now in orders by means of an examination, subscription, and rededication that would, in effect, *renew* their ministerial commitments (not orders). But it strikes me that it would be far more truly *self*-righteous to form the ministry of the new church out of our existing company (even by re-ordination) *without* some such reformation of its professed style and a renewal of its willing dedication. In any case, *ought* we to shrink from any "shortage" of ministries that might result from *this sort* of clerical self-reassessment?

Methodism
in the World
Christian Community

———†———

[1981] Speaking to the Uniting Church in Australia, Outler addresses the promise and problems of Methodists immersing themselves in a larger "uniting" church. He warns about the necessity to distinguish between heritage and nostalgia and discusses the reasons non-Methodists have trouble understanding Methodism. He interprets the "church-sect paradox" of Methodism as a negative example of its fragmentation and yet a positive demonstration of the ecumenically fruitful "principle of mingled memberships." According to Outler, a special vision of the Christian life epitomizes the Wesleyan heritage: a distinctive expectation of the presence and power of the Holy Spirit to transform persons and communities. Such a vision may yet have a vital ecclesiological impact on the world Christian community.

This is a great occasion for all of us here tonight; in some sense, it is actually a historic one. Some of us are Methodists from elsewhere in the world who have not yet found our way into a united church including Presbyterians and Congregationalists; some of you are partners of an exciting new venture in modern ecumenism; some of you were formerly Methodists, some not; Glenn Lucas of the United Church of Canada is from one of the oldest and most important united churches in this century—a fitting link between one of the first and one of the latest. Old lines of separation have happily been blurred, the sense of our true oneness in Christ is evident. Ever since I arrived in Australia I have felt a certain grace-filled "newness" in the air, and for it I thank God, with you!

It is also a great honor, and I am duly sensible of it, to be speaking to you on this occasion—this celebration, within the new Uniting Church in Australia, of one of the several traditions that are being mingled into your new church. You have labeled this a "Heritage Conference," and that is appropriate for it means that in this new church you are concerned not to lose the best of what you brought into the union. But I hope it also means that you have clearly distinguished, in your minds and hearts, the crucial difference between a sense of *heritage* (i.e., claiming the past for the future) and a sense of *nostalgia* (i.e., the mortgaging of the future to the past). With your heritage, I am deeply concerned; with your nostalgia, if any, I would wish to be merely sympathetic but not consoling.

Let us speak more specifically about the meaning of "heritage." Its basic sense is something from the past that belongs to you now by right (of birth or bequest). What makes all the difference, though, is whether one's heritage is chiefly a source of pride *or* a resource for *use*, whether it is being hoarded *or* shared, whether it is being mingled with other heritages, *or* whether it is exclusive by intention. In every religious group, one hears talk about something "distinctive"—a distinctive doctrine, or policy, or ethos. And almost always these so-called distinctive features are rather like scar tissue from older wounds of separation. The cause of Christian unity, then, is not served by tendencies to hang on too tightly to this heritage or that, or by claims that this "distinctive feature" or that is more important than it really is. Heritages are for sharing.

By the same token, however, there is only a net loss in any new church when the richness of its diverse heritages are abandoned or left to slide into oblivion. Just as we know all too well the *polemical* uses for church history, so also there are *ecumenical* uses of church history. When any once-living and fruitful tradition in the Christian community is lost, the whole body of Christ suffers a loss—and no tradition can rightly say to another, "I have no need of you." The first generation of a united church is difficult enough, but it is the second generation that is harder, and the third hardest of all—all our studies show this. But one of the things that helps most in these transitions is a traditioning of the best of the past on to the positive uses of the future, by appreciative people.

As a Methodist, I'm genuinely proud of the zeal and vision of the Australian Methodists in the great pioneering effort that I see represented by your new Uniting Church; it goes with the original genius of our tradition to be prepared for such commitments. We were not raised up to be a self-perpetuating church, but, much more significantly, to "spread scriptural holiness over these lands." But how are Christians who once bore the nickname "Methodist" to continue to cherish their heritage even as they also freely abandon some of their old, separatist "distinctive features" in a new and exciting church that bears all the signs of the Christian future in our time? The short answer is that it may not be easy but it will be crucial. For in the course of a fifty-year stint as a Methodist preacher and a forty-year stint as an ecumenical historian, I've noticed an odd thing about Methodists (in the nineteenth century till now in the twentieth): we are more susceptible to non-Methodist influences than we are inclined to abandon our divided and divisive polities. I know Methodists greatly affected by the Lutheran and the Reformed traditions but not at all interested in union with them; Methodists who are deeply involved with the Anglicans and Romans and Orthodox in their *liturgy* but rarely in their *polities*. This is why it interests me so much when Methodists (as in Canada and India and now Australia) break beyond the limits of interest and influence and take the plunge into institutional unity. John Wesley would be proud of you; Jabez Bunting almost certainly would not—but as between Wesley's approval and Bunting's disapproval, there is, of course, an easy choice.

But the other side of this same coin is that non-Methodists are so easily and so often baffled or misled by what they think they are seeing when they try to understand the Methodists— and, in my experience, they rarely do this unless they have to. For example, look at any of the sketches of Methodism in the denominational surveys or encyclopedias (even the new Catholic Encyclopaedia, in Schaff-Herzog, in *Religion in Geschichte und Gegenwart*, in Molland, Neve, Mayer, or Mead; the most important exception that I know of is in the sections on "The Methodists" and "The United Methodists" in the new Lutheran Survey, *Profiles in Belief*, where the description of the Methodists is truly remarkable; better than any of our own, I'm afraid! Important, other exceptions but somewhat less imperative interpretations may be found in Bernard Semmel, *The Methodist Revolution*, and Owen Chadwick's short sketch in *The Victorian Church*).

This difficulty of non-Methodists seeing us quite clearly is a historiographical problem and an ecumenical problem as well. Some of the answers are clear enough, and very much worth pondering, even by members of the Uniting Church with Methodist roots. One is that the Lutherans and the Calvinists wrote us off long ago as not being really serious or theologically sophisticated (and they had more warrant for this than one might have wished). William Burt Pope is the only Methodist theologian since Fletcher who might be nominated for inclusion in a *Who's Who* among the outstanding theologians in the past two centuries; and the fact is that even Pope is very rarely noticed in any of the standard histories of nineteenth-century theology. A second reason is that Methodism has a notorious record of triumphalism in its own historical literature and in its program of Wesley studies. This almost unselfconscious overconfidence is forever being pointed out to me by my non-Methodist friends and I'm often surprised to recognize what strikes them as triumphalism and what I had taken for granted as "pardonable pride."

A third thing that discourages so many non-Methodists from seeing us more clearly is what seems to them as a characteristic Methodist narcissism. Take the case in Wesley studies—so often by Methodists for Methodists; or analyze the example of the histories of Methodism, the Wesley hero cult, from Tyerman to Curnock, from Sugden to Telford and Simon. Or take all of those fatuous books about Wesley and the women. The horizons of this literature are almost all narrowly focused as if they were for Methodists only. Only in recent years have Wesley studies or Methodist church history been placed in the larger contexts of church history in general and in the history of doctrine in particular. And so only in recent years has serious interest been generated in what Wesley and the Methodists have to offer to the larger concerns of the Christian community over and beyond our pride of polity and our tendency toward muscular and/or emotional Christianity.

It has always been said that Methodists are pragmatists— they seek for what works and only then do we proceed to produce a theory that fits the results. Often enough we could simply point to the facts and let them speak for themselves. For example, we went from something under two hundred thousand in all the world in 1800—(from no more than fifty thousand in 1750) to around thirty million in 1900 with maybe another ten million since). But what happens when what once worked so well begins to wind down—when a zero-growth rate (or minus-growth-rate) develops? Certainly in the States and in Britain, there is a good deal of soul-searching going on—but without the historical and theological studies to supply our officials with the sort of deep probing, richly furnished intellectual or theoretical background that really fruitful soul-searching requires.

One of the most obvious of Methodism's paradoxes (viewed differently by insiders and outsiders) is that we are the only major church family in Christian history that began as an evangelical sect within a sacramental church and then evolved as a quasi-sacramental church (a proliferation of denominations) without an adequate self-understanding for doing so. The classical distinction between church and sect (made familiar by Troeltsch and Weber, and revised by Pope, Wilson, et. al.) never did apply to Methodism because in our case church principles and sectarian practices have been combined and recombined from the very beginning with never a fully grounded ecclesiology for guidance. Take infant baptism, for instance: what is the Methodist sacramental theory that really justifies this generally common practice? Or the Eucharist; there are Methodists with doctrines of "real presence" and Methodists with doctrines of "real absence." But on what grounds in either case? Or take ordination. The denomination I belong to has a clear and widely consented doctrine of "the priesthood of all believers"; but our doctrines of the representative or ordained ministry are not only rudimentary; even as they are enunciated, they are not very widely understood or devoutly believed. Methodism from the beginning has had a churchly view of the Christian responsibility for guiding the moral conscience of the state and of secular society—and yet also a sectarian conception of a voluntary association with prophetic and utopian values. We have also tried to combine the churchly view of evangelism (the welcome mat for whosoever wills) and the sectarian syndrome of proselytizing (the highways-and-hedges technique).

But on the other side, there is Methodism's strange record of bourgeois accommodation to secular cultures and their norms—a swift transition from a church of the lower classes to the middle classes in most of the countries where there is a middle class in the classical sense. There is, where I know it, our special Methodist passion for organizations (and some impressive gifts at it, too). We have a well-known record of centralized (not to say authoritarian) church government, an ambivalent history of professing a sensitivity to minority rights even as we ourselves live under the iron rule of parliamentary majorities (some of which, in my own United Methodist Church, are downright oppressive).

This church-sect paradox shows itself also in another way that often baffles our friends from outside. "The Methodists in all the world are one people," said Wesley more as a hope than a fact—and so we are, in a curious way. But whereas any conventional church-view places a high priority on organic union and whereas for the sects institutional organization matters less than "oneness in Christ," Methodists have tried to have it both ways. We have succeeded, too, sometimes in ways not quite intended. The World Methodist Council is an important communal link for us—yet it has no ecclesiastical jurisdiction whatsoever. There are sixty-four autonomous churches (give or take a few as in the aftermath of the United Methodist Church's latest actions) in eighty-seven countries, plus a fair number of Wesleyan-rooted denominations not in the United Methodist Church—Nazarenes, Salvationists, Pentecostalists, etc. In the very tentative roster of churches that would list themselves under the Methodist banner, there are twenty-four with reported memberships under a thousand; eighty-two with memberships in four figures under ten thousand; forty-one in five figures under a hundred thousand; sixteen in six figures under a million and only three with more than a million (not including the United Church of Canada, of course, in this sort of inventory). The largest of these, the United

Methodist Church, began with more than ten million and may reach it again, if our brave new words about evangelism bear fruit. But that is another story.

Invariably, when non-Methodists notice this remarkable fragmentation, they suppose that most of these divisions must reflect doctrinal issues. When told that practically none of them does (except on the point of "perfection" or "holiness") or that Methodists usually split along lines defined by ethos, social, ethnic, and structural issues, that Methodists run the gamut of the theological opinion within their own ranks, most of the non-Methodists I have known find this almost incomprehensible. But their reaction allows us to point to the positive and negative aspects of Methodist divisiveness (even as we admit that it needs much more critical historical analysis than it has yet received). Its chief negative aspect is its exhibition of Methodist obsession with institutional power and status—every autonomous church has its own hierarchy and curia, most of them top-heavy. Methodists would seem to have a special predilection for bureaucracy and curial power and this regularly poses difficulties in all serious or realistic ecumenical negotiations (including those between other Methodist churches!). But the positive side to all this fragmentation is its demonstration of the principle of readily mingled memberships (since most Methodists are actually "members one of another"—and we take this almost for granted).

This principle of mingled memberships is just now beginning to be taken seriously in current ecumenical discussions as the crucial first step toward mingled ministries and mingled sacraments, almost as if it were a new approach.

It is also mildly ambiguous to say that Methodists have rarely divided over doctrine. The fact is that the history of Methodist theology (another sadly underdeveloped field) is a story of moving away from its origins almost from the beginning. Our conventional histories begin with Wesley and assume an essential continuity thereafter. But studies like those of David Shipley, Dale Dunlap, Paul Sanders, Leland Scott, John Peters, Robert Chiles, *et. al.*, show a much more radical discontinuity between Wesley, and Watson and Miley and Pope and Knudson and Hildebrandt and Ogden, *et. al.*, than has ever been realized or explained. One of the failures of Methodist historiography (more startling to me the longer I live and work in Wesley's own sources) is the refusal to see him for what he thought he was—viz., an Anglican folk theologian, who filtered the Reformation to the Revival through an Anglican sieve (except on selected points such as political theory and the minority rights of an irregular ministry with an established church). On these points, he claimed Anglican tradition as well as scriptural precedent (and we might well face the fact that we, too, often respond as ineptly as Anglicans and Presbyterians when "extraordinary ministries" arise in our midst, e.g., the charismatics!).

Where does all this leave us and what does Methodism still have to bring to any prospective reunion of God's divided people? My own answer (partial, of course) begins with a recognition of the radical transformations of the Christian situation in the world since the second (or third) reformations of the sixteenth century, the religious wars of the seventeenth, the enlightenment of the eighteenth, the rise and arrest of the ideas of progress in the nineteenth and twentieth; the narcissist effects of the modern secularism and the revival of secular cults of self-improvement and self-salvation that are mushrooming about us everywhere (in the churches almost as much as outside). The short of a long story is that the old quarrels of the sixteenth century are no longer present life-and-death issues. The crucial problematic as to divine sovereignty and human responsibility has been altered past all recognition—so that the *sola fide* is no longer a credible whole answer, even less the high-minded moralism (Pelagianism, if you will) into which so much of Methodism seems to have slipped.

It may seem an anticlimax to some of you to conclude with a plea for *resourcement*—i.e., back to the sources and then forward; but there it is, that is my plea, and a lifetime of ecumenical historiography continues to confirm its potential fruitfulness. The evolution of Methodism (in doctrine, policy, and ethos) is unimpressive—theologically and ecumenically—and it will not be otherwise until we recover and transvaluate our very best heritage.

How might one phrase the gist of this heritage? To oversimplify (and appeal to Wesley for precedent in doing so): it is first and last a special vision of the Christian life as life in the Holy Spirit and as life in grace—the life of sacrificial love, to God and neighbor, responding to God's sacrificial love revealed in Jesus Christ and empowered by the Holy Spirit. What is crucially at stake is a special understanding of the Holy Spirit that would revive heart religion and social revolution with some of the "enthusiasm" that Methodists once had. Methodism at its best has a Christocentric pneumatology or pneumatological Christology, which the world Christian community needs, especially now, to have integrated into its classical traditions. Its promise and glory are the love of God in Christ shed abroad in our hearts by the Holy Spirit so that the absolute initiative in grace is always from God the Spirit and every positive human response is prompted by the Holy Spirit. This is the very essence of the idea of prevenience.

It was this pneumatology (and the ethos it generated) that validated the experience of "assurance of sins forgiven and of living in God's favor" (i.e., grace). It was this pneumatology that Wesley set as counterpoint to his stark doctrine of original sin, which allowed for his shift from a forensic to a therapeutic soteriology—a striking modern and ecumenical move. It was this pneumatology that lies behind the sacramental realism of Charles Wesley's eucharistic hymns since it is the Holy Spirit who consecrates the sacramental elements and who transsignifies their activity in the lives of the faithful. The church, then, is less the extension of the Incarnation than of the community of Pentecostal witness (this has been the good essence of revivalism, from then till now). *Ubi Spiritus Sanctus, ibi ecclesia Christi* [where the Holy Spirit is, there is the church of Christ]; Christian worship always, and rightly, expects the descent of the Dove!

Methodism thus has within it the makings of a pneumatological ecclesiology with immense import for the world Christian community. The church is *one* in the Spirit rather than in any of its institutional structures, it is *holy* in the Spirit, who calls and leads the faithful into that holy living without which none shall see the Lord. It is *catholic*, both in terms of Wesley's "catholic spirit" and in its radical commitment to actual inclusiveness; it is *apostolic* in the Spirit, who once turned a dispirited rabble into a company of witnesses and servants, and can work this same miracle again—as the Spirit has so often in the history of the Christian community.

Methodism, flaws and all, has a rightful place in the Christian community but by no principle are we committed to survival in perpetuity. Our original reason for being was to serve a clear and present need. Whenever and wherever there is no special need for our separate existence, we have no principled reason for continuing to be. Wesley would have approved the famous "Last Will and Testament" of the Springfield, Missouri, Presbytery in 1804, to the effect that "this body prepare itself to die, to be dissolved and sink into union with the Body of Christ at large." This is why I'm so excited by your boldness and faithfulness to your own Methodist heritage in joining this new Uniting Church in Australia. I hope you will not forget your heritage; don't let it be neglected or distorted in the larger riches of your new church. But I hope that you will do this with as much freedom and loyalty as Wesley brought to the Church of England in his time. Methodism is, and always has been, an interim church: free, on its own principles, to continue its mission as a denomination (or congeries of them) or, to follow the better way and as the Spirit opens the future, to lose our ecclesiastical life in order to save our larger ecumenical soul—provided only that the larger Christian communion be grounded in Scripture, pillared by Tradition and God-given Reason, and crowned with the garlands of experienced grace. What would it avail us if we gained the whole world, denominationally, and forfeited the chance to be a vital part of a church sufficiently catholic to provide all the means of grace for all, sufficiently evangelical to hold to Christ as Lord of the church and of the world, sufficiently willing to be reformed and reforming so that no institutional development would ever become sacrosanct as such.

Like Simeon of old, I have spent a lifetime in the ecumenical temple: waiting, hoping for a sign of the recovery of that unity that God wills for us all, "that the world may believe" (since ecumenism is nothing if not evangelistic). My chances now, as I know very well, are slim. But these investments in ecumenical historiography would seem less quixotic if I could hope and believe that other Methodist historians (and their colleagues in all the other churches) might come to share this vision of a "common Christian history" whose critical study might also help turn us all away from triumphalism and denominationalism to become volunteers in the quest for a renewed and renewing world Christian community in which the Father's manifest will for a whole human community in Christ through the Spirit might be realized and enjoyed here on earth, even as always and already it is done in heaven. Amen.

Epilogue:
Visions
and Dreams

Visions and Dreams; the Unfinished Business of an Unfinished Church

———†———

[1968] When the Methodist Church and The Evangelical United Brethren joined to form The United Methodist Church, Albert Outler was asked to preach the sermon at the Uniting Service. He chose Acts 2 as his text. The sermon celebrates the birthday of the new church by analogy with Pentecost as a day when the real work begins. Outler holds up the vision of a church truly catholic, evangelical, and reformed. He also delineates the ways we are not so yet and calls special attention to "the abject failure of the teaching church" in the modern world. Outler's meditation on the interactions of Pentecost and polity is an exemplary portrayal of the visions and dreams nurtured and disciplined in the Wesleyan tradition.

Brothers and Sisters in Christ:

Here we are this morning, gathered from all over the world to celebrate a birthday, *our* birthday as The United Methodist Church. In just a few moments now, we shall join in a ceremony symbolizing our new covenant of unity and mutual growth together. The aura of every newborn thing is an aura of hope. And so it is with us today. We stand here on a threshold. A new horizon looms ahead.

In some ears, it may sound fantastic to relate *this* day to the first Pentecost recorded in Acts 2—what with no rushing mighty wind, no tongues of fire, no glossolalia, etc. But actually, the lasting meaning of *that* Pentecost was its opening the way for others to follow after.

> And while the day of Pentecost was getting on, [the disciples] were all together with one accord in one place. . . . And they were filled with the Holy Spirit . . . and began to speak . . . as the Spirit gave them the power of utterance . . . about the great deeds of God. . . .

This is, of course, an abridgment of the longer text, with the marvels omitted and also those two bits of local color that still intrigue me: the one where Peter denies that the disciples are drunk because it was too early in the morning (about the same time of day as *now*!); and that other one about the three thousand new members added in one day. What a frustration it must have been for Peter to have all that happen, with no board to report it to!

Clearly, though, that first Pentecost was less significant for what happened *then* than for what came after. Pentecost *was the day when the real work of the church began*, when the Christian people accepted the agenda of their unfinished business in the world and began to get on with it! Those first Christians were not very well-furnished in terms of ecclesiastical apparatus. Their organization was shaky, their polity and discipline sketchy. Their theologians were in typical disagreement, and their most prominent lay leaders were Ananias and Sapphira!

THE CHURCH'S BIRTHDAY

Even so, *that* Pentecost was ever thereafter memorable as the church's *birthday*, as the day when Joel's prophecy was fulfilled—when the Holy Spirit would come and abide as the governing presence in the midst of God's People—and this memory remained, even when the rushing mighty wind subsided to homiletical zephyrs, when glossolalia was relegated to the margins of Christian experience, when the tongues of fire gave way to controversy and conflict. Pentecost is rightly remembered as the day when the Christian church was launched on its career *in* history, *for* the world. In every age, her performance has been scandalously short of her visions and dreams—and her plain imperatives. And yet also in every age since the first Pentecost, it is the Christian church that has marked off the crucial difference between humanity's best hope and its genuine despair.

I know as well as anyone that this analogy between that first birthday and this one of ours does not apply foursquare. Our new church does not represent a radical break with our several past histories nor is there a comparable intention toward a radically new future. Even so, the analogy between that first Pentecost and this one could be edifying to us, too. This is the day when *the real work of the UMC begins*. It is a day when doors are opened that heretofore were closed, when new possibilities of reformation and renewal are literally at hand.

The essence of the event is self-evident: it is the accomplished fact of the United Methodist Church. Where once, scarcely a generation ago, there were five churches, now there is one. Where once our differences kept us apart—with different languages and folkways—now they are overcome or at least contained within a larger circle of committed fellowship. We have been Christian brethren, after a fashion, for the better part of two centuries—but *separated* brethren. Now our memberships and ministries have been mingled without compromise or indignity; our separate traditions have been sublated and made one.

Obviously, no part of our venture in unity is really *finished* as yet. Our joy in *this* union ought to be tempered by our remembrance, in love, of those others of our Christian family, whom we acknowledge as such, and yet from whom we are still separated. Moreover, the various practical, domestic problems posed by our agenda in this Conference loom large and exigent. It will *not* be a debonair fortnight; few of us are likely to be content with the outcome. And yet here we are and this is our birthday. Here we turn a new page in modern church history—and, just as smugness is excluded from our celebration, so also is cynicism.

Let us then ask ourselves what this fact of a new church makes possible. What will it take to turn this beginning into the reality of its promise and of our hopes? We can offer our ungrudging gratitude and honor to all those whose toil and tears, faith and fortitude have led us to this hour—so long as we are all clear that none of their laurels (and certainly none of ours) is for *resting on*. We have much to be grateful for, nothing to be complacent about. Our joy this day is foretaste: foretaste of a future that can be even more creative than we have yet dared to ask or think.

This means that, as we turn from our ceremony of beginnings to the tasks that follow, our foremost need is for a vivid sense of the church we have been called to be. By what norms shall we seek to transform our covenant into genuine *koinonia*? By what principles are we willing to be guided in the agonies of growth that lie ahead? To what heavenly vision are we prepared to be obedient in the difficult days and years that even the blithest optimist can foresee?

One thing is for sure: what has served till now as our *status quo ante* will simply not suffice for the upcoming future. For all its great merits—for all its saints and heroes–the standing order is now too nearly preoccupied with self-maintenance and survival. The world is in furious and agonizing turmoil, incomprehensible and unmanageable. The church is in radical crisis, and in the throes of a profound demoralization, at every level: of faith and order, life and work. In such times, business as usual simply will not get our business done. Our own past golden age (the nineteenth century)—the heyday of pietism in a pre-urbanized society—has faded. Frontier people for tomorrow must be as dynamically adaptive to the *new* "new world" as our forebearers were in theirs.

There is, of course, a bit of glibness here—for the brute fact is that we have no clearly visible alternative to the *status quo* ready to hand, available merely for our choice and application. For all their advertisements, none of the new experiments in celebration of our own brave new world can honestly be hailed as the shape of things to come. Nor is it the case that any of our sister churches have had vouchsafed to them the blueprints for Zion's Ark, space-age model—though some (notably the Roman Catholics) have recently exposed themselves to more massive and more fruitful self-examination than we.

For freedom we have been set free, from the outdated past—but it begins to look as if we have been condemned *to* freedom as well: condemned to come up with something better than protests and complaints and self-righteous criticism of others; we are condemned to *responsible* prophecy, reform and renewal—or else to the fatal consequences of destructive discontent. If, in this new church of ours, we are to avoid "the dinosaur-syndrome" (with its zeal for furnishing later ages an abundance of fossils) or its opposite, "the Elijah complex" (with its self-pitying self-righteousness about our minority status), we *must* find our way forward in conscious concern for the continuum of the Christian tradition and history in which we stand with our forebearers always aware of God's habit of linking the past and the future by means of hopeful human actions in decisive *present* moments—like *this one!* We *must* learn to discipline our imaginations and inventions, not by our own constructive biases but by God's open-hearted mandates for pilgrim people, by patterns that will serve our *common* life in the body of Christ.

One version of the style of the new church that is to be has already been encapsulated in a phrase now familiar from the discussions of the Consultation on Church Union. It is a sort of motto that could qualify as a charter for authentic unity and effective mission: "We seek to be a church truly *catholic,* truly *evangelical,* truly *reformed.*" These words themselves are obviously not new; COCU has no copyright on this motto. Its significance lies in its summation of three essential dimensions and concerns of *any* company of persons calling and professing themselves Christian. Each of the terms has had a varied history of interpretation and misinterpretation; each has been a fighting word at one time or another. It is only when all three are taken and held *together*—each balancing and explaining the other two—that we can recognize their relevance as goal-points for the church we aspire to be: catholic *and* evangelical (*both,* not either/or); catholic, evangelical *and* reformed—viz., with both catholic and evangelical concerns brought under perennial reassessment and re-formation in each successive new age.

One of the virtues of the motto is that it suggests a rich range of meanings, without specifying any single one of them as obligatory upon all. Certainly the interpretation I now propose makes no claim to finality. My only concern is to interest you in trying to understand its possible import for us in the UMC and in our efforts to shape her future.

THE CHURCH CATHOLIC

The basic meaning of the word "catholic" is "whole," "universal," "open." It reminds us that true unity not only allows for diversity, it *requires* it. "Catholic" has never rightly meant "uniform," "lock-step," "produced by template." It means *"inclusive"*—a community in which all the members *"belong"* equally and by right of membership, in which all ministers share equally the basic office of representing the whole church, by right of ordination. It means "open"—a community whose boundaries are set by the Christian *essentials* (the *bare* essentials at that) in which it is bad faith for anyone to deny full membership to any other save by the canons of faith in Christ and the Christian discipline that derives from that confession. This rules out all distinctions based on race, sex, class, and culture—and so also all distinctions based on partisan emphases on this doctrine or that, this form of worship or that, this pattern of polity or that. Here is the plain teaching of Wesley's sermon on "Catholic Spirit"—a sermon we would all do well to recall and to update in terms that might fit our own condition. A church tormented and befuddled by racial strife is not yet truly "catholic." A church that cannot manage her global ties without "colonialism" or "autonomy" is not yet "truly catholic." A church that proudly (or humbly!) sets her own polity and folkways above those of other churches may be "united" but she is not yet "truly catholic." A church that opens her sacraments to all other Christians but is herself not yet eligible for sharing in the sacraments of some of the others is not yet "truly catholic." And if the main fault here lies, as we may think it does, with others fencing *us* from *their* sacraments, this does not alter the fact that we have rarely asked, with appropriate dignity, what is required of us, and of them, for the valid mingling of our memberships, ministries, and sacraments. It is also true that the other churches are not fully catholic either—and this is the ecumenical tragedy! But if we are to join them in the search for a more inclusive, integral, *"catholic"* fellowship in Christ, the least we can do is to commit ourselves to just such a fellowship in this new church of ours—and to open our hearts and minds to yet further bold ventures in quest of Christian unity.

THE CHURCH EVANGELICAL

But catholicity by itself is not enough. The church is called to mission, and her mission is both her message *and* the demonstration of that message in her corporate life. Her message is not *herself*, either—it is her witness to the *Christian evangel:* To the scandal and folly of Christ incarnate, Christ crucified, Christ resurrected, Christ transforming human life and culture, Christ in the world, Christ for the world; Christ in us, our hope of glory! Thus, the church we are called to be must be "truly evangelical"— a church ablaze with a passion that God's gospel shall be preached and heard and responded to in faith and hope and love by all who can be reached and instructed and gathered into the fellowship of God's covenanted people. The *fullness* of the gospel embraces all human concerns everywhere and always; but the *heart* of the gospel is startlingly simple: that God loves you and me and all people with a very special love and that Jesus Christ is the sufficient proof of this love to everyone who will receive and confess him as Savior and Lord. The gospel is the good news that it is God's love that pardons, heals, and reconciles, God's love that demands that we be fully human and opens up this possibility for us, God's love that can sanctify our memories and our hopes. And yet this same gospel also reminds us, in *every* human circumstance, that our salvation comes from God's sheer unmerited favor. In no sense can it ever be earned or bought or wheedled—it does not come by any merit or demerit, by any good works or bad, by any claim that we can bring on our own behalf. The word "evangelical" is concerned above all with *the faith that receives the gospel wholeheartedly and in trust;* it stresses faith as a gift *from* God, faith as our basic response *to* God, faith as the mortal foe of all human *pride*—and yet also faith as the loyal ally of all true human *dignity.* The church evangelical is, therefore, radically Christ-centered—disengaged from any final dependence on ecclesiastical apparatus of whatever sort, save only as it ministers to her central mission: that we may receive God's gift of saving grace in Christ and learn to live in the world in true communion with the Holy Spirit and with one another. The church evangelical is a proclaiming church—but it is also a *teaching church.* Wesley often pointed out that the difference between *his* movement and the others— equally zealous in proclamation—was his provision of *societies* in which converts came to learn the meaning of the gospel *in depth* and in *concrete life situations.*

We Methodists and EUBs alike—by profession and fond memory—are grateful heirs of evangelical fathers and mothers, but we can scarcely boast of having fully claimed their legacy. A church falling behind in the race with an exploding and huddling population is not truly evangelical, despite its self-advertisements. A church that counts her evangelical harvest chiefly in terms of members added to the rolls is not *truly* evangelical. A church the vast majority of whose members do not really understand the great issues entailed by "the Protestant principle"—God's sovereignty, justification by faith alone, the witness of the Spirit, the life of grace, the authority of the Scripture as the prime source of divine revelation, etc.—such a church is not only not truly evangelical, she is, indeed, partaker in the greatest tragedy of modern Christianity; *the abject failure of the teaching church.* Here we are—Christians by name and sign—organized to the teeth and involved in titanic labors of all sorts, and yet the generality of our people do not really know what the Christian faith purports, do not really believe in their hearts and minds what they profess with their lips, and, of those who do, there are few who can give a rational accounting of it to themselves and others. The proof of this turns up in every great upheaval—doctrinal, moral, social. The church evangelical must not be doctrinaire—but surely her people should be clear about the crucial priorities between God and humanity in the mystery of salvation and in the enterprise of our becoming fully human. Wesley and Asbury and Otterbein and Albright understood these priorities in their day and in their terms. Those days and those terms are not ours—but the same task remains: of calling everyone to the love *of God* above all else and of all else *in God.*

THE CHURCH REFORMED

And yet even the best conceptions of "catholicity" and "evangelical zeal" sag out of shape as history moves the church along through time and change. The provisional becomes permanent, creative experiments from an early age become vested interests in a later one, the pragmatic *warrant* for a given polity becomes defensive and self-maintaining. What once was a sign of "catholic spirit" becomes a new sectarianism; what once was an authentic evangelical concern becomes calcified into *theories about evangelism* that do not get the whole gospel preached and heard and appropriated for life in the secular city. And so the church, even as she seeks to be truly catholic *and* truly evangelical must also be truly *reformed*—constantly open to God's judgment upon the insidious idolatries of every successful venture, aware of the waning of every heyday—a church eager to be reformed, renewed: to have her spirit and power repristinated.

A church truly reformed is one that is open, intentionally and on principle, to creative change of every sort (in teaching, discipline, and administration)—not haphazard or reckless change, but not timid and grudging either. The church reformed lives by the Scriptures, for they alone provide a decisive appeal to the constitutive tradition of Christ without the dead hand of traditional*ism*; the Scriptures alone provide for radical mandated change without the gusts and shallows of human ingenuity. Their authority does not rest upon their letter nor yet with any arcane or coterie interpretation—but rather upon the public sense of the texts and their original intentions, enriched by the wisdom of the teaching church through all the ages, sifted by the canons of critical reason and vital Christian experience in the modern world.

But the church reformed is also under the judgment of the future. The eschatological orientation of faith is forever demanding that the old be constantly reexamined and reconstituted— always with an eye to the urgent, the needful, the effective. The reforming spirit calls for self-examination without self-just-ification, self-criticism without self-loathing, creative discontent rooted in the conviction that the *good* is the enemy of the best.

It may seem to some a mite unseasonable to suggest that the UMC needs to take conscious, urgent thought of being or becoming truly reformed, *just now*! We *are* a church re-formed: what with our new Plan and our newer Report and with ten more days to pull and haul away at their discussion, amendment, and adoption. Surely *this* is enough for the present moment. Well, Ye-s-s—in a way—but that's partly my point. This Plan and the Report in the form in which they will stand when we adjourn will doubtless be the very best we can do, under *all* the circumstances, etc., etc. But for how long will *that* be good *enough*? The answer: not much beyond the results being printed in the new *Discipline*. Wherefore, *now* is the time, as at that first Pentecost, for the young to see visions and for the old to dream dreams—visions and dreams that ask more of the Methodist people than we have ever asked before, visions and dreams that offer a richer, fuller life for all God's people, visions and dreams that see this "new" church *re*-newed yet again and again, not only "in the Spirit" but in her structures, functions, folkways.

This is not a proposal, not even indirectly, for any specific reform—yours or mine or anybody else's. It is, however, an open advocacy of the *idea* of reform and of "the Protestant principle" of *semper reformanda*. When more of us get accustomed to the notion that this new church of ours *can* be re-made for yet more effective mission, for still more authentic democracy and local initiative, for still more efficient, adventurous leadership—and that all this *can* be done and *should* be done forthwith!—then the pooled wisdom of our fellowship will surely be enabled to prove that rational, responsible change is a far more faithful pattern of obedience to Christ than the most devoted immobilism can ever be.

This, then, is our birthday—a day to celebrate, a day to remember, a day for high hopes and renewed commitments. This is a day when the eyes of the whole Christian community are focused on us. This *is* the day that the Lord has made. Let us *really* rejoice and be glad in it—glad for the new chance God now gives us: to be a *church united in order to be uniting, a church repentant in order to be a church redemptive, a church cruciform in order to manifest God's triumphant agony for humankind.*

Let us pray:

O God of unchangeable power and eternal light, look favorably on thy whole church, that wonderful and sacred mystery; and, by the tranquil operation of thy perpetual providence, carry out the work of our salvation; and let the whole world feel and see that things that were cast down are being raised up, that those things that had grown old are being made new, and that all things are returning to perfection, through him from whom they took their origin, even Jesus Christ our Lord. Amen.

Index of Names

Index of Subjects

Historiography 76, 130, 244, 247, 248, 250

Holiness 30, 52, 66–68, 92, 122, 140, 141, 168, 202, 207

Holy Club 44, 45, 78, 102, 123, 129, 147, 178

Holy living 64, 79–81, 83–86, 90, 93, 94, 108, 115, 117, 249

Holy Spirit 47, 50, 71, 105, 110, 135, 159–74, 168, 169, 235, 248–49

Homilies, Anglican 22, 27, 30, 46, 47, 66, 86, 104, 105, 200

Justification 27, 63–68, 81, 88–91, 115–20, 147

Kingswood 72, 91

Latin Christianity 92, 108, 121

Latitudinarianism 64, 82

Logic 33, 70, 106, 121, 198

Metousia theou 92, 105, 195

Ministerial Orders 98, 153, 227–30, 232–35, 238

Model Deed 23

Montanism 142

Moravians 27, 45, 46, 78, 84, 85, 166, 178, 200, 201

Mysticism 83, 122, 167

Mystics 93, 109

Nazarenes 146, 246

Nominalism 64, 86, 198, 199

Nonjurors 44, 101, 102, 204, 215

Opinions, theological 25, 30, 57, 58, 71, 102, 192, 193

Ordination 9, 49, 152, 186, 225, 229–39, 245, 258

Ordo salutis 25, 29, 47, 79, 101, 103, 105, 108, 167

Orthodoxy, Eastern 10, 11, 13, 25, 31, 44, 45, 46, 47, 51, 53, 54, 64, 92, 97–110, 121, 127, 135, 136, 163, 189, 192–93, 195, 203, 236

Oxford University 31, 58–60, 102, 165

Participation in God 32, 67, 92–94, 105, 117, 166, 195

Pelagianism 10, 32, 181, 195, 200, 203

Pentecostalists 73, 146, 223, 246

Perception, spiritual 7, 33, 169, 181

Perfection 51–53, 85, 109, 120–23, 139, 177, 182, 183, 202

Pietism 69, 77, 85, 93, 135, 166, 207, 256

Platonism 61, 106, 171

Polity 146, 149–50, 154, 156, 191, 217, 220, 223, 230, 245, 258, 260

Preaching 46, 48, 73, 85, 87, 178, 216

Predestination 47, 63, 89–91, 108, 118–19, 202

Primitivism 6, 16, 145, 148, 150, 152, 153, 156

Protestantism 26, 93, 156, 191, 193, 199

Psychotherapy 71, 176, 184

Puritans 63, 77, 87, 115, 191, 204

Quadrilateral, the Wesleyan 12, 16, 21–37, 101, 141

Quakers 163

Quietism 93

Reason 32–35, 69, 151

Reformation, Protestant 24, 70, 80, 148, 199, 220

Repentance 25, 44, 66, 79, 108, 115, 119–21, 140

Restrictive Rule 23, 152

Sacraments 215, 231–32, 258

Salvation Army 9

Sanctification 51–52, 68, 85, 94, 109, 120–23

Scripture 30–32, 101, 109, 114, 116, 148–51, 153–54, 163, 184, 209

Secularism 33, 60, 182, 194, 197, 208, 248

Sermons on Several Occasions 64, 100, 127

Sin 52, 66, 68, 88, 105, 109, 119, 121–23, 181–83, 194–96, 249

Synergism (cf. *facere quod in se est*) 46, 63, 64, 105, 182, 186, 195, 199–201, 206–8

Teaching
  Church 259–60
  Wesley's 139

Theological method 12, 21, 24, 26, 28, 35, 54

Theological pluralism 25, 118, 124

Theology 28, 36, 42–44, 54, 57–60, 193, 206–9, 221, 223, 244, 247

Thirty-Nine Articles 24, 86, 222

Tradition 31–32, 37, 75–95, 100–3, 110, 123–24, 137–38, 167, 181, 199, 236, 239, 243, 248, 250

Trent, Council of 65, 77, 89, 91, 118, 121